ULTIMATE
MANDARIN
CHINESE

BASIC–INTERMEDIATE

Also available from
LIVING LANGUAGE®

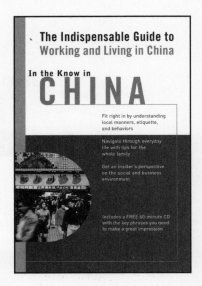

LIVING LANGUAGE®

ULTIMATE
MANDARIN
CHINESE

BASIC–INTERMEDIATE

WRITTEN BY

JENNIFER HUMPHRIES
AUDREY LI
CATHY WEI

EDITED BY

CHRISTOPHER A. WARNASCH

Published in the United States by Living Language,
A Random House Company. Living Language is a member of the Random
House Information Group.

www.livinglanguage.com

ISBN 1-4000-2102-2

Library of Congress Cataloging-in-Publication Data is available upon
request.

This book is available for special discounts for bulk purchases for sales
promotions or premiums. Special editions, including personalized covers,
excerpts of existing books, and corporate imprints, can be created in large
quantities for special needs. For more information. write to Special
Markets/Premium Sales, 1745 Broadway, MD 6-2, New York, New York
10019, or e-mail specialmarkets@randomhouse.com.

PRINTED IN THE UNITED STATES OF AMERICA

10 9 8 7 6

ACKNOWLEDGMENTS

Thanks to the Living Language team: Tom Russell, Elizabeth Bennett, Christopher Warnasch, Zviezdana Verzich, Suzanne McQuade, Amelia Muqaddam, Denise De Gennaro, Linda Schmidt, John Whitman, Alison Skrabek, Helen Kilcullen, Heather Lanigan, Fabrizio La Rocca, Guido Caroti, and Sophie Chin. Special thanks to everyone who assisted in the writing and development of this book: Professor Theresa Jen, Yuming Guo, Wenqing Zhou, and Ben Wang.

CONTENTS

ULTIMATE
MANDARIN
CHINESE

BASIC–INTERMEDIATE

INTRODUCTION

Living Language® Ultimate Chinese is a practical and enjoyable way to learn Chinese. The complete course consists of this text and eight hours of recordings. You can, however, use the text on its own if you already know how to pronounce Chinese.

With *Ultimate Chinese,* you'll start speaking Chinese from the very beginning. Each lesson begins with a dialogue about a common situation that you are likely to experience at home or abroad. You'll learn the most common and useful expressions for everyday conversation.

Key grammatical structures introduced in the dialogue are clearly explained in a separate section. The lessons build on one another. The material you've already studied is "recycled," or used again, in later lessons as you learn new words, phrases and grammatical forms. This method helps you increase your language skills gradually while reinforcing and perfecting the material learned previously.

In addition, brief notes on relevant cultural topics will add to your understanding of Chinese and Chinese-speaking people.

COURSE MATERIALS

THE MANUAL

Living Language® Ultimate Chinese consists of forty lessons, eight review sections and four reading sections. The review sections appear after every five lessons, and the reading sections after every ten.

Read and study each lesson before listening to the recordings. Or, try listening to the recorded dialogue first to see how much you understand without the help of reading the text or looking at the translations. This is an excellent way to test and practice comprehension.

Duìhuà (Dialogue): Each lesson begins with a dialogue presenting a realistic situation in a Chinese locale. The dialogue is followed by a translation in colloquial English. Note that while there are many regional dialects and accents, we will be using standard Chinese (Mandarin) grammar and vocabulary throughout the course.

Fāyīn (Pronunciation): In lessons 1 to 10, you will learn the correct pronunciation of vowels and diphthongs, as well as consonants and consonant combinations.

1

Yǔfǎ hé Yòngfǎ (Grammar and Usage): This section explains the major grammatical points covered in the lesson. The heading of each topic corresponds to its listing in the Table of Contents.

Hànzì (Characters): This section will gradually teach you how to recognize, read and write the most common and basic Chinese characters. About five new characters are introduced in each lesson, and the stroke order for each one is carefully demonstrated in the first twenty-five lessons.

Shēngcí (Vocabulary): In this section, you can review the words and expressions from the dialogue and learn additional vocabulary.

Wénhuà Zhùjiě (Cultural Note): These brief notes put the language in its cultural context. Cultural awareness will enrich your understanding of Chinese and your ability to communicate effectively.

Fùxí (Review): Review sections appear after every five lessons. These sections are similar to the exercises in format but integrate material of all the lessons you have studied to that point.

Yuèdú Liànxí (Reading Practice): The four reading passages are not translated. However, the material covered in the preceding lessons, along with the vocabulary notes that accompany the reading, will enable you to infer the meaning, just as you would when reading a newspaper abroad.

Appendices: There are four appendices—Common Measure Words, Types of Questions, Adverbs, and Particles.

Glossary: Be sure to make use of the two-way glossary in the back of the manual to check the meanings and connotations of new words.

Index: The manual ends with an index of all the grammar points covered in the lessons.

The appendices, glossary, and index make this manual an excellent source for future reference and study.

RECORDINGS (SETS A & B)

This course provides you with eight hours of audio practice. There are two sets of complementary recordings: The first is designed for use with the manual, while the second may be used without it. By listening to and imitating the native speakers, you will be able to improve your pronunciation and comprehension while learning to use new phrases and structures.

RECORDINGS FOR USE WITH THE MANUAL (SET A)

This set of recordings gives you four hours of audio practice in Chinese only, with translations in the manual. The dialogue of each lesson, the pronunciation sections of lessons 1 through 10, and the vocabulary section are featured on these recordings. All the words and expressions that are recorded appear in **boldfaced type** in your manual.

First, you will hear native Chinese speakers read the complete dialogue at a normal conversational pace without interruption; then you'll have a chance to listen to the dialogue a second time and repeat each phrase in the pauses provided.

Next, listen carefully to learn the sounds from the pronunciation sections. By repeating after the native speakers, you will gradually master the sounds.

Finally, the most important and commonly used vocabulary will also be modeled by the native speakers for you to repeat in the pauses provided.

After studying each lesson and practicing with Set A, go on to the second set of recordings (Set B), which you can use on the go — while driving, jogging, or doing housework.

RECORDINGS FOR USE ON THE GO (SET B)

The "On the Go" recordings give you four hours of audio practice in Chinese and English. Because they are bilingual, Set B recordings may be used without the manual, anywhere it's convenient to learn.

The forty lessons on Set B correspond to those in the manual. A bilingual narrator leads you through the four sections of each lesson.

The first section presents the most important phrases from the original dialogue. You will first hear the abridged dialogue at normal conversational speed. You'll then hear it again, phrase by phrase, with English translations and pauses for you to repeat after the native Chinese speakers.

The second section reviews and expands upon the vocabulary in the dialogue. Additional expressions show how the words may be used in other contexts. Again, you are given time to repeat the Chinese phrases.

3

In the third section, you'll explore the lesson's most important grammatical structures. After a quick review of the rules, you can practice with illustrative phrases and sentences.

The exercises in the last section integrate what you've learned and help you generate sentences in Chinese on your own. You'll take part in brief conversations, respond to questions, transform sentences, and occasionally translate. After you respond, you'll hear the correct answer from a native speaker.

The interactive approach on this set of recordings will teach you to speak, understand, and *think* in Chinese.

PĪNYĪN ROMANIZATION

The Chinese language does not have an alphabet. Each word is represented by a character, which may be composed of just one stroke (line) or as many as several dozen. To represent Chinese sounds for those who do not read characters, various systems of romanization have been devised. You will learn *pīnyīn*, the standard system used in China and the one most commonly used in the United States.

Each syllable in Chinese has an initial consonant sound and a final vowel sound. There are twenty-three initial sounds (consonants) and thirty-six final sounds (vowels or combinations of vowels and consonants). Here is how each sound is written in *pīnyīn*, with its *approximate* English equivalent.

INITIAL SOUNDS

CHINESE SOUND	ENGLISH EQUIVALENT
b	bear
p	poor
m	more
f	fake
d	dare
t	take
n	now
l	learn
z	yards
c	its
s	sing
zh	judge
ch	church
sh	shhhh!
r	rubber
j	and yet
q	won't you
x	shoe
g	get
k	cow
h	help

CHINESE SOUND	ENGLISH EQUIVALENT
y	<u>y</u>es
w	<u>w</u>ant

FINAL SOUNDS

a	m<u>a</u>
ai	m<u>y</u>
ao	p<u>o</u>ut
an	él<u>an</u>
ang	thr<u>ong</u>
o	<u>or</u>
ou	fl<u>oa</u>t
ong	l<u>ong</u>
e	n<u>e</u>rve
ei	d<u>ay</u>
en	<u>un</u>der
eng	m<u>ung</u>
i (after z, c, s, zh, ch, sh)	thunde<u>r</u>
i	<u>see</u>
ia	<u>yah</u>
iao	<u>meow</u>
ian	<u>yan</u>
iang	<u>yang</u>
ie	<u>ye</u>s
iu	<u>yo</u>-yo
iong	<u>young</u>
in	s<u>in</u>
ing	s<u>ing</u>
u	fl<u>u</u>
ua	s<u>ua</u>ve
uai	<u>wi</u>de
uan	<u>wan</u>
uang	<u>wong</u>
uo	<u>won</u>'t

ui	weigh
un	won
ü	rheumatic
üan	like ü above with an
üe	like ü above with net
ün	like ü above with an
er	are

TONE MARKS

Each syllable in Mandarin must be pronounced with a tone—there are four, plus a neutral tone. Here are the tone marks as they are written in *pīnyīn*:

first tone ▬

second tone ⁄

third tone ∨

fourth tone ⟍

Syllables pronounced with the neutral tone are unmarked. The tone marks are placed over the final vowel sound of a syllable. In the case of compound vowels (ai, uo, io), the tone is placed over the primary vowel.

Pronunciation of each of the four tones, as well as the neutral tone, is covered in Lesson 1.

DÌ YĪ KÈ
Lesson 1

HÁNXŪAN. Greetings.

A. DUÌHUÀ (Dialogue)

ZÀI LÙ SHÀNG.

On the way home, Mr. and Mrs. Li run into Ms. Wang, a former classmate of Mr. Li's.

LǏ XIĀNSHENG: **Wáng xiǎojie, hǎo jiǔ bú jiàn! Nǐ hǎo!**

WÁNG XIǍOJIE: **Nǐ hǎo! Hǎo jiǔ bú jiàn, Lǐ xiānsheng.**

LǏ XIĀNSHENG: **Nǐ zuìjìn máng ma?**

WÁNG XIǍOJIE: **Wǒ hěn máng. Nǐ ne?**

LǏ XIĀNSHENG: **Wǒ yě hěn máng.**

WÁNG XIǍOJIE: **Tā shì nǐ de tàitai* ma?**

LǏ XIĀNSHENG: **Shì. Tā shì wǒ tàitai, Yànfāng. Yànfāng, tā shì Wáng xiǎojie, wǒ de tóngxué.**

WÁNG XIǍOJIE: **Lǐ tàitai, nǐ hǎo ma?**

LǏ TÀITAI: **Wǒ hěn hǎo, xièxie. Wáng xiǎojie. Nǐ ne?**

WÁNG XIǍOJIE: **Wǒ yě hǎo. Xièxie.**

LǏ XIĀNSHENG: **Hǎo, hǎo, wǒmen zǒu le. Zàijiàn!**

WÁNG XIǍOJIE: **Zàijiàn, zàijiàn.**

ON THE STREET.

MR. LI: Miss Wang, I haven't seen you for a long time. Hello!

---

* Note that the word *tàitài* carries two fourth tones. However, in natural conversational Chinese, the second tone becomes neutral in some words. In this course, all such neutral tones are left unmarked, as in *tàitai*.

MISS WANG: Hello, Mr. Li! Long time no see.

MR. LI: Have you been busy lately?

MISS WANG: Quite busy, and you?

MR. LI: I've also been busy.

MISS WANG: Is this your wife?

MR. LI: Yes, this is my wife, Yanfang. Yanfang, this is Miss Wang, my class-mate.

MISS WANG: How are you, Mrs. Li?

MRS. LI: I'm fine, thank you, Miss Wang, and you?

MISS WANG: I'm fine too, thanks.

MR. LI: Good, good! Well, we'll be on our way. Good-bye.

MISS WANG: Bye-bye.

B. FĀYĪN (Pronunciation)

1. THE FOUR TONES

Every syllable in Chinese is pronounced with one of the four tones, or with the neutral tone. The first tone is pronounced at a relatively high pitch without variation in tone. The second tone is pronounced starting at a lower pitch which rises to the same pitch as the first tone, like in English when the pitch is raised at the end of a question. The third tone begins at a slightly higher pitch than the second tone, and dips even lower before returning to almost the same pitch as the first tone. The fourth tone starts at a high pitch and drops suddenly, like in English when the pitch falls at the end of a very emphatic statement.

first tone

second tone

third tone

fourth tone

Be careful to use the correct tone because, as you can see from the examples below, each sound can have a drastically different meaning depending on the tone used.

bī (to force)	**bí** (nose)	**bǐ** (to compare)	**bì** (wall)
dā (to build)	**dá** (to answer)	**dǎ** (dozen)	**dà** (big)
wēi (power)	**wéi** (small)	**wěi** (tail)	**wèi** (for)
yīng (cherry)	**yíng** (to win)	**yǐng** (shadow)	**yìng** (stiff)
wū (dark)	**wú** (nothing)	**wǔ** (five)	**wù** (error)
xī (west)	**xí** (to extinguish)	**xǐ** (to wash)	**xì** (drama)
qī (seven)	**qí** (to ride)	**qǐ** (to get up)	**qì** (steam)
qīng (light)	**qíng** (sunny)	**qǐng** (to invite)	**qìng** (to celebrate)

2. THE NEUTRAL TONE

Syllables which are pronounced with the neutral, or toneless tone, have no tone mark written over them in the *pīnyīn* system. Particles, such as *ma* and *ne* used in questions, are always pronounced with a neutral tone. The second syllables of reduplicated words are always pronounced with a neutral tone and the second syllables of some two-syllable words are toneless. Note the absence of tone marks in the following examples.

Nǐ hǎo <u>ma</u>?	How are you?
Xiè<u>xie</u>!	Thanks!
Tā shì Wáng xiǎo<u>jie</u>.	She is Miss Wang.

C. YŬFǍ HÉ YÒNGFǍ (Grammar and Usage)

1. WORDS AND SYLLABLES

In Chinese, each written character represents one syllable, and words are usually made up of one or two characters, sometimes more. Each word only has one form. Nouns take the same form whether single or plural. Verbs take the same form no matter who the subject is or when the action takes place; that is to say, verbs are not conjugated. Chinese uses single syllable particles to indicate various aspects of grammar, which in English might be indicated with prefixes, suffixes or verb tenses.

2. WORD ORDER FOR SIMPLE SENTENCES

The word order of a simple sentence is the same in Chinese as it is in English: the subject comes first, and then the predicate, or the verb.

Wǒ hěn hǎo, xièxie.
   I'm fine, thanks.

Tā shì wǒ tàitai.
   She is my wife.

3. NAMES AND TITLES

When presenting a full name in Chinese, the last name comes first and then the given name. Chinese given names are usually two syllables, but can also be one syllable. Last names are almost always one syllable.

Lǐ Yànfāng	Yanfang Li
Wáng Yǔ	Yu Wang

Titles come after names.

Wáng xiǎojie	Miss Wang
Wáng Xiǎoyīng xiǎojie	Miss Xiaoying Wang
Lǐ xiānsheng	Mr. Li
Huáng lǎoshī	Teacher Huang

4. ADJECTIVAL VERBS

Many adjectives in Chinese function as verbs. For example, the word *hǎo* means not only "good" but also "is good," "are good," etc. Therefore, when an adjectival verb is the main verb of a sentence, the verb "to be" is not used. *Hěn* (very) is often used before a single syllable adjectival verb, not to add to the meaning, but to provide a rhythmic balance to the sentence.

Wǒ hěn máng.
   I am busy.

Wǒ hěn hǎo.
   I am fine.

5. THE VERB *SHÌ* (TO BE)

Because of the existence of adjectival verbs in Chinese, the verb *shì* (to be) is used less often than in English. Sentences with *shì* are usually A = B sentences equating the subject (A) to another noun or pronoun (B).

Tā shì wǒ tàitai.
(A)   (B)
She is my wife.

Wáng Xiǎoyīng xiǎojie shì wǒ de tóngxué.
    (A)   (B)
Miss Xiaoying Wang is my classmate.

6. PRONOUNS AND POSSESSIVES

The same pronouns function as subjects and objects.

wǒ	I, me
nǐ	you
nín	you (polite form)
tā	he/she, him/her
wǒmen	we, us
nǐmen	you, all of you (general and polite form)
tāmen	they, them

The polite form *nín* is used to show respect. Young people use *nín* when speaking to those older than they are. *Nín* is also used when two people meet for the first time.

To form possessives, simply add the particle *de*. For example, *wǒ de* means "my" or "mine" and *tāmen de* means "their" or "theirs."

Tā shì nǐ de tàitai.
   She is your wife.

Wǒmen de lǎoshī hěn máng.
   Our teacher is busy.

De can also be added to names and other nouns to indicate possession. This corresponds to the "apostrophe s" in English.

Tā shì Lǐ Jūnmín de tàitai.
   She is Junmin Li's wife.

Huáng lǎoshī de tàitai hěn máng.
   Teacher Huang's wife is busy.

In casual conversation, the particle *de* is often omitted if it is attached to a pronoun.

Tā shì wǒ tàitai.
   She is my wife.

Wǒ tóngxué hěn máng.
   My classmate is busy.

7. SENTENCE FINAL QUESTION PARTICLES
MA AND *NE*

Chinese has several kinds of particles that have no meaning in and of themselves, but are added to the end of sentences to serve a variety of functions, such as signifying tense, suggestion or completion. The first particles you will learn are *ma* and *ne*, which are used at the end of sentences to form questions.

Most sentences can be turned into questions simply by adding the particle *ma* at the end.

Tā shì nǐ tàitai.
She is your wife.

Tā shì nǐ tàitai ma?
Is she your wife?

Nǐ hěn máng.
You are busy.

Nǐ máng ma?
Are you busy?

Note that *hěn* is not added to questions containing adjectival verbs.

The question particle *ne* is used in follow-up questions. Its implied meaning is "and what about [something or somebody]?"

Wǒ hěn máng. Nǐ ne?
I'm busy. And you?

Wǒ hěn hǎo. Nǐ ne?
I'm fine. How about you?

8. POSITION OF ADVERBS

Adverbs are always placed before the verb or adjectival verb that they modify.

Wǒ zuìjìn hěn hǎo.
I've been fine lately.

Tā tàitai yě máng ma?
Is his wife also busy?

D. HÀNZÌ (Characters)

There is no alphabet in Chinese. Each syllable is represented by a character that originally may have represented its meaning visually. In this course, you will begin to understand written Chinese by learning how to write some of the most useful words in characters.

The only way to learn a character is to memorize the sound, the meaning and how it is written. The way characters are written is very important; generally, the strokes, or lines, are written from the top left corner to the bottom right corner. With practice, the stroke order will become second nature.

Here are some characters from the dialogue. Practice writing them in the stroke order shown.

我 *wǒ* (I)

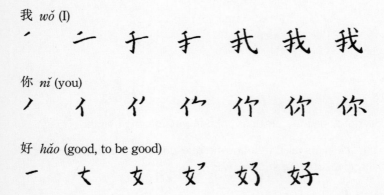

你 *nǐ* (you)

好 *hǎo* (good, to be good)

Look at the following short sentences to learn to recognize the characters.

你好！ *Nǐ hǎo!* (Hello!)

我好。 *Wǒ hǎo.* (I'm fine.)

E. SHĒNGCÍ (Vocabulary)

de	[possessive particle]
hǎo	good, fine
hǎo jiǔ bú jián	long time no see
hěn	very [used with adjectival verbs for balance]
lǎoshī	teacher
jiàn	to see
jiǔ	a long time
lù	street; road
ma	[question particle]
máng	to be busy

14

ne	[question particle]
nǐ	you
nǐmen	you (plural)
nín	you (formal)
shàng	on
shì	to be
tā	he/she, him/her
tāmen	they, them (plural)
tàitai	Mrs., wife
tóngxué	classmate
wǒ	I, me
wǒmen	we, us
xiānsheng	Mr., husband
xiǎojie	Miss, young woman
xièxie	thank you
yě	also
zài	[indicates position]
zàijiàn	good-bye
zǒu	to walk; to leave
zuìjìn	recently, lately

LIÀNXÍ (Exercises)

A. Choose the best Chinese word for the following situations.

1. What might you say when you see someone you haven't seen in a while?

   a. *Nǐ máng ma?*   b. *Hǎo jiǔ bú jiàn.*   c. *Zàijiàn.*

2. What do you say as a simple greeting?

   a. *Nǐ hǎo ma?*   b. *Zàijiàn.*   c. *Xièxie.*

3. What is the correct way to say Mr. Li in Chinese?

   a. *xiānsheng Lǐ*   b. *Lǐ*   c. *Lǐ xiānsheng*

4. How do you say good-bye?

    a. *zàijiàn*   b. *xièxie*   c. *hǎo*

B. Change the following sentences into questions using the particle *ma*.

1. *Tā shì Wáng xiānsheng.*
2. *Nǐmen zǒu.*
3. *Lǐ tàitai hěn máng.*
4. *Wáng xiǎojie hěn hǎo.*

C. Choose the appropriate response to the questions or sentences in column A from column B.

A	B
1. *Nǐ hǎo ma?*	a. *Wǒ yě hǎo.*
2. *Nǐ zuìjìn máng ma?*	b. *Wǒ hǎo.*
3. *Tā shì nǐ de xiānsheng ma?*	c. *Wǒ hěn máng.*
4. *Nǐ ne?*	d. *Tā shì wǒ xiānsheng.*

D. Translate the following from *pīnyīn* into English.

1. *Wǒ de xiānsheng zuìjìn hěn máng.*
2. *Wáng tàitai yě hǎo, xièxie.*
3. *Lǐ xiǎojie shì wǒ de tóngxué.*

E. Write the characters for the underlined words.

1. *Wǒ hěn <u>hǎo</u>, nǐ ne?*
2. *Tā shì <u>wǒ</u> de xiānsheng.*
3. *<u>Nǐ</u> zuìjìn máng ma?*

WÉNHUÀ ZHÙJIĚ (Cultural Note)

When Chinese friends run into each other on the street, they commonly greet each other by saying *Nǐ hǎo!* or *Nǐ hǎo ma?* if they want to strike up a conversation. If acquaintances are passing on the street and don't wish to stop, they might say *Nǐ chīfàn le ma?* (have you eaten?), or *Nǐ qù nǎr?* (where are you going?), or make a simple query on the activity of the other person, such as "oh, you are going to class?" Although these questions may seem prying to an American, a response is not expected and people are not trying to find out all the details of your everyday life. Male friends might shake hands when they run into each other and, increasingly, women are shaking hands as well. When strangers meet for the first time, handshaking is not as necessary as it is in the West, although when business people meet for the first time the exchange of business cards is obligatory. Kissing or hugging of any kind is rarely seen in public.

DÁÀN (Answer Key)

A. 1.b 2.a 3.c 4.a

B. 1. *Tā shì Wáng xiānsheng ma?* 2. *Nǐmen zǒu ma?* 3. *Lǐ tàitai máng ma?* 4.*Wáng xiǎojie hǎo ma?*

C. 1.b 2.c 3.d 4.a

D. 1. My husband has been very busy lately. 2. Mrs. Wang is also fine, thanks. 3. Miss Li is my classmate.

E. 1.好 2.我 3.你

DÌ ÈR KÈ
Lesson 2
NÍN ZUÒ SHÉNME GŌNGZUÒ? What do you do?

A. DUÌHUÀ (Dialogue)

ZÀI WǍNHUÌ.

Mr. Zhang starts a conversation with a stranger at a party.

ZHĀNG XIĀNSHENG: **Nín hǎo! Qǐngwèn, nín xìng shénme?**

GĀO XIĀNSHENG: **Wǒ xìng Gāo, wǒ jiào Zhuāng, nín ne?**

ZHĀNG XIĀNSHENG: **Wǒ xìng Zhāng, jiào Jìngzé.**

GĀO XIĀNSHENG: **Zhāng xiānsheng, nín zuò shénme gōngzuò?**

ZHĀNG XIĀNSHENG: **Wǒ zuò shēngyi.**

GĀO XIĀNSHENG: **O. Nín zài shénme gōngsī zuò shēngyi?**

ZHĀNG XIĀNSHENG: **Zài Měiguó Màoyì Gōngsī. Nín yě zuò shēngyi ma?**

GĀO XIĀNSHENG: **Bù. Wǒ bú zuò shēngyi. Wǒ jiāoshū.**

ZHĀNG XIĀNSHENG: **Nín jiāo shénme?**

GĀO XIĀNSHENG: **Wǒ zài Yǔyán Xuéyuàn jiāo wàiguórén Hànyǔ.**

ZHĀNG XIĀNSHENG: **Gāo lǎoshī, wǒ hěn gāoxìng rènshi nín.**

GĀO XIĀNSHENG: **Wǒ yě hěn gāoxìng rènshi nín.**

AT A PARTY.

MR. ZHANG: Hello. May I ask your surname?

MR. GAO: My surname is Gao. My first name is Zhuang. And you?

MR. ZHANG: My surname is Zhang, my first name is Jingze.

MR. GAO: Mr. Zhang, what kind of work do you do?

18

MR. ZHANG: I'm in business.

MR. GAO: Oh. At which company do you do business?

MR. ZHANG: At the American Trading Company. Are you (do you work) in business also?

MR. GAO: No, no, I'm not in business. I teach.

MR. ZHANG: What do you teach?

MR. GAO: I teach foreigners Chinese at the Language Institute.

MR. ZHANG: Teacher Gao, it's very nice to meet you.

MR. GAO: It's very nice to meet you, too.

B. FĀYĪN (Pronunciation)

1. INITIAL SOUNDS B, P, D, T, G, K

b	like the English <u>b</u>	**bān** to move; **bèi** to memorize; **bǎo** full
p	like the English p	**pǎo** to run; **pàng** fat; **pá** to climb
d	like the English <u>d</u>	**dōu** all; **děng** to wait; **dà** big
t	like the English <u>t</u>	**tīng** to listen; **tōu** to steal; **tà** to step on
g	like the English g	**gè** each; **gǎn** dare; **gào** to tell
k	like the English <u>k</u>	**kè** class; **kào** to lean on; **kǔ** bitter

2. TWO THIRD TONES TOGETHER

When two syllables that are both pronounced with the third tone follow each other directly in a sentence, the first syllable always changes to the second tone. For example, *hěn* (very) and *hǎo* (good) both take the third tone but in the sentence *Tā hěn hǎo* (he is fine), *hěn* takes the second tone. In the text, the initial third tone is marked as the third tone even when it is pronounced as a second tone. Here are some more examples.

Nǐ hǎo ma? (How are you?)
Hǎo jiǔ bú jiàn. (Long time no see.)

C. YŬFǍ HÉ YÒNGFǍ
(Grammar and Usage)

1. TALKING ABOUT NAMES: *XÌNG* VS. *JIÀO*

The verbs *xìng* and *jiào* both mean "to be named," but *xìng* is used exclusively with last names, while *jiào* is used with first names or whole names.

Wǒ xìng Wáng.
  My last name is Wang.

Wǒ jiào Xiǎoyīng.
  My first name is Xiaoying.

Wǒ jiào Wáng Xiǎoyīng.
  My name is Wang Xiaoying.

When meeting people for the first time, it is more polite to ask for their last name, *Nín xìng shénme?* (What is your surname?), or *Nín guì xìng?* (What is your honorable last name?) and then to ask for their first name, *Nín jiào shénme* (What is your first name?).

2. DIRECT AND INDIRECT OBJECTS

As in English, some Chinese verbs can take direct objects, indirect objects or both. The word order in such sentences is similar to the word order in English.

Wǒ zuò shēngyi.
  I do business.

Wǒ jiāo Hànyǔ.
  I teach Chinese.

Wǒ jiāo wàiguórén.
  I teach foreigners.

Wǒ jiāo wàiguórén Hànyǔ.
  I teach foreigners Chinese.

3. NEGATION WITH *BÙ*

The particle *bù* placed directly before a verb conveys negation. Note that when *bù* negates a single syllable verb, *hěn* (very) is not used.

Wǒ shì Měiguórén.   *Wǒ bú shì Měiguórén.*
  I am American.   I am not American.

Wǒ jiāoshū.
I teach.

Wǒ bù jiāoshū.
I don't teach.

Wǒ hěn máng.
I'm busy.

Wǒ bù máng.
I'm not busy.

4. DELETION OF SUBJECTS AND OBJECTS

In Chinese, subjects and objects can simply be deleted if they are understood from the context.

Wǒ xìng Gāo, wǒ jiào Zhuāng, nín ne?
Xìng Zhāng, jiào Jīngzé.
My last name is Gao and my first name is Zhuang, and you?
[My] last name is Zhang, [my] first name is Jingze.

When answering questions, subjects and objects are understood and often deleted. Positive responses can be just the verb and negative responses can be just the verb negated with *bù*.

Tā shì nǐ tàitai ma?
Shì.
Is she your wife?
Yes, [she is my wife].

Nǐ máng ma?
Bù máng. or *Máng.*
Are you busy?
No, [I'm not busy]. or Yes, [I'm busy].

5. QUESTION WORD *SHÉNME*

There are several question words in Chinese that function differently than the sentence final particles *ma* and *ne*, which you have already learned. *Shénme* can be used in two ways to ask "what?" It can replace the direct or indirect object under question in which case the position of *shénme* in the sentence is the same as what it replaces:

Nín jiāo shénme?
What do you teach? [You teach what?]

Wǒ jiāo Hànyǔ.
I teach Chinese.

Nín jiào shénme?
What is your first name? [Your first name is what?]

Wǒ jiào Jīngzé.
My name is Jingze.

Shénme can also modify a direct or indirect object to ask "what kind of?" or "which?" Here, *shénme* is placed directly before the object in question.

Nǐ zài shénme gōngsī gōngzuò?
Which company do you work for?

Nǐ zùo shénme gōngzuò?
What kind of work do you do?

6. ADVERBIAL PHRASES OF LOCATION USING *ZÀI*

Adverbial phrases of location consist of the preposition *zài* (at) and a place-name; the entire phrase is usually put before the verb.

Wǒ zài Měiguó jiāoshū.
I teach in America.

Tā zài Màoyì Gōngsī zuò shēngyi.
He does business at the Trading Company.

D. HÀNZÌ (Characters)

There are two different systems for writing Chinese characters—a traditional system and a simplified system. The traditional forms of characters contain more strokes than the simplified forms, which were introduced in China in the 1940s and 1950s in order to, obviously, simplify the writing system. Many characters are the same in both systems. In mainland China, only the simplified forms of characters are used, while in Taiwan and Hong Kong the traditional forms are predominant. In this book, you will learn the stroke order for the simplified forms, but when a traditional form exists you will see it in parentheses.

Here are more words for you to learn to write in characters. Note that the word for "teacher" has both a traditional and a simplified form. Follow the stroke order shown.

不 *bù* (not)

是 *shì* (to be)

老师 (老師)　　　　　*lǎoshī* (teacher)

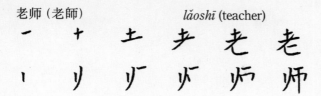

Compare the following two sentences.

我是老师。

Wǒ shì lǎoshī (I am a teacher.)

我不是老师。

Wǒ bú shì lǎoshī (I am not a teacher.)

E. SHĒNGCÍ (Vocabulary)

bù	not
gāoxìng	glad, happy
gōngsī	company
gōngzuò	work, job
guì	honorable
Hànyǔ	Chinese language
Hànzì	Chinese characters
jiào	to be called, to be (first) named
jiāo	to teach
jiāoshū	to teach in a school
màoyì	trade
Měiguó	America
Měiguórén	American person
qǐng	please, to invite
qǐngwèn	may I ask?
rén	person
rènshi	to recognize, to know (a person)
shēngyi	business
shénme	what
shū	book
wàiguó	foreign country
wàiguórén	foreign person
wǎnhuì	a party
wèn	to ask
xìng	to be (last) named, last name

xuéyuàn	institute
yǔyán	language
zài	at
zuò	to do (for work)

LIÀNXÍ (Exercises)

A. Answer the following questions in the negative.

1. *Nǐ xìng Wáng ma?*
2. *Nǐ shì lǎoshī ma?*
3. *Nǐ zuò shēngyi ma?*
4. *Nǐ jiào Lǐ Míng ma?*

B. Negate the following affirmative statements.

1. *Wǒ jiào Zhāng Aìméi.*
2. *Lǐ xiānsheng zuìjìn zuò shēngyi.*
3. *Tā shì wàiguórén.*
4. *Zhāng tàitai hěn máng.*

C. Combine the pairs of phrases using *zài* (at) to make a complete sentence and then translate into English.

EXAMPLE: *Tā gōngzuò. Yǔyán Xuéyuàn.*
         Tā zài Yǔyán Xuéyuàn gōngzuò.
         She works at the Language Institute.

1. *Wǒ zuò shēngyi. Měiguó.*
2. *Wǒ lǎoshī jiāoshū. Yǔyán Xuéyuàn.*
3. *Tā zuò shēngyi. Měiguó Màoyì Gōngsī.*

D. Translate the following sentences into *pīnyīn*.

1. What do you do?
2. What do you teach?
3. I am very glad to know you, too.
4. I teach foreigners to do business.

E. Match the English to the Chinese characters.

1. 你不是老师。   a. I'm a teacher.
2. 我不好。   b. You aren't a teacher.
3. 我是老师。   c. Hello.
4. 你好！   d. I'm not fine.

WÉNHUÀ ZHÙJIĚ (Cultural Note)

Chinese society is particularly sensitive to age and status, and this is reflected in the ways in which people address one another. Only close friends are on a first name basis. Only friends who are extremely close will use nicknames like *Xiǎo Wáng* (Little Wang) and *Lǎo Lǐ* (Old Li). Otherwise, a last name and a title, or just a title, are required when employees address employers, when students address teachers and when younger people address their elders. There is a certain amount of respect accorded in these relationships in the opposite direction as well: employers and teachers will address those of lower status and rank with their whole name, last name first, rather than just the first name. Children are also taught to respect adults who are strangers by calling them *āyí* (auntie) or *shūshu* (uncle).

Given all the respect between people in China, it may be surprising to a foreigner to be called *lǎowài* (old outsider) by strangers as they walk down the street. This nickname is not meant to offend but rather as a term of endearment. Even when it is shouted on the streets in China, it just means that people are curious to get a look at you.

DÁÀN (Answer Key)

A. 1. *Wǒ bú xìng Wáng.* 2. *Wǒ bú shì lǎoshī.* 3. *Wǒ bú zuò shēngyi.* 4. *Wǒ bú jiào Lǐ Míng.*

B. 1. *Wǒ bú jiào Zhāng Àiméi.* 2. *Lǐ xiānsheng zuìjìn bú zuò shēngyi.* 3. *Tā bú shì wàiguórén.* 4. *Zhāng tàitai bù máng.*

C. 1. *Wǒ zài Měiguó zuò shēngyi.* I do business in the United States. 2. *Wǒ lǎoshī zài Yǔyán Xuéyuàn jiāoshū.* My teacher teaches at the Language Institute. 3. *Tā zài Měiguó Màoyì Gōngsī zuò shēngyi.* He works at the American Trade Company.

D. 1. *Nǐ zuò shénme gōngzuò?* 2. *Nǐ jiāo shénme?* 3. *Wǒ yě hěn gāoxìng rènshi nín.* 4. *Wǒ jiāo wàiguórén zuò shēngyi.*

E. 1.b 2.d 3.a 4.c

DÌ SĀN KÈ
Lesson 3
JIĀRÉN. The Family.

A. DUÌHUÀ (Dialogue)

ZÀI CHÁGUǍN.

Xiaoying is having tea with Amy Stone, an American who is teaching English in Beijing.

XIǍOYĪNG: **Aìméi, qǐngwèn, nǐ de jiā yǒu jǐ ge rén?**

AÌMÉI: **Wǒ jiā yǒu liù ge rén. Yǒu māma, bàba, gēge, mèimei, dìdi hé wǒ. Tāmen dōu zhù zài Měiguó Niǔyuē Shì.**

XIǍOYĪNG: **Nǐ de fùmǔ zuò shénme gōngzuò?**

AÌMÉI: **Wǒ mǔqīn dāng dàifu, wǒ de fùqīn jiāo gāozhōng xuéshēng. Wǒ mèimei dàxué bìyè yǐhòu, xiǎng xuéxí yīshù. Wǒ jiārén dōu shì lǎoshī huòzhě dàifu.**

XIǍOYĪNG: **Nǐ xiǎng bù xiǎng tāmen?**

AÌMÉI: **Wǒ dāngrán xiǎng tāmen. Nǐ de jiārén dōu zhù zài Běijīng ma?**

XIǍOYĪNG: **Wǒ fùmǔ dōu tuìxiū le, zhù zài Běijīng. Wo chángchang qù kàn tāmen. Wǒ yě yǒu liǎng ge jiějie. Tāmen yě zài Běijīng gōngzuò. Wǒ méiyǒu xiōngdì.**

AÌMÉI: **Wǒ xīwàng yǒu jīhuì rènshi nǐ de jiārén!**

AT A TEAHOUSE.

XIAOYING: Amy, will you tell me how many people are in your family?

AMY: There are six people in my family—my mother, father, older brother, younger sister, younger brother and me. They all live in the United States in New York City.

XIAOYING: What do your parents do for a living?

AMY: My mother is a doctor and my father teaches high school students. When my younger sister graduates from college, she is thinking about studying medicine. The people in my family are all either doctors or teachers.

XIAOYING: Do you miss them?

AMY: Of course I miss them. Does your family all live in Beijing?

XIAOYING: My parents are both retired and living in Beijing. I go to see them often. I also have two older sisters who work in Beijing, too. I don't have any brothers.

AMY: I hope I have the chance to meet your family!

B. FĀYĪN (Pronunciation)

1. INITIAL SOUNDS Z, C, S, ZH, CH, SH, J, Q, X

z	like the <u>ds</u> in yar<u>ds</u>	**zài** again; **zǎo** early; **zuǒ** left
c	like the <u>ts</u> in i<u>ts</u> but with a strong puff of air	**cǎo** grass; **cóng** from; **cài** vegetables
s	like the English <u>s</u>	**sān** three; **sè** color; **suǒ** lock
zh	like the <u>j</u> in june but shorter and crisper	**zhuō** table; **zhōu** state; **zhàn** station
ch	like the <u>ch</u> in <u>ch</u>urch but with the tongue curled further back	**chá** tea; **chōu** to smoke, to draw; **chū** to go out
sh	like the <u>sh</u> in <u>sh</u>out but with the tongue curled further back	**shōu** to receive; **shā** to kill; **shū** book
j	like the <u>d and y</u> combination in "and <u>y</u>et" but with the tongue against the lower teeth	**jiā** home; **jìn** come in; **jǐ** some
q	like the <u>t and y</u> combination in "won'<u>t you</u>" but with the tongue against the lower teeth	**qì** air; **qiū** autumn; **qún** skirt

| x | like the s and y combination in "yes you" but with the tongue against the lower teeth | **xī** west; **xiě** to write; **xuě** snow |

2. TONE CHANGES WITH *BÙ*

The negation particle *bù* is pronounced in the fourth tone, but when it is followed by another fourth tone it takes the second tone. This change is marked in the text.

Wǒ bú zuò shēngyi. (I don't do business.)

C. YǓFǍ HÉ YÒNGFǍ
(Grammar and Usage)

1. MEASURE WORD *GÈ*

In Chinese, when expressing how many of a person or a thing, a measure word needs to be used in between the number and the noun. Different types of nouns require different measure words, and these will be introduced in subsequent lessons. *Gè* is the most common measure word and is used with people as well as with other general nouns. When in doubt about a specific measure word, *gè* can be substituted.

*Wǒ yǒu yí ge dìdi.**
I have one younger brother.

Wǒ de sān ge mèimei dōu zài Niǔyūe zhù.
My three young sisters all live in New York.

2. NUMBERS 0–10

líng	zero
yī	one
èr	two
sān	three
sì	four
wǔ	five
liù	six

---

* *Note:* Although *gè* is fourth tone, it is most often pronounced and written without a tone.

qī	seven
bā	eight
jiǔ	nine
shí	ten

3. *ÈR* VS. *LIǍNG*

In counting, *èr* is the word for two. However, when a noun is being measured or counted, *liǎng* is used instead of *èr*.

yī, èr, sān
   one, two, three

Wǒ yǒu liǎng ge dìdi.
   I have two younger brothers.

4. NEGATION OF *YǑU* (TO HAVE)

You have already seen that *bù* is used to negate verbs. The exception is the verb *yǒu* (to have). *Yǒu* is negated by putting *méi* in front of it.

Wǒ méiyǒu Měiguó péngyou.
   I don't have American friends.

Tā méiyǒu mèimei.
   He doesn't have any younger sisters.

Nǐ méiyǒu jiějie.
   You don't have an older sister.

5. QUESTION WORD *JǏ*

The question word *jǐ* (how many) must always be used with a measure word. In answering this type of question, simply replace *jǐ* with the correct number.

Nǐ yǒu jǐ ge gēge?
   How many older brothers do you have?

Wǒ yǒu liǎng ge gēge.
   I have two older brothers.

6. CONJUNCTION *HÉ*

The conjunction *hé* (and) functions differently in Chinese than in English. *Hé* is only used to connect two nouns and, unlike English, cannot be used to connect verbs or phrases.

Wǒ hé wǒ māma dōu dāng lǎoshī.
My mother and I are both teachers.

Tā yǒu yí ge gēge hé yí ge mèimei.
He has an older brother and a younger sister.

7. THE ADVERB *DŌU*

The adverb *dōu* (all, both) is placed after the subject and before the verb. It is used more commonly in Chinese than "all" is used in English, especially if the subject of a sentence is plural and contains the conjunction *hé*.

Wǒmen dōu shì lǎoshī.
We are all teachers.

Tā hé tā tàitai dōu hěn máng.
He and his wife are both busy.

When *yě* and *dōu* are used in the same sentence, *yě* comes before *dōu*.

Wǒmen yě dōu shì lǎoshī.
We are all teachers also.

D. HÀNZÌ (Characters)

In China, you will see numbers written in figures, e.g., 1, 2, 3 . . . , on buses, train schedules, etc. Numbers written in characters are also common, so it is worth being able to recognize and write them.

一   *yī* (one)

二   *èr* (two)

三   *sān* (three)

四   *sì* (four)

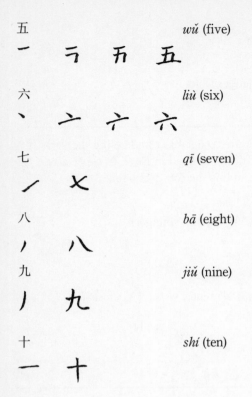

五   *wǔ* (five)

一   丂   五   五

六   *liù* (six)

丶   亠   六   六

七   *qī* (seven)

丿   七

八   *bā* (eight)

丿   八

九   *jiǔ* (nine)

丿   九

十   *shí* (ten)

一   十

E. SHĒNGCÍ (Vocabulary)

bàba	dad
bìyè	to graduate
cháguǎn	teahouse, tea room
chángchang	often
dàifu	doctor
dāng	work as, serve as
dāngrán	of course
dìdi	younger brother
dōu	all
fùqīn	father
fùmǔ	parents
gāozhōng	high school
ge	[general measure word]
gēge	older brother
hé	and
huòzhě	or

jǐ	how many
jiějie	older sister
jiěmèi	sisters (older or younger)
jīhuì	opportunity
māma	mom
méi	[particle for negation]
mèimei	younger sister
mǔqīn	mother
Niǔyuē	New York
shì	city
tuìxiū	to retire
xiǎng	to miss, to want to
xiōngdì	brothers (older or younger)
xīwàng	hope
xuéxí	to learn, to study
yīshēng	doctor
yīshù	medicine
yǒu	to have
zhù	to live

LIÀNXÍ (Exercises)

A. Make the negative sentences positive and the positive sentences negative.

1. *Tā shì wǒ bàba.*
2. *Tā bù máng.*
3. *Wǒ dìdi bú zài Běijīng jiāoshū.*
4. *Gāo xiānsheng yǒu yí ge mèimei.*
5. *Wǒ méiyǒu gōngzuò.*

B. Turn the following statements into questions using *jǐ*.

1. *Wǒ yǒu yí ge mèimei.*
2. *Wǒ xiānsheng de jiā yǒu wǔ ge rén.*
3. *Tā yǒu sān ge lǎoshī.*

C. Combine the following sentences using *dōu*.

1. *Wǒ shì lǎoshī. Wǒ jiějie yě shì lǎoshī.*
2. *Wáng xiǎojie jiào Yīng. Lǐ tàitai yě jiào Yīng.*

3. *Tā xiànzài zuò màoyì. Wǒ xiànzài yě zuò màoyì.*
4. *Zhāng xiǎojie yǒu yí ge jiějie. Lín xiānsheng yě yǒu yí ge jiějie.*
5. *Tā bú zuò shēngyi. Tā tàitai yě bú zuò shēngyi.*

D. Translate the following sentences into Chinese *pīnyīn*.

1. Do your mother and father both work?
2. Is that your older brother?
3. I don't have a younger sister.
4. How many people are there in your family?
5. I have one younger brother.

E. Write the Chinese characters for the numbers one through ten.

WÉNHUÀ ZHÙJIĚ (Cultural Note)

In a traditional Chinese family, members of every generation lived together in the same house or in adjacent houses. In order to specify family relationships within these close quarters, family terms in Chinese are much more exact than they are in English. As you know, there are different words for older sister, *jiějie*, and younger sister, *mèimei*, as well as for older brother, *gēge*, and younger brother, *dìdi*. It gets even more complicated. Where we use "uncle" to refer to many different people, for example, in Chinese there are different words for "the oldest uncle on the father's side," *dàbó*, and for "all uncles on the mother's side," *jiùjiu*. Today, the tradition of children taking care of retired parents lives on. Elderly parents live with one of their children, often the oldest son, and it is not uncommon for the parent of a retired parent to live there also. Familial situations are beginning to change, however, with the government-imposed limit of one child per couple. The new generation of only children might find the responsibility of caring for parents to be too much of a burden without the help of siblings. Other solutions are being explored—nursing homes and retirement communities—but it may be that the traditional concept of duty that children feel for their parents is one that even modern practicalities can't change.

DÁÀN (Answer Key)

A. 1. *Tā bú shì wǒ bàba.* 2. *Tā hěn máng.* 3. *Wǒ dìdi zài Běijīng jiāoshū.*
4. *Gāo xiānsheng méiyǒu mèimei* 5. *Wǒ yǒu gōngzuò.*

B. 1. *Nǐ yǒu jǐ ge mèimei?* 2. *Nǐ xiānsheng de jiā yǒu jǐ ge rén?* 3. *Tā yǒu jǐ ge lǎoshī?*

C. 1. *Wǒ hé wǒ jiějie dōu shì lǎoshī.* 2. *Wáng xiǎojie hé Lǐ tàitai dōu jiào Yīng.* 3. *Tā hé wǒ xiànzài dōu zuò màoyì.* 4. *Zhāng xiǎojie hé Lín xiānsheng dōu yǒu yí ge jiějie.* 5. *Tā hé tā tàitai dōu bú zuò shēngyi.*

D. 1. *Nǐ māma hé nǐ bàba dōu gōngzuò ma?* 2. *Nà shì nǐ de gēge ma?* 3. *Wǒ méiyǒu mèimei.* 4. *Nǐ jiā yǒu jǐ ge rén.* 5. *Wǒ yǒu yí ge dìdi.*

E. 一二三四五六七八九十

DÌ SÌ KÈ
Lesson 4
GUÓJÍ. Nationalities.

A. DUÌHUÀ (Dialogue)

ZÀI BÀNGŌNGSHÌ.

David Stone, an American working in Beijing, asks Song Xuezhi about a new foreign colleague in his office.

DÀWÈI: **Sòng Xuézhì, nǐ jiànguò wǒmen de xīn tóngshì ma? Tā shì nǎ guó rén?**

XUÉZHÌ: **Wǒ bú rènshi tā, kěshì wǒ zhīdào tā bú shì Měiguó rén. Tā dàgài shì Déguórén. Wǒmen de gōngsī xiànzài yào gēn Déguó duō zuò mǎimài, suǒyǐ wǒmen yīnggāi yǒu Déguó de zhuānjiā.**

DÀWÈI: **Tā shénme shíhòu yào lái, nǐ zhīdào bù zhīdào?**

XUÉZHÌ: **Dàgài zhège yuè yào lái. Zhè shì tā dì yí cì lái Zhōngguó, suǒyǐ wǒmen dōu yīnggāi qǐng tā chīfàn, huānyíng tā.**

DÀWÈI: **Hǎo. Wǒmen yě yīnggāi qǐng wǒmen de Rìběn tóngshì.**

XUÉZHÌ: **Hěn hǎo.**

AT THE OFFICE.

DAVID: Song Xuezhi, have you met our new colleague? What country is he from?

XUEZHI: I haven't met him, but I know he isn't American. He's probably German. Our company wants to do more business with Germany, so we should have a German expert.

DAVID: When is he coming, do you know?

XUEZHI: Probably this month. It's his first time in China, so we should all invite him out to dinner to welcome him.

DAVID: Okay. We should also invite our Japanese colleague.

XUEZHI: Great!

B. FĀYĪN (Pronunciation)

1. INITIAL SOUNDS *M, F, N, L*

m	like the English m	**mā** mother; **mén** door; **míng** bright
f	like the English f	**fàn** food; **fēng** wind; **fù** father
n	like the English n	**nán** male; **nǚ** female; **nǎ** which
l	like the English l	**lěng** cold; **lā** to pull; **lán** blue

2. TONE CHANGES WITH *YĪ*

Yī (one) is pronounced in the first tone when it is just a number, but when it is followed by other syllables the tone can change—it is pronounced in the second tone before a fouth tone, in the fourth tone before another first tone and in the fourth tone before a first, second or third tone. Since *gè* takes the fourth tone, the tone of *yī* changes to the second tone before *gè*, even when *ge* is not pronounced with a strong tone. The tones are changed in these ways as necessary in the text.

Zhè shì dì yí kè.
This is lesson one.

Wǒ chī yìxiē jiǎozi.
I am eating some dumplings.

Wǒmen yìqǐ qù.
We are going together.

Tā yǒu yí ge lǎoshī.
He has one teacher.

C. YǓFǍ HÉ YÒNGFǍ
(Grammar and Usage)

1. ALTERNATIVE QUESTIONS

You have already learned to use the question particle *ma* at the end of a sentence to form a question. Another common question construction is "verb-not-verb," found in the usual verb position in a sentence. Thus, *Nǐ shì Měiguórén ma?* (Are you American?) can also be expressed as *Nǐ shì bú shì Měiguórén?*

Other examples:

Tā máng bù máng?
   Is she busy?

Nǐ zhīdào bù zhīdào?
   Do you know?

Tā yǒu méiyǒu mèimei?
   Does she have a younger sister?

2. DEMONSTRATIVES

When the demonstratives *zhè* (this) and *nèi* (that) are used to modify a noun, a measure word, such as *ge*, must be used.

Zhège gōngsī yào gēn Déguó duō zuò mǎimài.
   This company wants to do more business with Germany.

Nèige yuè wǒ méiyǒu shíjiān.
   I don't have any time that month.

Demonstratives can also serve as the subject of a sentence, but in this case *nà* is used for "that" instead of *nèi*. Notice that no measure word is used in this case.

Zhè shì wǒ de māma.
   This is my mother.

Nà shì wǒ de mèimei.
   That is my younger sister.

3. QUESTION WORD *NǍ*

The question word *nǎ* has two functions. It can mean "where?" when placed at the end of a simple sentence. When in this position, *nǎ* is pronounced either *nǎr* (in the Northern accent) or *nǎli* (in the Southern accent).

Tā zhù zài nǎr?
   Where does she live?

Nǐ qù nǎli?
   Where are you going?

You learned about adverbial phrases of location with *zài* in lesson 2. You can replace the location name with *nǎr* or *nǎli* to form a question.

Wáng xiǎojie zài Běijīng Dàxué xuéxí Hànyǔ.
Miss Wang studies Chinese at Beijing University.

Wáng xiǎojie zài nǎr xuéxí Hànyǔ?
Where does Miss Wang study Chinese?

Nǎ can also ask "which," as in the following examples where *nǎ* replaces a place-name or a demonstrative.

Tā shì nǎ guó rén?
Which country is he from?

Nǎge shì nǐ de?
Which one is yours?

4. ADVERBIAL PHRASES OF TIME

You have already learned that adverbial phrases of location with *zài* are placed before the verb. This is also the case with adverbial phrases of time.

Wǒmen xīn tóngshì míngtiān yào lái.
Our new colleague is coming tomorrow.

Nǐ xiàge yuè yǒu kòng ma?
Do you have time next month?

When a sentence contains adverbial phrases of both time and place, the rule is that time comes before place.

Tā jīnnián zài Běijīng xuéxí.
He is studying in Beijing this year.

5. MODAL VERBS *YÀO* AND *YĪNGGĀI*

In English, modal verbs are verbs such as "can," "could," "should" and "must," which are followed directly by another verb. Modal verbs in Chinese also come before the main verb. Take *yào* (to want to) and *yīnggāi* (should) as examples:

Wǒmen yīnggāi qǐng tā chī wǎnfàn.
We should ask him to dinner.

Wǒmen gōngsī yào zuò màoyì.
Our company wants to do some trade.

6. CONJUNCTIONS *KĚSHÌ* AND *SUŎYĬ*

The conjunction *kěshì* (but) and *suŏyĭ* (therefore, so) are used to connect two clauses. They can also be placed at the beginning of a sentence to respond to a previous idea, much as in English.

Wŏ bú rènshi tā, kěshì wŏ zhīdào tā bú shì Měiguórén.
   I don't know him, but I know he isn't American.

Kěshì wŏ bù zhīdào!
   But I don't know!

Tā shì Měiguórén, suŏyĭ tā bú shì Déguó rén.
   He's American, so he isn't German.

Suŏyĭ, wŏmen yào zŏu.
   Therefore, we're going.

7. ORDINAL NUMBERS

To express "first, second, third . . . ," place the word *dì* in front of any number. You will notice that the lessons in this book are numbered in this way; *dì wŭ kè* literally means "the fifth lesson."

Zhè shì nĭ dì yí cì lái Zhōngguó ma?
   Is this your first time in China?

Wŏ dì sān ge lăoshī hěn hǎo.
   My third teacher is really good.

D. HÀNZÌ (Characters)

It is common in Chinese to see one syllable forming a part of several different words, all of which are similar in meaning. For example, when *guó* (country) is paired with *zhōng* (middle) you have the country name "China." *Guó* (country) with *měi* (beautiful) becomes the country name "America." It is easy to see this when you look at the characters.

国 （國）   *guó* (country)

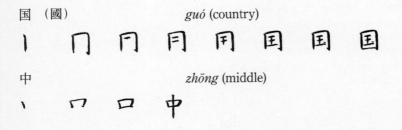

中   *zhōng* (middle)

40

美   *měi* (beautiful)

中国（中國）   *Zhōngguó* (China)

美国（美國）   *Měiguó* (America)

Here are two most useful characters and some sentences for practice.

人   *rén* (person)

他   *tā* (he)

她   *tā* (she)

他是中国人。

    Tā shì Zhōngguórén. (He is Chinese)

我是美国人。

    Wǒ shì Měiguórén (I am American)

E. SHĒNGCÍ (Vocabulary)

bànfǎ	method
chīfàn	to eat
dàgài	probably
Déguó	Germany
Déguórén	German person
Fǎguó	France
Fǎguórén	French person
guójí	nationality
huānyíng	to welcome
jiàn	to see
jīnnián	this year
kěshì	but
mǎimài	business, trade
nǎ	which

nà/nèi	that
qǐng	to invite
Rìběn	Japan
shàngge	last
shíhòu	time
suǒyǐ	therefore
tóngshì	colleague
xiàge	next
xiànzài	now
xīn	new
yào	to want to, to plan to
yīnggāi	should
yuè	month
zhīdào	to know
Zhōngguó	China
zhuānjiā	expert
zuò mǎimài	to do business

SUPPLEMENTARY VOCABULARY 1: PLACE-NAMES

Note that while two-syllable country names contain the syllable *guó* (country), three-syllable country names do not. *Zhōu* means "continent."

Déguó	Germany
Éguó	Russia
Fǎguó	France
Fēizhōu	Africa
Hánguó	Korea
Jiānádà	Canada
Měiguó	America, USA
Nán Měizhōu	South America
Ōuzhōu	Europe
Rìběn	Japan
Yǎzhōu	Asia
Yìdàlì	Italy
Yīngguó	England
Yuènán	Vietnam
Xībānyá	Spain
Zhōngguó	China

42

LIÀNXÍ (Exercises)

A. Change the following questions with ma into alternative questions.

    1. *Nǐ shì wàiguó zhuānjiā ma?*
    2. *Nǐ yǒu mèimei ma?*
    3. *Nǐmen yào chīfàn ma?*
    4. *Nǐ xiàge yuè yǒu kòng ma?*

B. Place the adverbial time phrases into the proper position in the sentences according to the clues in parentheses.

    1. *Wǒmen xīn tóngshì yào lái.* (tomorrow)
    2. *Nǐ yǒu méiyǒu kòng?* (next month)
    3. *Tā māma qǐng wǒ chīfàn.* (today)
    4. *Wǒ zài Běijīng gōngzuò.* (now)

C. Translate the following sentences into *pīnyīn* using the modal verbs *yào* or *yīnggāi*.

    1. You should eat.
    2. I want to eat.
    3. You should study in Beijing this year.
    4. I want to study in Beijing this year.

D. Write the Chinese characters for the underlined words.

    1. *Wǒ jiā yǒu <u>wǔ</u> ge rén.* (There are five people in my family.)
    2. *Tā shì <u>Zhōngguórén</u>.* (She is Chinese.)
    3. *Wǒ <u>bú shì</u> Zhōngguórén.* (I'm not Chinese.)
    4. *<u>Tā</u> bú shì <u>Měiguórén</u>.* (He is not American.)
    5. *<u>Wǒ lǎoshī shì Měiguórén</u>.* (My teacher is American.)

E. Translate the following into English.

    1. 中国人好。
    2. 我是美国人。
    3. 他是美国人。

WÉNHUÀ ZHÙJIĚ (Cultural Note)

When foreigners go to China to work for a company or a university, they are often called *wàiguó zhuānjiā* (foreign experts) and accorded privileged treatment as well as spacious housing and office space. It is also not uncommon for a foreign visitor to be given a welcoming dinner in his/her honor and to be assigned a local helper to be shown about town. Although this might be uncomfortable for foreigners working in China, most Chinese people aren't bothered by the discrepancy between the local living situation and the lives led by visitors. The general conception is that if foreigners travel a long way to live in China, they should be treated with gratitude and made as comfortable as possible. At the same time, it rests upon the visitor to express appreciation for being treated so well. It is a good idea to bring small gifts from home to give to guides, drivers and others who might help you during your stay. And, of course, to throw a dinner party for your colleagues and hosts goes a long way in expressing thanks and maintaining a good relationship with those you meet in China.

DÁÀN (Answer Key)

A. 1. *Nǐ shì bú shì wàiguó zhuānjiā?* 2. *Nǐ yǒu méiyǒu mèimei?* 3. *Nǐmen yào bú yào chīfàn?* 4. *Nǐ xiàge yuè yǒu méiyǒu kòng?*

B. 1. *Wǒmen xīn tóngshì míngtiān yào lái.* 2. *Nǐ xiàge yuè yǒu méiyǒu kòng?* 3. *Tā māma jīntiān qǐng wǒ chīfàn.* 4. *Wǒ xiànzài zài Běijīng gōngzuò.*

C. 1. *Nǐ yīnggāi chīfàn.* 2. *Wǒ yào chīfàn.* 3. *Nǐ jīnnián yīnggāi zài Běijīng xuéxí.* 4. *Wǒ jīnnián yào zài Běijīng xuéxí.*

D. 1.五 2.中国 3.不是 4.他，美国人 5.我老师是美国人。

E. 1. Chinese people are great. 2. I am American. 3. He is American.

DÌ WǓ KÈ
Lesson 5
SHÍJIĀN. Time.

A. DUÌHUÀ (Dialogue)

ZÀI YÒUÉRYUÁN.

Mrs. Wang and Mrs. Lin are waiting to pick up their children at kindergarten.

WÁNG TÀITAI: **Lín tàitai, xiànzài jǐdiǎn zhōng?**

LÍN TÀITAI: **Liùdiǎn shífēn. Yòuéryuán jīntiān wǎn yìdiǎnr xiàkè. Nǐ zuìjìn zěnmeyàng?**

WÁNG TÀITAI: **Xiànzài wǒ tǐng máng. Wǒ měitiān zǎoshàng liùdiǎn bàn qǐchuáng. Xiān chī zǎofàn ránhòu sòng háizi lái yòuéryuán. Qīdiǎn shífēn shàngbān. Wǒ méiyǒu shíjiān zuò biéde shì.**

LÍN TÀITAI: **Xiàbān yǐhòu zuò shénme? Jǐdiǎn shuìjiào?**

WÁNG TÀITAI: **Wǒ huíjiā yǐhòu, chī wǎnfàn, qīnglǐ fángzi, gēn wǒ àirén tán yì tán huòzhě kàn diànshì. Yǒu de shíhòu wǒmen qù wàibiān chī yìdiǎn fàn. Kěshì yǒu háizi, yě yǒu gōngzuò bù róngyì.**

LÍN TÀITAI: **Wǒ tóngyì.**

WÁNG TÀITAI: **Tāmen lái le. Zàijiàn!**

AT THE KINDERGARTEN.

MRS. WANG: Mrs. Lin, what time is it?

MRS. LIN: It's 6:10. Kindergarten is getting out a bit late today. How've you been?

MRS. WANG: I'm quite busy now. Everyday I get up at 6:30. First I have breakfast and then bring my child to kindergarten. I get to work at 7:10. I don't have time to do anything else.

MRS. LIN: What do you do after work? What time do you get to bed?

MRS. WANG: After I get home, I have dinner, clean the house, talk with my husband or watch TV. Sometimes we go out to eat. But having a kid and a job at the same time isn't easy.

MRS. LIN: I agree.

MRS. WANG: Here they come. Bye!

B. FĀYĪN (Pronunciation)

1. SEMIVOWEL INITIAL SOUNDS

h	like the guttural German <u>ach</u> with the back of the tongue raised and air forced through	**hé** and; **hàn** sweat; **hěn** very
y	like the English <u>y</u>	**yě** also; **yuǎn** far; **yī** one
w	like the English <u>w</u>	**wǒ** I; **wèn** to ask; **wǔ** five

2. *R* SOUNDS

When *r* is in the initial position, it is pronounced like the *r* in the run except that the tongue is curled and presses above the upper teeth and the lips are in a "smile" position.

r **rén** person; **rè** hot; **ruǎn** soft

The same sound is also heard in the final position of a syllable if the initial sound is *zh, ch, sh* or *r* and the final sound is represented in *pīnyīn* with *i*. Note that this pronunciation is regional. The final *i* is pronounced this way only in the north of China, especially in Beijing. In the south of China and in Taiwan, the tongue is never curled back so the final *i* sound is more similar to the <u>e</u> in sh<u>e</u>. Since the *r* sound is what is used in standard Mandarin pronunciation, it is the one you will learn here.

zhǐ paper
chī to eat
shì to be
rì sun

The final sound *er* is pronounced like the English <u>are</u>.

èr two

46

C. YǓFǍ HÉ YÒNGFǍ
(Grammar and Usage)

1. NUMBERS 11–99

To form the numbers 11–99, simply combine the word for the first digit with the word for the second digit.

11	*shíyī (shí + yī)*
15	*shíwǔ (shí + wǔ)*
20	*èrshí (èr + shí)*
29	*èrshíjiǔ (èr + shí + jiǔ)*
34	*sānshísì (sān + shí + sì)*
56	*wǔshíliù (wǔ + shí + liù)*
78	*qīshíbā (qī + shí + bā)*
99	*jiǔshíjiǔ (jiǔ + shí + jiǔ)*

2. TELLING TIME

When talking about clock time, these expressions are useful.

Xiànzài shì jǐdiǎn (zhōng)?
   What time is it now?

Xiànzài shì jǐdiǎn jǐfēn?
   What time it is now? (What hour and what minute?)

xiànzài shì . . .
   It is now . . .

Diǎn or *diǎn zhōng* mean "hour" and *fēn* means "minute." Time is counted in the same way as it is in English, on a twelve-hour clock.

yìdiǎn or *yìdiǎn zhōng*
   one o'clock

liùdiǎn or *liùdiǎn zhōng*
   six o'clock

sānfēn
   three minutes

èrshí wǔfēn
   twenty-five minutes

liǎngdiǎn shísìfēn
    2:14

The word *kè* is also used, with a number, for a quarter of an hour, and *bàn* is used for a half an hour (two quarters of an hour is not used).

sāndiǎn yíkè
    3:15

sāndiǎn bàn
    3:30

When the time is more than 45 minutes past the hour, the word *chà* (short of) can be used to express the number of minutes until the next hour.

liùdiǎn chà shífēn
    ten minutes to six

liùdiǎn chà yíkè
    a quarter to six

The following words are used to indicate the time of day. In a sentence, they are placed before the clock time.

zǎoshàng
    morning (usually before 10:00)

shàngwǔ
    morning (usually after 10:00)

zhōngwǔ
    noon

xiàwǔ
    afternoon

wǎnshàng
    evening

Xiànzài shì zǎoshàng qīdiǎn èrshífēn.
    Now it's 7:20 in the morning.

Wǒ dìdi shàngwǔ shíyīdiǎn chà yíkè shàngkè.
    My younger brother attends class at a quarter to eleven in the morning.

3. BEFORE AND AFTER

Yǐqián (before) and *yǐhòu* (after) are placed in a sentence directly after a time or event.

bādiǎn yǐqián
  before 8:00

shídiǎn sìshífēn yǐhòu
  after 10:40

chī zǎofàn yǐqián
  before eating breakfast

xiàbān yǐhòu
  after getting off work

Nǐ chī wǎnfàn yǐhòu zuò shénme?
  What do you do after having dinner?

Shàngbān yǐqián, wǒ sòng háizi qù yòuéryuán.
  Before work, I send my kid to kindergarten.

4. THE EXPRESSION *DE SHÍHÒU*

The expression *de shíhòu* means "while [doing something]." It is placed between two phrases that are occuring at the same time. Examine the following examples:

Wǒ chīfàn de shíhòu, kàn diànshì.
  While I eat, I watch TV.

Tā máng de shíhoù, bú shuìjiào.
  When he's busy, he doesn't sleep.

Yǒu de shíhòu means "sometimes." This expression generally comes directly before or after the subject of a sentence.

Yòuéryuán yǒu de shíhòu wǎn yìdiǎnr xiàkè.
  Kindergarten sometimes gets out a bit late.

Yǒu de shíhòu, wǒ kànshū.
  Sometimes I read a book.

5. VERB REDUPLICATION

Verbs are repeated in a sentence to indicate that an action is being done "a little bit" or to a lesser degree. This can also soften the tone of a command or a suggestion.

Wǒmen tántan.
    We're talking a little.

Wǒ qīnglǐ qīnglǐ fángzi.
    I'm just cleaning the house a bit.

The word *yī* can also be inserted between the two syllables of a repeated single syllable verb without changing the meaning.

Wǒmen tán yì tán.
    We're talking a little.

6. THE ADVERB *YÌDIĂN(R)*

When *yìdiǎn(r)* (a little bit) is used after a verb and before an object, the implication is also that something is being done just a little. This usage is more literal that what is implied by verb reduplication.

Yòuéryuán jīntiān wǎn yìdiǎn(r) xiàkè.
    Kindergarten is getting out a bit late today.

7. VERB-OBJECT VERBS

Some two syllable verbs are verb-object compounds; that is, the first syllable is a true verb and the second syllable is an object. This is important to know because these verbs function differently in a sentence than do regular two syllable verbs. With regular two syllable verbs like *rènshi* (to recognize), adverbs come before the verb in a sentence. With verb-object verbs like *chīfàn* (to eat), adverbs are placed between the first and second syllables.

Wǒ yě rènshi nǐ.
    I also recognize you.

Wǒmen chī yìdiǎn(r) fàn.
    We are eating a little.

D. HÀNZÌ (Characters)

Practice writing these new characters.

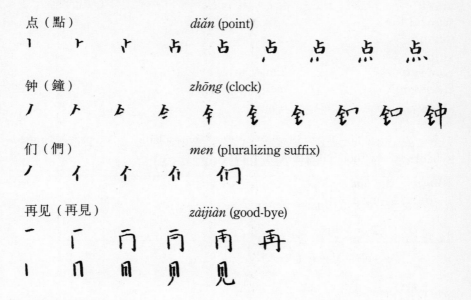

点（點）   *diǎn* (point)

钟（鐘）   *zhōng* (clock)

们（們）   *men* (pluralizing suffix)

再见（再見）   *zàijiàn* (good-bye)

E. SHĒNGCÍ (Vocabulary)

àirén	spouse, sweetheart
chīfàn	to eat
diǎn	[measure word for time, o'clock]
diànshì	television
fángzi	house
gēn	with
háizi	child/children
huíjiā	to go home
jīntiān	today
kàn	to watch
měitiān	every day
qǐchuáng	to get out of bed
qīnglǐ	to clean
shàngbān	to start work
shàngkè	to start class
shuìjiào	to go to sleep
tóngyì	to agree
wàibiān	outside

wǎnshàng	evening
xiàbān	to get out of work
xiàwǔ	afternoon
xiàkè	to get out of class
xiànzài	now
yǐhòu	after
yǐqián	before
yòuéryuán	kindergarten
zǎoshàng	morning
zhōng	o'clock

LIÀNXÍ (Exercises)

A. Write the time in Chinese pīnyīn.

EXAMPLE: 9:15 A.M.
   zǎoshàng jiǔdiǎn shíwǔfēn.

1. 8:00 A.M.
2. 12:00 P.M.
3. 4:55 P.M.
4. 7:30 A.M.

B. Fill in the blanks according to the English in parentheses.

A: *Qǐngwèn, xiànzài shì* _____? (what time)
B: *Xiànzài qīdiǎn* _____. (6:45) *Nǐ yǒu kòng ma?*
A: _____. (no). *Wǒ hěn* _____, *yě hěn* _____. (busy, tired)
B: *Nǐ huíjiā xiūxi* _____. (rest a little)

C. Match the *pīnyīn* to the character.

1. 再见   a. *Měiguó*
2. 美国   b. *nǐ hǎo!*
3. 老师   c. *sāndiǎn zhōng*
4. 三点钟   d. *zàijiàn*
5. 你好！   e. *lǎoshī*

52

D. Translate the following into English.

1. *Xiànzài shì bādiǎn chà yíkè.*
2. *Wǒmen míngtiān zǎoshàng qīdiǎn bàn chīfàn.*
3. *Tāmen wǔdiǎn érshí wǔfēn yào chīfàn.*

WÉNHUÀ ZHÙJIĚ (Cultural Note)

A typical workday in Mainland China begins earlier than in the United States. Many employees start work as early as 7:30 in the morning, take a two-hour lunch break at noon and work again until 5:30 or so. The two-hour lunch break is a time-honored tradition all over China, perhaps due to a traditionally agrarian society where a rest during the heat of the day was a necessity. From twelve to two in the afternoon, many workers today in China head home for lunch and a nap. Offices are generally closed during this time, but even if they remain open you may still find people napping at their desks or surprised that you would think of doing business between the hours of twelve and two!

DÁÀN (Answer Key)

A. 1. *zǎoshàng bādiǎn* 2. *zhōngwǔ* 3. *wǎnshàng wǔdiǎn chà wǔfēn* 4. *zǎoshàng qīdiǎn bàn*

B. *jǐdiǎn / chà yíkè / Méiyǒu / máng, lèi / xiūxi*

C. 1.d 2.a 3.e 4.c 5.b

D. 1. It's a quarter to eight. 2. We'll eat tomorrow morning at 7:30. 3. They want to eat at 5:25.

FÙXÍ 1 (Review 1)

A. Make these sentences negative.

    1. *Lǎoshī xiàge yuè dào Měiguó qù.*
    2. *Wǒ jiā yǒu sān ge rén.*
    3. *Wǒ chīfàn de shíhòu, wǒ kàn diànshì.*
    4. *Nèige rén xìng Wáng.*

B. Ask alternative questions to elicit these answers.

    1. *Wǒ hěn máng.*
    2. *Nà shì wǒ de.*
    3. *Wǒ zài Měiguó jiāoshū.*
    4. *Wǒmen gōngsī yào zuò mǎimài.*

C. Choose from the question words in parentheses to match the English translation.

    1. *Tā de jiā yǒu _____ ge rén? (ma, nǎ, jǐ)*
       How many people are in his family?
    2. *Jīntiān shì xīngqīyī _____? (ma, nǎ, jǐ)*
       Is today Monday?
    3. *Nǐ de mǔqīn shì _____ guó rén? (ma, nǎ, jǐ)*
       What nationality is your mother?

D. Choose the correct word.

    1. *Wǒ _____ Běijīng jiāoshū.*
       a. *yě* b. *zài* c. *bù*
    2. *Wǒmen tán _____.*
       a. *tán* b. *máng* c. *rén*
    3. *Tā wǎnshàng liùdiǎn _____ chīfàn.*
       a. *chī* b. *bàn* c. *yǒu*

E. Write the equivalents in Chinese *pīnyīn*.

    1. Miss Wang, I haven't seen you in a long time.
    2. I teach foreigners Chinese in Beijing.
    3. Of course I miss my family.
    4. That is my mother.

F. Write the English equivalents.

1. 他是美国人。
2. 我不是老师。
3. 你好！
4. 再见！再见！
5. 七点钟

G. Write the underlined words in Chinese characters.

1. *Wǒ de <u>lǎoshī</u> bú shì <u>Měiguórén</u>.*
2. *Xiànzài jǐdiǎn <u>zhōng</u>?*
3. *Wǒ jiā yǒu <u>wǔ</u> ge <u>rén</u>.*
4. *<u>Wǒmen</u> sìdiǎn bàn qù.*

DÁÀN (Answer Key)

A. 1. *Lǎoshī xiàge yuè bú dào Měiguó qù.* 2. *Wǒ jiā méiyǒu sān ge rén.* 3. *Wǒ chīfàn de shíhòu bú kàn diànshì.* 4. *Nèige rén bú xìng Wáng.*

B. 1. *Nǐ máng bù máng?* 2. *Nà shì shéi de?* 3. *Nǐ zài Měiguó zuò shénme?* 4. *Wǒmen gōngsī yào zuò shénme?*

C. 1. *jǐ* 2. *ma* 3. *nǎ*

D. 1.B 2.A 3.B

E. 1. *Wáng xiǎojie, hǎojiǔ bújiàn.* 2. *Wǒ zài Běijīng jiāo wàiguórén Hànyǔ.* 3. *Wǒ dāngrán xiǎng wǒ de jiā.* 4. *Nà shì wǒ de mǔqīn.*

F. 1. He is American. 2. I am not a teacher. 3. Hello! 4. Good-bye! Good-bye! 5. Seven o'clock

G. 1.老师，美国 2.钟 3.五，人 4.我们

DÌ LIÙ KÈ
Lesson 6
JIǍOZI. Dumplings.

A. DUÌHUÀ

SHENGRÌ.

Meiru arranges a birthday party for her little brother and calls her brother's classmate Wenxiong to invite him.

MÉIRÚ: **Zhège xīngqīrì shì wǒ dìdi de shēngrì. Nǐ kě bù kěyǐ lái wǒmen jiā chī jiǎozi hé miàntiáo?**

WÉNXIÓNG: **Dāngrán kěyǐ. Suīrán wǒ gāng rènshi nǐ dìdi, kěshì wǒmen yǐjīng shì hǎo péngyou. Tā jīnnián duōdà suìshù?**

MÉIRÚ: **Tā jīnnián èrshísān suì. Nǐ de shēngrì shì jǐyuè jǐhào?**

WÉNXIÓNG: **Wǒ de shēngrì shì jiǔyuè shíbāhào. Wǒ yě mǎn èrshí sān suì.**

MÉIRÚ: **Wǒ dìdi shuō nǐ xǐhuan chī jiǎozi. Nǐ yě huì bāo jiǎozi ma?**

WÉNXIÓNG: **Jiǎozi shì wǒ zuì xǐhuan chī de fàn, kěshì wǒ bú huì bāo. Nǐ yào jiāo wǒ zěnme zuò ma?**

MÉIRÚ: **Hǎo, xīngqī rì wǒmen yìqǐ bāo jiǎozi ba!**

WÉNXIÓNG: **Hǎo, xīngqī rì jiàn!**

A BIRTHDAY.

MEIRU: This Sunday is my little brother's birthday. Can you come over to our house for a dumpling and noodle dinner?

WENXIONG: Of course I can come. Even though I've only known him a short time, your brother's already a good friend. How old will he be this year?

MEIRU: He'll be twenty-three. When is your birthday?

WENXIONG: My birthday is September 18. I'm twenty-three also.*

* See this lesson's Cultural Note for an explanation of *mǎn*.

56

MEIRU: My brother says you like to eat dumplings. Do you also know how to make them?

WENXIONG: Dumplings are my favorite thing to eat, but I can't make them. Do you want to teach me?

MEIRU: Okay. On Sunday, let's all make dumplings together.

WENXIONG: Great, I'll see you on Sunday!

B. FĀYĪN

1. FINAL SOUNDS WITH *A*

a	like the English <u>a</u> in m<u>a</u>	**mā** mother; **bà** father; **tā** him
ai	like the <u>y</u> in m<u>y</u>	**lái** to come; **dài** to bring; **cāi** to guess
ao	like the <u>ou</u> in p<u>ou</u>t	**dào** to go; **cǎo** grass; **nǎo** brain
an	like the <u>a</u> sound above with an *n* attached	**fàn** food; **mǎn** full; **tán** to discuss
ang	like the <u>a</u> sound above with an *ng* attached	**fàng** to place; **tāng** soup; **bāng** to help

C. YǓFǍ HÉ YÒNGFǍ

1. DAYS OF THE WEEK

Xīngqī means week. For the days of the week, simply add the numbers one through six to the word *xīngqī*. For Sunday, add *rì* (sun) or *tiān* (day), not *qī* (seven).

xīngqīyī	Monday
xīngqīèr	Tuesday
xīngqīsān	Wednesday
xīngqīsì	Thursday
xīngqīwǔ	Friday
xīngqīliù	Saturday
xīngqīrì	Sunday
xīngqītiān	Sunday

Use the verb *shì* (to be) when talking about what day it is.

Jīntiān shì xīngqīwǔ.
Today is Friday.

Otherwise, the words for days are placed before the verb and before any other adverb in the sentence.

Wǒmen xīngqīsān yìqǐ chīfàn ba.
Let's eat together on Wednesday.

2. DATES

Talking about dates in Chinese is just as straightforward as talking about days. *Yuè* means month, and *yīyuè* is January, *èryuè* February, all the way through *shíèryuè*, December!

Note the difference between the names of months and expressing a certain number of months. To express a number of months, the measure word *ge* is needed:

yīyuè	January
yí ge yuè	one month

Wǒ liǎng ge yuè yǐhòu dàxué bìyè.
I am going to graduate in two months.

Rì and *hào* both mean day, but *rì* is mainly used in the written language and *hào* is more colloquial. The first day of the month is *yī hào*, the second day, *èr hào*, etc., until the thirty-first day, *sānshí hào*.

jiǔyuè bāhào (or *rì*)
September 8

For counting purposes, use the word *tiān* for day; no measure word is needed because *tiān* functions in this capacity as well.

liǎng tiān
two days

shíèr tiān
twelve days

Dates are expressed with the year first, then the month, then the day.

yījiǔbābānian, yīyuè shíyīhào
January 11, 1988

Dates function in a sentence in the same way as do days of the week.

Jīntiān shì bāyuè sìhào.
Today is August fourth.

58

Wǒmen bāyuè sìhào yìqǐ chīfàn ba.
Let's eat together on August 4th.

Wǒ de shēngrì shì yījiǔliùbānián, jiǔyuè shíwǔhào.
My birthday is September 15, 1968.

3. MORE ADVERBS OF TIME

Other useful expressions for days, weeks and months are the following. You have already learned that these are placed in a sentence before the verb and before other adverbs.

qiántiān	the day before yesterday
zuótiān	yesterday
jīntiān	today
míngtiān	tomorrow
hòutiān	the day after tomorrow
shàngshang ge xīngqī	the week before last
shàngge xīngqī	last week
zhège xīngqī	this week
xiàge xīngqī	next week
xiàxia ge xīngqī	the week after next
shàngshang ge yuè	the month before last
shàngge yuè	last month
zhège yuè	this month
xiàge yuè	next month
xiàxia ge yuè	the month after next
qiánnián	the year before last
qùnián	last year
jīnnián	this year
míngnián	next year
hòunián	the year after next

4. MORE USES OF THE QUESTION WORD *JǏ*

To ask the date, use the question word *jǐ*. As with other questions of this type (see lesson 3), place *jǐ* in the same position as the number in question.

Jīntiān shì jǐyuè jǐhào?
What is the date today?

Jīntiān shì xīngqījǐ?
What day is it today?

5. ASKING AGE

Both *nǐ duō dà suìshù?* and *nǐ jǐ suì?* (how old are you?) are used to ask age. The first expression is used for older people and in polite speech, the latter is used more informally as with small children. To answer these questions, just use the verb *suì* (to be aged) as follows.

Wǒ wǔ suì le.
   I'm five.

Tā sānshíyí suì le.
   She is thirty-one.

6. *KĚYǏ* VS. *HUÌ*

Kěyǐ and *huì* both mean "to be able to" but with different connotations. *Kěyǐ* implies that a person is able to do something because they have the time, inclination or permission. *Huì* implies that one is able to do something because of a natural or learned talent.

Wǒ de gēge huì shuō Zhōngguóhuà.
   My brother can speak Chinese.

Tā bù kěyǐ dào Rìběn qù.
   He can't go to Japan.

Nǐ míngtiān kěyǐ lái wǒmen jiā ma?
   Can you come to our house tomorrow?

Nǐ huì bú huì bāo jiǎozi?
   Do you know how to (can you) make dumplings?

7. QUESTION WORD *ZĚNME*

The question word *zěnme* (how) can only be used in conjunction with a verb and directly precedes the verb in a sentence.

Zěnme zuò?
   How is it done?

Nǐ zhīdào zěnme yòng kuàizi ma?
   Do you know how to use chopsticks?

Nǐ zěnmeyàng?
   How are you doing?

8. SUGGESTION PARTICLE *BA*

The sentence final particle *ba* turns a statement into a suggestion or command.

Wŏmen zŏu ba!
   Let's go!

Nĭ shōushi shōushi nĭ de wūzi ba!
   Clean your room!

Shuìjiào ba!
   Go to sleep!

Wŏmen xīngqìrì yìqĭ bāo jiăozi ba!
   Let's all make dumplings together on Sunday!

As you already know, the use of verb reduplication with suggestions and commands serves to soften the tone.

Nĭ zuòzuo nĭ de gōngkè ba!
   Why don't you do your homework? / How about doing your homework?

D. HÀNZÌ

Here are some useful characters for learning how to read dates.

星期　　　　　　　　　*xīngqī* (week)

月　　　　　　　　　　*yuè* (month)

号　　　　　　　　　　*hào* (day)

今天   *jīntiān* (today)

ノ   人   仝   今

一   二   于   天

Look at these sentences to see how these characters are used.

今天是星期五。

Jīntiān shì xīngqīwǔ.

    Today is Friday.

今天是六月二十四号。

Jīntiān shì liùyuè èrshísìhào.

    Today is June 24.

E. SHĒNGCÍ

ba	[suggestion particle]
bāo	to wrap
dàxué	college
fángjiān	room
gāng	just
huì	to be able to, can
jiǎozi	dumplings
kěyǐ	to be able to, can
miàntiáo	noodles
péngyou	friend
rì	sun, day
shàngxué	go to school
shēngrì	birthday
shōushi	to clean, tidy up
suì	age
suīrán	although
suìshù	age

tiān	day
xǐhuan	to like
xīngqī	week
xīngqīyī	Monday
xīngqīèr	Tuesday
xīngqīsān	Wednesday
xīngqīsì	Thursday
xīngqīwǔ	Friday
xīngqīliù	Saturday
xīngqītiān	Sunday
zěnme	how
Zhōngguóhuà	Chinese language (spoken)
zuì	most
zuì xǐhuan	favorite

LIÀNXÍ

A. Answer the following questions based on Xiaoying's weekly schedule.

xīngqīrì—kàn diànshì
xīngqīyī—shàngxué
xīngqīèr—shàngbān
xīngqīsān—qù Jūnmín jiā chīfàn
xīngqīsì—shàngbān
xīngqīwǔ—méi shì
xīngqīliù—zuò yùndòng

1. What day does Xiaoying go to work?
2. What day is Xiaoying free?
3. What day does Xiaoying exercise?
4. What day does Xiaoying go to school?
5. What day does Xiaoying watch TV?
6. What day does Xiaoying go to Junmin's house?

B. Place either *kěyǐ* or *huì* in the blanks as appropriate.

1. *Wǒ* _____ *bāo jiǎozi.*
2. *Tā bú* _____ *shuō Zhōngguóhuà.*

3. *Wǒ jīntiān bù* _____ *shàngbān.*

4. *Wǒ māma* _____ *lái nǐ jiā chīfàn.*

C. Translate the following into *pīnyīn.*

1. Let's go on October 14.
2. See you Sunday.
3. Why don't you clean your room?
4. What day of the week is it today?

D. Translate the following into English.

1. 今天是星期五。
2. 再见！再见！
3. 今天是十二月一号。
4. 星期一好。

WÉNHUÀ ZHÙJIĚ

Although birthdays aren't celebrated with as much gusto in China as they are in the United States, Chinese people might honor a birthday with a special meal of dumplings and noodles. Noodles are a particularly auspicious birthday food, as their length symbolizes longevity. Handmade dumplings, because of the complicated process involved in making them, are only served on special occasions such as Chinese New Year, birthdays and weddings. It is also not uncommon for Chinese people to arrange a dumpling party for foreign guests. Making dumplings alone can be a tedious process, but a group working together can wrap dumplings and talk together all day.

In China, a year is not traditionally added to a person's age on their birthday, but during the Spring Festival (*Chūnjié*), what we call Chinese New Year. Thus, everyone gains a year in age at the same time. Also, the day babies are born, they are considered to be one year old. So, when Westerners are turning one year old, Chinese children are already turning two.

In the dialogue, one of the speakers used the term *mǎn* when giving his age. *Mǎn* in this sense means a full age, without adding any of the traditional Chinese elements. Thus, *mǎn èrshí sān suì* means "a full twenty-three years old" in the Western sense. By contrast, *xū* means "false age," or the age calculated with the traditional Chinese element of already being one year old at birth and having added a year during the Spring Festival.

A. 1. Tuesday and Thursday 2. Friday 3. Saturday 4. Monday 5. Sunday
6. Wednesday

B. 1. *huì* 2. *huì* 3. *kěyǐ* 4. *kěyǐ*

C. 1. *Wǒmen shíyuè shísìhào qù ba.* 2. *Xīngqīrì jiàn.* 3. *Nǐ shōushi shōushi fángjiān ba.* 4. *Jīntiān shì xīngqījǐ?*

D. 1. Today is Friday. 2. Good-bye! Good-bye! 3. Today is December first.
4. Monday is good.

DÌ QĪ KÈ
Lesson 7
FÁNGZI. Houses.

A. DUÌHUÀ

Qǐng péngyou chīfàn.

Wenlin invites David and Amy over to her house for dinner.

WÉNLÍN: **Huānyíng, huānyíng. Qǐng jìn.**

DÀWÈI: **Xièxie. Nǐ jiā zhēn piàoliang. Wǒmen kě bù kěyǐ cānguān?**

WÉNLÍN: **Bù hǎo yìsi, tài luàn le!**

ÀIMÉI: **Nǐ tài kèqi le. Wénlín, zhège fángzi yǒu jǐ jiān wūzi?**

WÉNLÍN: **Zhège fángzi yǒu liǎng ge fángjiān, hái yǒu chúfáng hé cèsuǒ. Zhè shì kètīng, nàr shì wòshì. Qǐng zuò, qǐng zuò!**

ÀIMÉI: **Nǐ de fángzi bǐ wǒmen de fángzi shūfu!**

DÀWÈI: **Duì a, zhèr de chuānghu zhēn duō, fángzi hěn liàng. Zhè tào shāfā bǐ wǒmen de shūfu.**

WÉNLÍN: **Xièxie, wǒ yě tǐng xīhuan de. Nǐmen è ma? Nǐ yào chī yìdiǎn(r) shénme?**

ÀIMÉI: **Bú yòng, bú yòng!**

INVITING FRIENDS FOR DINNER.

WENLIN: Welcome, welcome. Come in!

DAVID: Thanks. Your house is really pretty. Can we look around?

WENLIN: Oh, I'm too embarrassed, the place is a mess!

AMY: You are too polite. Wenlin, how many rooms does this house have?

WENLIN: This house has two rooms, plus a kitchen and bathroom. This is the living room and over there is the bedroom. Please, have a seat.

AMY: Your house is much more comfortable than ours.

DAVID: Oh yes, there are so many windows in this room that the house is quite bright. This couch is more comfortable than ours.

WENLIN: Thank you. I really like it, too. Are you hungry? Do you want to eat a little something?

AMY: Don't worry about it!

B. FĀYĪN

1. FINAL SOUNDS WITH *O*

o	like the <u>o</u> in <u>or</u> but with a slight *w* sound between the consonant and the *o*	**wǒ** I; **mó** to rub; **pò** broken
ou	like the <u>oa</u> in fl<u>oa</u>t	**tōu** to steal; **zhōu** state; **sōu** to search
ong	like the <u>ong</u> in thr<u>ong</u>	**tóng** same; **nóng** farm; **hóng** red

C. YǓFǍ HÉ YÒNGFǍ

1. MEASURE WORDS

You have already learned the general measure word *ge*. Many objects are assigned specific measure words according to their category. For example, flat objects like paper and tables take the measure word *zhāng*, and long, thin objects like noodles and roads take the measure word *tiáo*. Here is a list of common measure words and the types of objects they are used with.

bǎ	objects with a handle (knives, toothbrushes, chairs)
bāo	a pack of something (cigarettes)
běn	a volume (books, magazines)
jiān	rooms
jù	a spoken phrase (questions, remarks)
kuài	a piece of something (soap, land)
tào	a set of something (furniture)
tiáo	very long, twisty objects (roads, noodles)
zhāng	flat, rectangular objects (table, piece of paper)
zhī	long, thin objects (pencils, pens)

Specific measure words are used in the same position as the general measure word *ge*, between the number and the noun being counted.

Zhè jiān wūzi zhēn luàn.
   This room is really messy.

Tā yǒu liǎng tào shāfā.
   She has two sofas.

2. THE *TÀI . . . LE* CONSTRUCTION

The particle *le* is one of the most gramatically complex little words in Chinese. You will learn about its many different uses in subsequent lessons. But for now, know that *tài . . . le* is a fixed expression that serves to stress a particular quality, as we might use "much too," or, more colloquially, "so," in English. *Tài* (too) comes directly before the stressed adjectival verb and the particle *le* comes directly after the verb.

Wǒ de fángzi tài luàn le!
   My house is much too messy!

Wǒ tài è le!
   I'm so hungry!

3. MAKING COMPARISONS WITH *BǏ*

A simple way of making comparisons is to use A *bǐ* B + adjective or adjectival verb.

Wǒ bǐ tā è.
   I am hungrier than she is.

Wǒ de māma bǐ nǐ de lǎoshī máng.
   My mother is busier than your teacher.

Zhè ge fángjiān bǐ nèige fángjiān shūfu.
   This room is more comfortable than that room.

If the verb used in this type of sentence is used in conjunction with an amount, the amount follows the verb.

Wǒ bǐ wǒ mèimei dà sì suì.
   I am four years older than my sister.

Wǒ de lǎoshī bǐ wǒ wǎn bànge xiǎoshí.
   My teacher was a half hour later than I was.

68

4. *ZHÈR* AND *NÀR* AS SUBJECT

When *zhèr* and *nàr* are used at the beginning of a sentence in the subject position to mean "here" or "there" respectively, they must be pronounced with the *r* sound, even though the characters are written in the same way as the demonstratives *zhè* and *nà*.

Zhèr shì cèsuǒ.
 Here is the bathroom.

Nàr shì Běijīng Yǔyán Xuéyuàn.
 There is the Beijing Language Institute.

5. SENTENCE FINAL PARTICLE *A*

A is used at the end of a sentence to express agreement, or when exclaiming on the obvious.

Zhè jiān wūzi zhēn shūfu.
Shì a!
 This room is really comfortable.
 It sure is!

Nǐ tài máng a!
 You are so busy!

D. HÀNZÌ

The words for "man" and "woman" are useful to know wherever you travel, especially if they are paired with "restroom." In China, many rooms are labeled with *jiān* (room), so this is another useful character to know.

男　　　　　　　　　　*nán* (man)

女　　　　　　　　　　*nǚ* (woman)

厕所　　　　　　　　　*cèsuǒ* (restroom)

房间（房間）　　　　　*fángjiān* (room)

丶　丶　冖　戸　戸　戸　房　房

丶　亠　门　闩　问　问　间

房子　　　　　　　　　*fángzi* (house)

フ　了　子

E. SHĒNGCÍ

bǐ	[comparison word]
bǐjiào	relatively
cānguān	to visit, to look around
cèsuǒ	bathroom, toilet
chúfáng	kitchen
chuānghu	window
è	to be hungry
gānjìng	to be clean
jiān	[measure word for rooms]
kèqi	polite
kètīng	living room
le	[particle of many uses]
liàng	to be bright
luàn	to be messy
piàoliang	pretty
shāfā	sofa
shūfu	comfortable
tài	too
tào	[measure word for sets]
wòshì	bedroom
wūzi	a room
tǐng	extremely
yòng	to use
zhēn	really

SUPPLEMENTARY VOCABULARY 2: HOUSE TERMS

chuáng	bed
dēng	lamp
dēngpào	lightbulb
dìtǎn	rug
jìngzi	mirror
línyù	shower
lóushàng	upstairs
lóuxià	downstairs
máojīn	towel
qiáng	wall
shūzhuō	desk
tǎnzi	blanket
wèishēngjiān	bathroom
shuǐcáo	sink
xǐyīfáng	laundry room
yǐzi	chair
zhuōzi	table

LIÀNXÍ

A. What are the appropriate measure words for the following?

1. *wòshì*
2. *zhuōzi*
3. *shāfā*
4. *yǐzi*
5. *wūzi*
6. *bǐ*

B. Translate the following sentences into *pīnyīn* using the comparison word *bǐ*.

1. Your house is messier than mine.
2. My mother is prettier than your little sister.
3. This sofa is more comfortable than that one.
4. Sunday is better than Monday.

C. Translate the following into English.

1. *Wǒ de fángjiān tài luàn le!*
2. *Zhèr shì wòshì.*
3. *Nǐ jiā bǐjiào dà.*
4. *Zhè tào shāfā zhēn shūfu. Shì a!*

D. Write the English equivalents.

1. 女厕所
2. 男厕所
3. 你的房子不好。

WÉNHUÀ ZHÙJIĚ

Until very recently, all Chinese people could only get a place to live from their *dānwèi* or work unit. Teachers were given a place to live by their school or university, and businesses provided apartments to their employees. The size of the apartment depends on seniority or position; but generally because space is so scarce in China, most families only have two- or three-room apartments. It is not uncommon for a family of three to live in one small room, sharing a bathroom and kitchen with other families. Now that it is becoming increasingly common for people to work on their own or start their own businesses, more apartments are available to be rented, but they are difficult to find and can be expensive.

DÁÀN

A. 1. jiān 2. zhāng 3. tào 4. bǎ 5. jiān 6. zhī

B. 1. *Nǐ de jiā bǐ wǒ de luàn.* 2. *Wǒ māma bǐ nǐ mèimei piàoliang.* 3. *Zhè tào shāfā bǐ nèi tào shūfu.* 4. *Xīngqīrì bǐ xīngqīyī hǎo.*

C. 1. My room is much too messy! 2. Here is the bedroom. 3. Your home is relatively large. 4. This sofa is really comfortable. Sure is!

D. 1. Women's toilet. 2. Men's toilet. 3. Your house is not good.

DÌ BĀ KÈ
Lesson 8
ZUÒ CHŪZŪCHĒ. Taking a Taxi.

A. DUÌHUÀ

YǑUYÍ SHĀNGDIÀN.

David and Amy want to go to the Friendship Store from Beijing University.

SĪJĪ: Xiānsheng, xiǎojie, nǐmen zuò chē ma?

DÀWÈI: Wǒmen yào dào Yǒuyí Shāngdiàn. Nǐ qù bú qù?

SĪJĪ: Wǒ qù. Kěshì, Yǒuyí Shāngdiàn lí zhèr hěn yuǎn. Nǐ yào duō gěi yìdiǎnr qián.

AÌMÉI: Dàwèi, wǒ kàn wǒmen zuò gōnggòng qìchē hùozhě qí zìxíngchē ba.

DÀWÈI: Aìméi, fàngxīn. Wǒ péngyou gàosù wǒ zuò chūzūchē yào zhùyì biǎo.

SĪJĪ: Kěshì, xiànzài qìchē hěn duō, jiāotōng yě hěn jǐ . . .

AÌMÉI: Cóng Běijīng Dàxué dào Yǒuyí Shāngdiàn zuò dìtiě yě bú tài fāngbiàn.

DÀWÈI: Suàn le. Suàn le. Wǒ zhǎo biéde chūzūchē.

SĪJĪ: Hǎo ba! hǎo ba! Wǒ qù Yǒuyí Shāngdiàn. Qǐng liǎng wèi shàngchē ba.

AÌMÉI: Nǐ yào kāi biǎo a!

SĪJĪ: Hǎo.

THE FRIENDSHIP STORE.

DRIVER: Sir, miss, do you want a cab?

DAVID: We're going to the Friendship Store. Will you go there?

73

DRIVER: I'll go. But the Friendship Store is quite a ways from here, you'll have to pay more.

AMY: David, I think we should take the bus or ride bikes.

DAVID: Don't worry, Amy, my friend told me that when we take a cab we just need to watch the meter.

DRIVER: But there are so many cars on the road, and so much traffic . . .

AMY: To take the subway from Beijing University to the Friendship Store is also inconvenient.

DAVID: Forget it, I'll find another cab . . .

DRIVER: Fine! Fine! I'll go to the Friendship Store. Get in.

AMY: Start the meter.

DRIVER: Fine.

B. FĀYĪN

1. FINAL SOUNDS WITH *E*

e	like the e in serve	**kè** class; **de** (particle); **le** (particle)
ei	like the ay in day	**děi** must; **bēi** cup; **měi** pretty
en	like the un in under	**mén** door; **gēn** with; **zhēn** true
eng	like the ung in mung	**mèng** dream; **shēng** to be born; **lěng** cold

C. YŬFǍ HÉ YÒNGFǍ

1. "TO RIDE": *ZUÒ* VS. *QÍ*

The verb *zuò* (to sit or to ride) is used with forms of transportation that the passenger physically gets into, such as cars, trains and subways. *Qí* (to ride astride) is used with forms of transportation that the passenger straddles, such as bicycles, motorcycles and horses.

Wǒmen zài Niǔyuē zuò dìtiě.
We take the subway in New York.

Nǐ zuò gōnggòng qìchē qù shàngbān ma?
Do you take the bus to work?

Wǒ xǐhuan qí zìxíngchē.
   I like to ride bicycles.

2. DIRECTIONAL PHRASES WITH *DÀO . . . QÙ/LÁI*

To express that a person is coming or going to a place, the following pattern is used:

   Subject + *dào* (to go, come to) + place + *qù* (go)/*lái* (come)

Wǒ dào Yǒuyí Shāngdiàn qù.
   I am going to the Friendship Store.

Wǒ de lǎoshī dào Yǔyán Xuéyuàn lái.
   My teacher is coming to the Language Institute.

When returning to a place use *huídào.*

Māma huídào jiā le.
   Mom came home.

When the subject is going or coming to a place to do something, the verb or the verb phrase that describes the action is placed at the end of a sentence.

Tā dào Yǒuyí Shāngdiàn qù mǎi dōngxi.
   He is going to the Friendship Store to buy things.

Wǒ de lǎoshī dào wǒ jiā lái chīfàn.
   My teacher is coming to my house to eat.

3. DIRECTIONAL PHRASES WITH *CÓNG . . . QÙ/LÁI/HUÍ*

To indicate coming or going from a place to another use the following pattern:

   Subject + *cóng* (from) + place + *qù* (go) *lái* (come)

Wǒ cóng Yǒuyí Shāngdiàn lái.
   I am coming from the Friendship Store.

Wǒ cóng wǒ jiā lái.
   I am coming from my home.

You can also combine sentences with *dào* and sentences with *cóng* to talk about coming or going from one place to another by using the following pattern:

Subject + *cóng* + place + *dào* + place + *qù/lái*

Wǒ cóng Běijīng Dàxué dào Yǒuyí Shāngdiàn qù.
I am going from Beijing University to the Friendship Store.

Tā cóng tā jiā dào bàngōngshì lái.
He is coming from home to the office.

These sentences can also end with a verb or verb phrase describing the action a person goes or comes to a place to do.

Wǒ cóng Běijīng Dàxué dào Yǒuyí Shāngdiàn qù mǎi dōngxi.
I'm going from Beijing University to the Friendship Store to buy things.

4. USING *LÍ* TO EXPRESS DISTANCE BETWEEN TWO PLACES

Lí (between) is used in between two place-names, which are then followed by a distance term, such as *yuǎn* (far) or *jìn* (close) to express the amount of physical space between these two places.

Běijīng Fàndiàn lí zhèr yuǎn ma?
Is the Beijing Hotel far from here?

Běijīng Fàndiàn lí zhèr hěn yuǎn.
The Beijing Hotel is quite far from here.

Gōngsī lí dàxué yuǎn bù yuǎn?
Is the company far from the college?

Gōngsī lí dàxué hěn jìn.
The office is quite close to the college.

NiǔYuē Shì lí BōShìDùn duōshǎo lǐ lù?
How many miles is New York City from Boston?

NiǔYuē Shì lí BōShìDùn sānbǎi lǐ lù.
New York City is 300 miles from Boston.

5. *SHÀNG* AND *XIÀ*

Shàng (on, over) and *xià* (off, under) are used in a variety of ways. You learned in lesson 5 that *shàngkè* means "to start class" and *xiàkè* means "to finish class." You also learned in lesson 6 that *shàngge xīngqī* means "last week" and *xiàge xīngqī* means "next week." *Shàng* can also mean "to get into a vehicle" and *xià* can mean "to get out of a vehicle."

Qǐng nǐ shàng qìchē.
    Please get into the car.

Wǒ yào xià gōnggòng qìchē.
    I want to get out of the bus.

D. HÀNZÌ

Practice the following characters.

上   *shàng* (on, over)

丨　　丄　　上

下   *xià* (off, under)

一　　丁　　下

坐   *zuò* (to sit)

丿　　人　　从　　从　　坐　　坐　　坐

汽车（汽車）   *qìchē* (car)

丶　　冫　　氵　　汽　　汽　　汽　　汽

一　　七　　车　　车

出租车（出租車）   *chūzūchē* (taxi)

乚　　凵　　屮　　出　　出

丿　　二　　千　　禾　　禾　　和　　和　　租　　租

地铁   *dìtiě* (subway)

丿　　人　　仁　　仲　　他

丿　　人　　钅　　钅　　钅　　钅　　钅　　铁

铁　　铁

E. SHĒNGCÍ

biǎo	meter
biéde	other
BōShìDùn	Boston
chē	car
chūzūchē	taxi
cóng	from
dìtiě	subway
fāngbiàn	convenient
fàngxīn	to relax
gàosù	to tell
gōnggòng qìchē	public bus
jǐ	crowded
jiāotōng	traffic
jìn	nearby
kāi	to start
lí	distance from
lǐ	miles
qí	to ride astride
qìchē	automobile, car
qián	money
shàngchē	to get in the vehicle
shāngdiàn	store
suàn le!	forget it!
wèi	[polite measure word for people]
xiàchē	to get out of the vehicle
yǒuyí	friendship
Yǒuyí Shāngdiàn	Friendship Store
yuǎn	far
zhùyì	pay attention to
zìxíngchē	bicycle
zuò	to ride, to sit [for transportation]

LIÀNXÍ

A. Fill in the blank with either *zuò* or *qí*.

1. *Wǒ xǐhuan _____ zìxíngchē.*
2. *Nǐ _____ chūzūchē dào Běijīng Dàxué qù ma?*
3. *Wǒmen _____ gōnggòng qìchē qù ba!*

B. Make the following into sentences using *lí* to express distance.

1. *Yǒuyí Shāngdiàn Běijīng Shīfàn Dàxué hěn jìn*
2. *Shànghǎi Xiānggǎng wǔbǎi lǐ lù*
3. *Měiguó Zhōngguó yuǎn*
4. *Wǒ de jiā tā de jiā sān lǐ lù.*

C. Translate into English.

1. *Wǒ huíjiā qù.*
2. *Chūzūchē cóng fàndiàn dào lǚguǎn lái.*
3. *Wǒ qí zìxíngchē cóng wǒ jiā dào dàxué lái.*
4. *Wǒ zuò dìtiě dào bàngōngshì qù.*

D. Write the Chinese characters for the words below.

1. subway
2. car
3. taxi

E. Fill in the blanks with the appropriate Chinese character according to the English equivalent.

1. 我今天 _____ 汽车。 (I rode in the car today.)
2. _____ 坐地铁。 (They take the subway.)
3. 我 _____ 出租车。 (I am getting out of the cab.)

During the past few years, taxis have proliferated in China. In fact, the streets of Beijing are so crowded, not only with taxis but with personal cars and buses, that traffic jams are inevitable at all times of day. As in most large cities of the world, taxi drivers have been known to try to cheat their passengers, either by insisting that the meter is broken or that a service charge is necessary for trips over a long distance. Use your common sense in China, make sure the meter is on and ask for a receipt after your trip.

Buses are inexpensive and convenient options all over China. The large buses are the cheapest, but there are also small minivans which are more comfortable but also more expensive. When you get on the bus, make your way to the ticket seller, who sits near the back of the bus. Fares depend on how far you are going; if you tell the ticket seller your destination, he or she will charge you the appropriate amount. Of course, you can follow the Chinese example and rent a bike, but keep your eyes open for the traffic—the rule of the road seems to be that the biggest vehicle has the right of way, so don't take chances!

DÁÀN

A. 1. *qí* 2. *zuò* 3. *zuò*

B. 1. *Yǒuyí Shāngdiàn lí Běijīng Shīfàn Dàxué hěn jìn.* 2. *Shànghǎi lí Xiānggǎng wǔbǎi lǐ lù.* 3. *Měiguó lí Zhōngguó hěn yuǎn.* 4. *Wǒ de jiā lí tā de jiā sān lǐ lù.*

C. 1. I'm going home. 2. The taxi came from the restaurant to the hotel. 3. I ride my bike from home to come to school. 4. I ride the subway to go to work.

D. 1. 地铁 2. 汽车   3. 出租车

E. 1. 坐 2. 他们 3. 下

DÌ JIǓ KÈ
Lesson 9

WÈNLÙ. Asking for Directions.

A. DUÌHUÀ

DÀO YÍHÉYUÁN.

Mr. Zhang is a tourist in Beijing on his way to visit the Summer Palace.

ZHĀNG: **Lǎojià, cóng zhèr qù Yíhéyuán zěnme zǒu?**

MÒSHĒNGRÉN: **Yíhéyuán lí zhèr bú jìn. Bié zǒulù. Nǐ zuò gōnggòng qìchē cóng zhèr dào Yíhéyuán qù.**

ZHĀNG: **Hǎo. Qìchē zhàn zài nǎr?**

MÒSHĒNGRÉN: **Nǐ wàng qiánbiān zǒu yì tiáo jiē, dào hónglǜdēng yǐhòu wàng yòu zhuǎn, qìchēzhàn jiù zài yòubiān.**

ZHĀNG: **Xièxie nín.**

MÒSHĒNGRÉN: **Bié kèqi.**

ZÀI GŌNGGÒNG QÌCHĒZHÀN QIÁNMIÀN.

ZHĀNG: **Duìbùqǐ, xiānsheng. Zhè lù chē dào Yíhéyuán ma?**

MÒSHĒNGRÉN: **Nǐ xiān zuò zhè lù chē ránhòu yào huànchē.**

ZHĀNG: **Zài nǎr huàn?**

MÒSHĒNGRÉN: **Nǐ zài Běijīng Dòngwùyuán xiàchē, zài huàn sān sān èr lù qìchē.**

ZHĀNG: **Xiéxie.**

GOING TO THE SUMMER PALACE.

ZHANG: Would you please tell me how to get to the Summer Palace from here?

STRANGER: The Summer Palace is not close. Don't walk. Take the bus from here to the Summer Palace.

ZHANG: Okay. Where is the bus stop?

STRANGER: Go straight up this street, turn right after the traffic light and the bus stop is on your right.

ZHANG: Thanks.

STRANGER: Sure.

IN FRONT OF THE BUS STOP.

ZHANG: Excuse me, does this bus go to the Summer Palace?

STRANGER: You can first take this bus and then you need to change.

ZHANG: Where should I transfer?

STRANGER: Get off at the Beijing Zoo and then get on bus 332.

ZHANG: Thank you.

B. FĀYĪN

1. FINAL SOUNDS WITH *I*

i	like the <u>ee</u> in s<u>ee</u>	**bǐ** pen; **mǐ** meter; **pí** leather
ia	like <u>yah</u> with a stronger initial *ee* sound	**jiā** home; **liǎ** two; **qià** exact
iao	like the <u>eow</u> in m<u>eow</u>	**miáo** to describe; **liáo** to chat; **diào** to fish
ian	like <u>yan</u> but with a stronger initial *ee* sound	**tiān** day; **diǎn** dot; **liǎn** face
iang	like <u>yang</u> but with a stronger initial *ee* sound	**jiāng** river; **liǎng** two; **qiáng** strong
ie	like the <u>ye</u> in <u>yes</u>	**tiě** iron; **bié** don't; **dié** to fall
iu	like the <u>yo</u> in <u>yo</u>-yo	**qiū** autumn; **diū** to lose; **liú** to flow
iong	like the end of be<u>long</u> without the *l*	**xióng** bear; **qióng** poor

in	like the <u>in</u> in s<u>in</u>	**qín** diligent; **jìn** come; **lín** forest
ing	like the <u>ing</u> in s<u>ing</u>	**xìng** surname; **líng** zero; **míng** first name

2. The *I* SOUND AFTER *S, C* AND *Z*

When the *i* comes after *s, c* or *z*, it is not pronounced. That is, *si, ci* and *zi* sound like their respective initial sounds (see lesson 3) on their own.

sǐ to die
cí expression
zì word

C. YǓFǍ HÉ YÒNGFǍ

1. GIVING DIRECTIONS

Here are some useful constructions for giving directions.

Wàng qián zǒu.
   Go straight ahead.

Nǐ xiān wàng qián zǒu sān tiáo jiē.
   You first need to go forward three streets (three more blocks).

Wàng yòu zhuǎn.
   Turn right.

Wàng zuǒ zhuǎn.
   Turn left.

Yìzhí zǒu.
   Go straight.

Xiān wàng yòu zhuǎn, ránhòu yìzhí zǒu.
   First turn right, then go straight.

Zài hónglǜdēng wàng zuǒ zhuǎn.
   Turn left at the traffic light.

2. PHRASES OF LOCATION

Biān and *miàn* are interchangeable words meaning "side" that are used in conjunction with place-names.

qiánbiān or *qiánmiàn*
   front side, in front of

Gōngsī jiù zài qiánbiān.
The company is just up ahead.

Tā jiā zài huǒchēzhàn de qiánbiān.
Her home is in front of the train station.

hòubiān or *hòumiàn*
back side, in back of, behind

Gōngsī jiù zài hòubiān.
The company is right in the back.

Tā jiā zài huǒchēzhàn de hòubiān.
His home is behind the train station.

Miàn is not normally used with *zuǒ*, left, and *yòu*, right. Use *biān* instead.

Tā zài wǒ de yòubiān.
He is on my right.

Běijīng fàndiàn zài nǐ de yòubiān.
Beijing Hotel is on your right hand side.

shàngbiān or *shàngmiàn*
top side, on, over, above

Fàn zài zhuōzi shàng.
The food is on the table.

xiàbiān or *xiàmiàn*
bottom, under, beneath, below

Shōujù zài yǐzi xiàbiān.
The receipt is under the chair.

lǐbiān or *lǐmiàn*
inside, in

Tā zài chē lǐmiàn.
He is in the car.

zhōngjiān
middle [note the use of *jian*]

Cāntīng de zhōngjiān shì zhuōzi.
In the middle of the dining room is a table.

3. DIRECTIONAL PHRASES WITH MEANS OF TRANSPORTATION

To express that a person is coming, going or returning to a place by a certain means of transportation, use the following pattern:

> Subject + *zuò . . . qí* + means of transportation + *cóng*
> + place + [*dào* + place] + *qù/lái*

Wǒ qí zìxíngchē cóng wǒ jiā dào dàxué qù.
I ride my bike from my house to college.

Tā xǐhuan zuò gōnggòng qìchē cóng jiā dào xuéxiào qù.
She likes to take the bus from home to school.

Or you can simply use the following constructions:

Wǒ zuò gōnggòng qìchē qù huǒchēzhàn.
I take the bus to the train station.

Tā zuò chūzūchē lái shàngbān.
He comes to work by taxi.

Māma qí zìxíngchē huíjiā.
Mom rides her bike to come home.

4. NEGATIVE SUGGESTION PARTICLE *BIÉ*

For negative suggestions or commands, use *bié* before the verb.

Nǐ bié zǒulù.
Don't walk.

Bié dào Yǒuyí Shāngdiàn qù!
Don't go to the Friendship Store!

Bié kèqi.
Don't be polite. [You're welcome.]

5. POLITENESS TERMS

There are several ways to preface an inquiry to a stranger, such as asking for directions or the time. The most common way is to say *duìbùqǐ* (excuse me). You will also hear *máfán nǐ* (I'm sorry to bother you), *qǐngwèn* (may I ask) or *láojià* (may I trouble you).

Duìbùqǐ, cóng zhèr dào Yíhéyuán zěnme zǒu?
Excuse me, how do I get to the Summer Palace from here?

Máfán nǐ, xiànzài jǐdiǎn zhōng?
    Sorry to bother you, but what time is it?

Qǐngwèn, nín xìng shénme?
    May I ask your name?

Láojià, cóng zhèr qù Běijīng zěnme zǒu?
    Excuse me, how do I get to Beijing?

D. HÀNZÌ

Practice the following characters.

很   *hěn* (very)

ノ   ｜   ｲ   ｨ   彳   彳   彳   彳   彳

在   *zài* (at)

一   ナ   ナ   右   右   在

路   *lù* (road)

丶   ｜   口   ロ   卩   足   足   足   足

趵   趵   路   路

北京   *Běijīng* (Beijing)

丨   ⺆   ⺌   北   北

丶   ⼆   宀   古   古   亨   京   京

谢谢 （謝謝）   *xièxie* (thank you)

丶   讠   讠   订   讷   讷   讷   讷   讷

谢   谢   谢

E. SHĒNGCÍ

bié	don't
cóng	from
dòngwù	animal
dòngwùyuán	zoo

duìbùqǐ	excuse me
hòu	back, behind
hónglǜdēng	traffic light
huàn	to change
kèqì	to be polite
láojià	excuse me, may I trouble you?
mòshēngrén	stranger
qián	front
tiáo	[measure word for roads]
wàng	to, toward
wènlù	to ask directions
yòu	right
yuán	park
Yíhéyuán	the Summer Palace
zěnme	How?
zhàn	station
zhí	straight
zhuǎn	turn
zuǒ	left

LIÀNXÍ

A. Change the following statements into alternative questions.

1. *Tā de gōngsī bù yuǎn.*
2. *Huǒchēzhàn hěn jìn.*
3. *Zuò chūzūchē bù piányi.*
4. *Wǒmen xiànzài xiàchē ba.*
5. *Tā jīntiān zuò gōnggòng qìchē.*

B. Write the English equivalents.

1. *Wǒ huíjiā xiūxi, xiūxi.*
2. *Nǐ zài hónglǜdēng wàng yòu zhuǎn.*
3. *Wǒ zuò chē qù Běijīng Shīfàn Dàxué.*
4. *Wǒ cóng wǒ péngyou jiā lái zhèr.*
5. *Dàwèi zài qìchēzhàn děng péngyou.*
6. *Měifēn jiǔdiǎn zuò chē lái shàngbān.*
7. *Míngtiān shì wǒ mèimei de shēngrì.*

C. Fill in the blanks with the most appropriate word according to the clues in parentheses.

1. *Xiānsheng, _____, zhè shì Běijīng Fàndiàn ma?* (may I ask)
2. *Búshì. Běijīng Fàndiàn zài _____.* (in front).
3. *Fàndiàn _____ zhèr yuǎn ma?* (distance from)
4. *Qǐng gàosù wǒ _____ nàr.* (how to go there)
5. *Nǐ _____ qián zǒu yì tiáo jiē, kàn dào hónglǜdēng wàng yòu _____, jiù shì Yǒuyí Shāngdiàn.* (toward, turn)

D. Write the English equivalents.

1. 地铁
2. 汽车
3. 在北京
4. 谢谢
5. 在路上

WÉNHUÀ ZHÙJIĚ

When asking for directions in China, keep in mind the polite terms *qǐngwèn* (may I ask), *duìbùqǐ* (excuse me), *láojià* (may I trouble you) and *xièxie* (thank you). Be careful, though; perhaps even despite good intentions on the part of the direction giver, it is not uncommon for people in China to give you incomplete or erroneous directions. There are people in every country who don't like to admit when they don't know the answer to something; in China, this includes when people don't know where a place is. The ticket takers on the bus will certainly tell you when your stop is approaching, and although some taxi drivers will take you for a wild ride they generally know where they are going. You can find reliable maps in English in most major cities, so try exploring on foot. However, some maps don't do justice to the huge size of many cities so make sure you don't get stuck walking too far!

DÁÀN

A. 1. *Tā de gōngsī yuǎn bù yuǎn?* 2. *Huǒchēzhàn jìn bú jìn?* 3. *Zuò chūzūchē piányi bù piányi?* 4. *Wǒmen xiànzài xià bú xiàchē?* 5. *Tā jīntiān zuò bú zuò gōnggòng qìchē.*

B. 1. I'm going home to rest a little. 2. Turn right at the stoplight. 3. I'm taking a car to Beijing Normal University. 4. I came here from my friend's house. 5. David is waiting at the bus stop for a friend. 6. Meifen is coming to work by car at 9 o'clock. 7. Tomorrow is my little sister's birthday.

C. 1. *qǐngwèn* 2. *qiánbiān* 3. *lí* 4. *zěnme qù* 5. *wàng, zhuǎn*

D. 1. subway 2. car 3. in Beijing 4. thank you 5. on the street

DÌ SHÍ KÈ
Lesson 10

HÀNZÌ. Chinese Characters.

A. DUÌHUÀ

TÁN SHŪFǍ.

David Stone meets a neighbor outside of his building.

ZHĀNG: **Shí xiānsheng, nǐ de Zhōngguóhuà shuō de zhēn biāozhǔn, méiyǒu yìdiǎnr wàiguó kǒuyīn.**

DÀWÈI: **Nǎli, nǎli, bù gǎndāng.**

ZHĀNG: **Nǐ gēn shéi xué Zhōngwén?**

DÀWÈI: **Wǒ yǐqián zài Měiguó xué Zhōngwén. Wǒ de Zhōngwén lǎoshī yào wǒmen duō shuō, duō kàn. Xiànzài zài Běijīng, wǒ měitiān dōu shuō Zhōngguòhuà.**

ZHĀNG: **Zhōngwén zì ne? Nǐ huì xiě, huì kàn ma?**

DÀWÈI: **Wǒ rèn zì rèn de bú cuò, kěshì Zhōngguó zì bù hǎo xiě, wǒ xiě de bù duō.**

ZHĀNG: **Nǐ rènshi duōshǎo Hànzì?**

DÀWÈI: **Chàbùduō qī, bā bǎi ge zì.**

ZHĀNG: **Bù shǎo. Nǐ yīnggāi xué shūfǎ. Xué shūfǎ de shíhòu nǐ yě kěyǐ duō zhīdào Zhōngwén zì yǒu shénme yìsi. Bǐfang shuō "ài" zì zài shàngmiàn yǒu yì zhī shǒu, zhōngjiān yǒu yí ge xīn, xiàmiàn yǒu yì zhī jiǎo. Yìsi shì yí ge rén, zǒu hěn yuǎn de lù, yòng shǒu bǎ tā de xīn gěi tā ài de rén.**

DÀWÈI: **Zhōngwén zì zhēn yǒu yìsi!**

TALKING ABOUT CALLIGRAPHY.

ZHANG: Mr. Stone, your Chinese is quite good (standard). You don't have any foreign accent at all.

DAVID: No, no. You are too polite.

ZHANG: Who taught you Chinese?

DAVID: I studied Chinese in the United States. My Chinese teacher wanted us to speak and read a lot. Now that I'm in Beijing, I speak Chinese every day.

ZHANG: How about Chinese characters? Can you read and write?

DAVID: I can read quite well. However, Chinese characters are difficult to write and I don't write too many.

ZHANG: How many characters do you know?

DAVID: About seven or eight hundred.

ZHANG: Not bad! You should study Chinese calligraphy. That way you might be able to start to understand where the characters come from. For example, the character for "love" has a hand on top, a heart in the middle and a foot on the bottom. The original meaning was that a person would take his heart in his hands and carry it a long distance to give to the person he loves.

DAVID: Chinese characters really are interesting.

B. FĀYĪN

1. FINAL SOUNDS WITH *U*

u	like the <u>u</u> in fl<u>u</u>	**mù** wood; **zhù** to live; **chū** to go out.
ua	like the <u>ua</u> in s<u>ua</u>ve	**huā** flower; **zhuā** to catch; **shuā** to brush
uai	like the <u>wi</u> in <u>wi</u>de	**huài** bad; **kuài** piece; **shuāi** to tumble
uan	like the Spanish name <u>Juan</u>	**tuán** round; **chuān** to wear; **luàn** disorganized
uang	like the <u>ong</u> in th<u>ong</u> with a strong *u* at the beginning	**huáng** yellow; **zhuàng** shape; **chuáng** bed
uo	like the <u>wo</u> in <u>wo</u>n't	**cuò** wrong; **huó** life; **zuò** to do
ui	like the <u>wei</u> in <u>wei</u>gh	**zuì** sin, crime; **suì** age; **guǐ** ghost
un	like the <u>on</u> in w<u>on</u> but with a shorter *o* sound	**shǎn** to twinkle; **kùn** tired; **hūn** to faint

2. FINAL SOUNDS WITH *Ü*

The *ü* sound in Chinese is pronounced like the German *hübsch* or the French *tu*. If you're unfamiliar with this sound, try to say <u>ee</u> as in s<u>ee</u> with your lips puckered. The dots over the *u* are omitted in words spelled with *j*, *q*, *x* and *y*, but remain in words spelled with *n* and *l*. The *üan* sound is the *ü* sound plus the <u>en</u> like in p<u>en</u>. The *üe* sound is *ü* plus the <u>e</u> like in d<u>e</u>bt. The *ün* sound is the *ü* sound plus <u>n</u>.

nǚ woman; **lǚ** travel; **qù** to go; **yǘ** fish

yuán source; **xuǎn** to choose; **quán** spring (of water)

nüè malaria; **lüè** to plunder; **yuè** to jump; **xuě** snow

qún skirt; **jūn** equal; **yún** even

C. YǓFǍ HÉ YÒNGFǍ

1. DESCRIBING AN ACTION WITH V-*DE* + ADJECTIVE

When describing how an action is done, *de* is used directly after the verb and the adjective of manner follows the verb. This *de* is pronounced the same as the possessive particle *de* that you learned about in lesson 1, but is written differently (see the character section).

Wǒ xiě de hěn hǎo.
   I write very well.

Tā kàn de bú cuò.
   He reads well.

An object cannot occur between *de* and the verb. The verb must be repeated in order to accommodate both an object and *de*.

Wǒ xiě zì xiě de hěn hǎo.
   I write characters very well.

Tā shuō Zhōngguóhuà shuō de hěn biāozhǔn.
   She speaks Chinese very well (with a standard accent).

2. THE PREPOSITION *BĂ*

Although the preposition *bă* cannot be translated into English, it implies a sense of disposal, of taking something and giving it away or bringing it somewhere else. In sentences with *bă,* the direct object is brought forward to a position in front of the verb so that the word order becomes Subject + *bă* + direct object + verb + other elements. The verb cannot stand alone, if it is not followed by an indirect object, the verb can be reduplicated or the particle *le* can be added.

Qǐng nǐ bă fángjiān shōushi shōushi.
   Please clean the room.

Tā bă jiăozi chī le.
   She ate the dumplings.

Wǒ yào bă yì běn shū gěi nǐ.
   I want to give you a book.

Tā bă tā de xīn gěi tā de tàitai.
   He gave his heart to his wife.

3. EXPRESSING LARGE NUMBERS

Large numbers in Chinese are categorized differently then they are in English.

yìbăi	one hundred
yīqiān	one thousand
yíwàn	one ten thousand
băiwàn	one million (one hundred ten thousands)
qiānwàn	ten million (one thousand ten thousands)
liăngbăi èrshíqī (or *èrbăi èrshíqī*)	227
bāwàn sānqiānsì (băi)	83,400
wǔbăi qīshíwàn sānqiān èr (băi)	5,703,200

4. ESTIMATING NUMBERS

When estimating numbers in English, the conjunction "or" is often used. In Chinese, all that is needed is a comma between "uncertain" numbers.

Wǒ rènshi qī, bābăi ge zì.
   I recognize seven or eight hundred characters.

Wǒ bù zhīdào tā yǒu liăng, sān ge dìdi.
   I don't know if she has two or three younger brothers.

5. QUESTION WORD *DUŌSHĂO*

The question word *duōshăo* is similar to *jĭ* in that it asks "how much." However, when *duōshăo* is used, a measure word is not required. Generally, *jĭ* is used to inquire about small numbers and *duōshăo* is reserved for larger numbers.

Nĭ yŏu duōshăo qián?
　　How much money do you have?

Tā rènshi duōshăo Hànzì?
　　How many Chinese characters does he recognize?

6. QUESTION WORD *SHÉI*

As with other question words of this type, *shéi* (who) appears in a sentence in the same position as the word which replaces it in the answer.

Nĭ shì shéi?
Wŏ shì Huáng Yànfāng.
　　Who are you?
　　I am Yanfang Huang.

Nĭ gēn shéi xuéxí Zhōngguóhuà?
Wŏ gēn tā xuéxí Zhōngguóhuà.
　　Who did you study Chinese with?
　　I studied Chinese with him.

D. HÀNZÌ

The parts of Chinese characters often have the same meanings from one character to another. In this lesson's dialogue, you read about the character *ài* (love) 爱, which is written in the traditional way like this: 愛

　　The traditional forms of characters usually show the various parts more clearly. In this character, you can see that 手 means "hand," 心 means "heart" and 脚 means "foot." So the character for "love" originally meant that someone carried their heart in their hand over a long distance in order to give it to someone. If you see the same elements in another character, you can be sure that they have an effect on the meaning.

Study the following characters.

说（説）　　　　　　　*shuō* (to speak)

丶　讠　讠　讠　讠　讠　说　说

话 （話）　　　　　*huà* (to speak, language)

丶　讠　讠　计　计　话　话

字　　　　　　　*zì* (character)

丶　丷　宀　宁　字

个 （個）　　　　　*gè* (general measure word)

丿　人　个

爱 （愛）　　　　　*ài* (love)

丿　丷　丷　心　心　爫　爫　孚　爱　爱

E. SHĒNGCÍ

ài	love
biāozhǔn	standard
bǐfang shuō	for example
bú cuò	not bad
bù gǎndāng	you're welcome
chàbùduō	about
cuò	wrong
duō	many
duōshǎo	how many
Hànzì	Chinese characters
huà	speech
jiǎo	foot
kèběn	textbook
kǒuyīn	accent
měitiān	every day
měinián	every year
rèn, rènshi	recognize
shǎo	few
shǒu	hand
shuō	to speak
tán	to discuss
shuōhuà	to speak
shūfǎ	calligraphy
xīn	heart

xué	to study
yǒu yìsi	interesting
yìsi	meaning
yòng	to use
Zhōngguòhuà	Chinese (spoken)
Zhōngwén	Chinese (written)
zì	word, characters

LIÀNXÍ

A. Fill in the blanks according to the English equivalents.

1. *Nǐ de Zhōngwén shuō _____ hěn hǎo.*
   You speak Chinese very well.
2. *Nǐ de Zhōngwén méiyǒu wàiguó _____.*
   Your Chinese doesn't have a foreign accent.
3. *Wǒ _____ dú Zhōngwén.*
   I can read Chinese.
4. *Nǐ _____ jiāo wǒ xiě Zhōngguó zì ma?*
   Could you teach me how to write Chinese characters?
5. *Wǒ de lǎoshī yào wǒmen _____ kàn, _____ shuō.*
   My teacher wants us to read and speak more.

B. Use the words in parentheses to make sentences using *de* and an adjective to describe the action of the verb.

1. *Tā xiě. (hěn hǎo)*
2. *Tā shuō Yīngwén. (biāozhǔn)*
3. *Wǒ gēge zǒu lù. (kuài)*
4. *Tā māma bāo jiǎozi. (hǎo chī)*

C. Write in Chinese *pīnyīn* using the preposition *bǎ*.

1. Please give me the Chinese book.
2. I'm giving him the money.
3. Give the lamp to your mother!

D. Write the following in Chinese characters.

1. I love you.
2. He is American.
3. fifty characters
4. I am speaking.
5. He is getting out of the car.

WÉNHUÀ ZHÙJIĚ

Chinese calligraphy is one of the four ancient arts of China, along with brush painting, opera and classical poetry. The art of calligraphy does not simply consist of drawing stylized versions of Chinese characters. The art expresses a reverence for the long evolution of the written language and the deeper meanings behind each character. To watch a calligrapher at work is quite an inspiration—the brush is held vertically up from the paper with all five fingers keeping balance. The artist uses his whole body to move the brush on the paper and write a character or a poem in one long fluid motion. Many different styles of calligraphy are practiced today in China, from the most straightforward to various "grass" styles, which can be difficult even for a native speaker of Chinese to interpret.

DÁÀN

A. 1. *de* 2. *kǒuyīn* 3. *huì* 4. *kěyǐ* 5. *duō, duō*

B. 1. *Tā xiě de hěn hǎo.* 2. *Tā shuō Yīngwén shuō de hěn biāozhǔn.* 3. *Wǒ gēge zǒulù zǒu de hěn kuài.* 4. *Tā māma bāo jiǎozi bāo de hǎochī.*

C. 1. *Qǐng bǎ Zhōngwén shū gěi wǒ.* 2. *Wǒ bǎ qián gěi tā.* 3. *Nǐ bǎ dēng gěi nǐ de māma!*

D. 1. 我爱你。 2. 他是美国人。 3. 五十个字。 4. 我说话。 5. 他下汽车。

FÙXÍ 2

A. Fill in the blanks with either *zuò* or *qí.*

1. *Nǐ _____ chē ma?*
2. *Wǒ māma _____ zìxíngchē shàngbān.*
3. *Tā _____ gōnggòng qìchē dào Yǒuyí Shāngdiàn qù.*

B. Choose from the measure words in parentheses to complete the sentences.

1. *Nǐ shuō jǐ _____ huà ba. (jù, jiàn, bǎ)*
2. *Zhè _____ shū hěn yǒu yìsi. (bǎ, běn, kuài)*
3. *Qǐng nǐ bǎ yī _____ zhǐ gěi wǒ. (zhāng, kuài, ge)*
4. *Nèi _____ shāfā hěn shūfu. (bǎ, tiáo, tào)*

C. Fill in the particle (*ba, ma, a*) needed to match the English equivalents.

1. *Nǐ qù zuò gōngkè _____ ?*
   Why don't you go do your homework?
2. *Nǐ xǐhuan chī jiǎozi _____ ?*
   Do you like dumplings?
3. *Yǒuyí Shāngdiàn zhēn yuǎn _____ !*
   Yes, the Friendship Store is really far!

D. Choose the appropriate question word from column two to complete the sentences in column one.

One	Two
1. *Tā shì _____ ?*	a. *jǐ*
2. *Tā yǒu _____ ge háizi?*	b. *ma*
3. *Nǐ shuō Zhōngguóhuà _____ ?*	c. *shéi*

E. Write the following in *pīnyīn.*

1. China is quite far from the United States.
2. I want to go home.
3. I came from China.
4. He is going from Beijing University to the Friendship Store.

98

F. Write the English equivalents.

1. 再见！再见！
2. 星期一
3. 房子
4. 汽车
5. 五点钟

G. Fill in the blanks according to the English.

1. 我 _____ 美国 _____ 。
   I am American.
2. 请 _____ 。
   Please sit down.
3. 我会说中国 _____ 。
   I can speak Chinese.
4. 他要坐 _____ 。
   He wants to take the subway.

DÁÀN

A. 1. *zuò* 2. *qí* 3. *zuò*

B. 1. *jù* 2. *běn* 3. *zhāng* 4. *tào*

C. 1. *ba* 2. *ma* 3. *a*

D. 1. C 2. A 3. B

E. 1. *Zhōngguó lí Měiguó hěn yuǎn.* 2. *Wǒ yào huíjiā.* 3. *Wǒ cóng Zhōngguó lái.*
4. *Tā cóng Běijīng Dàxué daò Yǒuyí Shāngdiàn qù.*

F. 1. Good-bye! Good-bye! 2. Monday 3. house 4. car 5. five o'clock

G. 1. 是，人 2. 坐 3. 话 4. 地铁

YUÈDÚ LIÀNXÍ 1 (Reading Practice 1)

Wǒ dìdi shì lǎoshī. Tā xiànzài zài Zhōngguó jiāoshū. Wǒ hěn xiànmù tā, yīnwèi wǒ méiyǒu jīhuì lǚyóu. Wǒ dìdi chángchang shuō tā xiǎng wǒ hé wǒ jiārén, kěshì wǒ zhīdào tā dǎsuàn zài biéde guójiā zhù hěn cháng shíjiān. Wǒ xīngqī yī dào wǒ gōngsī qù. Gōngzuò hěn zhòngyào, kěshì shēnghuó yě hěn zhòngyào.

xiànmù	to be envious of
yīnwèi	because
dǎsuàn	to plan
gōngzuò	to work
shēnghuó	life
zhòngyào	to be important

DÌ SHÍYĪ KÈ
Lesson 11
MǍI DŌNGXI. Shopping.

A. DUÌHUÀ

ZÀI BǍIHUÒ SHĀNGDIÀN

Wenlin and her friend, Mingfen, are shopping for clothes.

DIÀNYUÁN: **Xiǎojie, nǐmen xiǎng kànkan shénme dōngxi?**

WÉNLÍN: **Wǒmen guàngguang. Míngfēn, nǐ kàn, nà jiàn chènshān hǎo kàn ma?**

MÍNGFĒN: **Búcuò. Duìbùqǐ, nèi jiàn chènshān duōshǎo qián?**

DIÀNYUÁN: **Sìshí jiǔ kuài bā máo sì fēn qián.**

MÍNGFĒN: **Nǐ zhèr de chènshān tài guì le!**

DIÀNYUÁN: **Zhè jiàn piányi, zhǐ yào èrshí kuài wǔ máo.**

WÉNLÍN: **Míngfēn, nǐ xǐhuan zhè jiàn ma?**

MÍNGFĒN: **Zhè jiàn tài xiǎo le, wǒ bù xǐhuan. Wǒmen kànkan lǐngdài ba. Zhè tiáo bú cuò. Qǐngwèn, zhè tiáo lǐngdài zěnme mài?**

DIÀNYUÁN: **Qī kuài bā máo wǔ yì tiáo.**

MÍNGFĒN: **Wǒmen xiǎng mǎi sì tiáo. Néng bù néng piányi yìdiǎnr?**

DIÀNYUÁN: **Duìbùqǐ, wǒmen zhèr bù jiǎngjià.**

WÉNLÍN: **Míngfēn, wǒ bù xiǎng mǎi le. Wǒmen zǒu ba.**

MÍNGFĒN: **Hǎo, wǒmen qù kànkan duìmiàn de xīguā. Xiànzài hěn piányi, sān máo qián yì jīn.**

WÉNLÍN: **Hǎo, wǒmen zǒu.**

AT THE DEPARTMENT STORE.

CLERK: Ladies! What would you like to see?

WENLIN: We are just browsing. Mingfen, look! Do you think that blouse is pretty?

MINGFEN: Not bad. Excuse me, how much is that blouse?

CLERK: Forty-nine kuai, eight mao and four fen.

MINGFEN: Your shirts are too expensive.

CLERK: This one is cheaper, only twenty kuai and five mao.

WENLIN: Mingfen, do you like this one?

MINGFEN: It's too small. I don't like it. Let's take a look at the ties. This tie isn't bad. How much does it cost?

CLERK: Ties are seven kuai, eight mao and five fen each.

MINGFEN: We want four. Can you charge us a little less?

CLERK: I'm sorry, we don't bargain here.

WENLIN: Mingfen, I don't want to buy anything. Let's go.

MINGFEN: Okay. We'll look at the watermelons across the street. Right now watermelons are really cheap, only three mao a jin.

WENLIN: Let's go.

B. YǓFǍ HÉ YÒNGFǍ

1. MORE ABOUT MEASURE WORDS

In lesson 7, you learned measure words for several types of objects. Some measure words, in addition to indicating the type of object, also indicate the amount or number of the object.

yì jīn xīguā
    one "jin"* of watermelon

liǎng shuāng wàzi
    two pairs of socks

* One "jin" is equivalent to ½ kilogram.

102

Wǒ méiyǒu wǔ kuài qián.
I don't have five yuan.

Wǒ yào mǎi sān jīn píngguǒ.
I want to buy three "jīn" of apples. [one and a half kilograms]

2. TALKING ABOUT MONEY AND PRICES

The basic unit of currency in China is the *yuán*, which is divided into *jiǎo* (1/10 *yuán*) and *fēn* (1/100 *yuán*). Colloquially, *yuán* are called *kuài* and *jiǎo* are called *máo*.

sānshí kuài yì máo bā fēn
thirty kuai, one mao, eight fen

Qián, or money, can be used when referring to a price, but is ususally deleted in conversation.

sānshí yuán yì jiǎo bā fēn (qián)
thirty yuan, one jiao, eight fen

In colloquial conversation, the money terms *jiǎo* or *fēn* can be deleted if at the end of the price term.

sānshí kuài yì máo bā
thirty kuai, one mao, eight fen

Use the verb *yào* (to want) or *shì* (to be) when indicating the cost of an item. *Yào* and *shì* can be deleted without affecting the meaning.

Zhè jiàn chènshān yào sānshí kuài qián.
This shirt is thirty yuan.

Zhè jiàn chènshān sānshí kuài qián.
This shirt is thirty yuan.

When talking generally about the price of a type of item, the price can come between the item and its measure word or at the end of a sentence after the item and its measure word.

Lǐngdài qī kuài bā máo wǔ yì tiáo.
Ties are seven kuai eight mao five fen each.

Yì tiáo lǐngdài qī kuài bā máo wǔ.
One tie is seven kuai eight mao five fen.

The question word *duōshǎo* (how many) is used when asking about the price of an item.

Zhè jiàn chènshān (yào) duōshǎo qián?
  How much is this shirt?

Lǐngdài duōshǎo qián yì tiáo?
  How much does each tie cost?

However, in many parts of China you will hear the colloquial *zěnme mài*; literally, "how is it sold."

Zhè jiàn chènshān zěnme mài?
  How much for this shirt?

3. TO BUY AND TO SELL (*MǍI* and *MÀI*)

You need to be careful when saying *mǎi* (to buy) or *mài* (to sell) because these words have the same sound—except that *mǎi* (to buy) takes the third tone and *mài* (to sell) takes the fourth tone. This is just one example of how the tone of a word radically effects the meaning.

Nǐ yào mǎi zhège ma?
  Do you want to buy this?

Nǐ yào mài zhège ma?
  Do you want to sell this?

4. NOUN OR PRONOUN + *ZHÈR* OR *NÀR*

Zhèr or *nàr* comes after a noun or pronoun to indicate the location of that noun or pronoun.

Wǒ xǐhuan nǐ zhèr.
  I like your place here. [i.e., someone's home or business]

Nǐ fùmǔ nàr yǒu méiyǒu yòuéryuán?
  Is there a kindergarten where your folks live?

Nǐ zhèr yǒu chènshān ma?
  Do you have shirts here?

5. MODAL VERBS OF DESIRE

Yào (to want) and *xiǎng* (would like) can both be used as modal verbs expressing desire. Remember that modal verbs are used in conjunction with a main verb.

Wǒ xiǎng huíjiā.
I would like to go home.

Wǒ xiǎng mǎi nèi tiáo lǐngdài.
I would like to buy that tie.

Wǒ yào huíqù.
I want to go back.

Wǒ bù xiǎng qù kàn duìmiàn de xīguā.
I don't want to look at the watermelons across the street.

C. HÀNZÌ

If you see the characters for *shāngdiàn* on a sign in China, you will most likely be looking at some kind of department store.

商店　　　　　　　　*shāngdiàn* (store)

Here are some characters that are useful for recognizing the amounts on price tags in China.

元　　　　　　　　*yuán* (yuan)

分　　　　　　　　*fēn* (fen)

毛　　　　　　　　*máo* (mao)

块（塊）　　　　　*kuài* (kuai)

钱（錢）　　　　　*qián* (money)

In China, you might see prices written in characters on cards that are placed near the items for sale.

四十九块八毛四分钱
forty-nine kuai, eight mao and four fen

三毛钱
three mao

五十元
fifty yuan

D. SHĒNGCÍ

bǎihuò shāngdiàn	department store
chènshān	shirt
diànyuán	retail salesperson
dōngxi	thing
fēn	cent
guàng	to browse
guì	expensive
hǎo kàn	good-looking
jiǎngjià	to bargain
jiǎo	ten cents
kuài	dollar
lǐngdài	necktie
piányi	inexpensive
píngguǒ	apple
mài	to sell
mǎi	to buy
mǎimài	to do business
máo	ten cents
wàzi	socks
xīguā	watermelon
yuán	dollar, yuan

LIÀNXÍ

A. Answer the following questions based on the dialogue.

1. *Míngfēn hé Wénlín qù nǎr?*
2. *Míngfēn méiyǒu mǎi shāngdiàn de chènshān? Wèishénme?*
3. *Zhè jiā bǎihuò shāngdiàn jiǎngjià ma?*

B. Fill in the blanks with the most appropriate words.

1. A: *Xiǎoméi, wǒmen qù Yǒuyí Shāngdiàn _____, hǎo ma?* (to browse)
   B: *Hǎo a.*
2. A: *Xiǎojie, zhè _____ chènshān duōshǎo qián?*
   B: _____ (89.99)

C. Match the appropriate answers to the following statements.

1. *Qǐngwèn nǐ yào mǎi shénme?*   a. *Hěn hǎokàn.*
2. *Zhèi tiáo lǐngdài yào wǔbǎi kuài qián.*   b. *Wǒ bù xiǎng chī.*
3. *Nǐ xǐhuan wǒ de shāfā ma?*   c. *Tài guì le.*
4. *Nǐ yào chī shénme?*   d. *Wǒmen guàngguang.*

D. Match the *pīnyīn* to the character.

1. *liù kuài*   a. 上地铁
2. *sāndiǎn zhōng*   b. 三点钟
3. *wǒ shì Měiguórén*   c. 三元五毛八分
4. *xīngqītiān*   d. 星期天
5. *sān yuán wǔ máo bā fēn*   e. 我会说中国话。
6. *shàng dìtiě*   f. 六块
7. *wǒ huì shuō Zhōngguóhuà*   g. 我是美国人。

E. Translate the above examples of *pīnyīn* into English.

WÉNHUÀ ZHÙJIĚ

Bargaining is commonplace in China, particularly at the outdoor markets. In fact, many clothing or electronic merchants who set up shop in the street expect to bargain and enjoy it. At places like the famous silk market in Beijing, you will be quoted prices that are twice as much as what the merchant expects to receive. Be persistent; if you give up bargaining too soon, you lose respect as well as money.

Chinese cities are also full of farmers from the countryside selling their produce in the street. Bargaining is not as common when buying produce mainly because the prices are so low to begin with and the few pennies that you might be able to save mean so much more to a farmer. Bargaining is not allowed at most state-run stores and department stores. If you see the prices posted for items in stores, this usually means that they are fixed and trying to bargain won't get you anywhere.

DÁÀN

A. 1. *Tāmen qù bǎihuò shāngdiàn.* 2. *Yīnwèi chènshān tài guì le!* 3. *Zhè jiā bǎihuò shāngdiàn bù jiǎngjià.*

B. 1. *guàngguang* 2. *jiàn, bāshíjiǔ kuài jiǔ máo jiǔ*

C. 1.d 2.c 3.a 4.b

D. 1.f 2.b 3.g 4.d 5.c 6.a 7.e

E. 1. six kuai 2. three o'clock 3. I am American. 4. Sunday 5. three yuan five mao eight fen 6. to get on the subway 7. I can speak Chinese.

DÌ SHÍÈR KÈ
Lesson 12
ZÀI LǙGUǍN. At a Hotel.

A. DUÌHUÀ

ZÀI LǙGUǍN GUÌTÁI.

Wang Bing arrives in Beijing for a business trip and checks into his hotel.

WÁNG: **Wǒ jiào Wáng Bīng. Wǒ de gōngsī bāng wǒ dìngle yì jiān fángjiān.**

GUÌTÁI: **Huānyíng nín, Wáng xiānsheng. Qǐngwèn, nín yí ge rén lái ma? Yào dānrén fáng háishì shuāngrén fáng?**

WÁNG: **Wǒ zhǐ yǒu yí ge rén, yào dānrén fáng.**

GUÌTÁI: **Zhù duōjiǔ?**

WÁNG: **Wǒ zhù liǎng ge xīngqī.**

GUÌTÁI: **Wǒmen xiànzài zhǐ shèngxia yí ge dānrén fángjiān, zài sān lóu, kěshì méi yǒu kōngtiáo. Yī lóu yǒu liǎng ge kōng fángjiān, dōu yǒu kōngtiáo. Kěshì, shì shuāngrén fáng. Nín yào nǎ yì zhǒng?**

WÁNG: **Qíguài! Wǒ dìng de fángjiān shì yǒu kōngtiáo de dānrén fángjiān!**

GUÌTÁI: **Zhēn duìbùqǐ. Zhè jǐ ge xīngqī lǚkè tài duō. Běijīng měi ge lǚguǎn dōu kěmǎn le.**

WÁNG: **Nàme, shuāngrén fáng de jiàqián zěnme suàn?**

GUÌTÁI: **Měitiān duō jiā sānshí kuài qián ba. Zhēn bàoqiàn!**

WÁNG: **Dǎoméi! Hǎo ba! Hǎo ba! Běijīng de xiàtiān tài rè, wǒ jiù zhù shuāngrén fáng ba.**

GUÌTÁI: **Hǎo. Nǐ de fángjiān shì yī yī liù hào. Zhè shì fángjiān yàoshi.**

WÁNG: **Xièxie.**

_____

AT THE HOTEL'S FRONT DESK.

WANG: My name is Wang Bing. My company reserved a room for me.

DESK CLERK: Welcome, Mr. Wang. May I ask, are you traveling alone? Do you need a single room or a double room?

WANG: I am here by myself, so I need a single room.

DESK CLERK: How long will you be staying?

WANG: I'll be staying two weeks.

DESK CLERK: There's only one single room left right now. It's on the third floor, but it doesn't have air-conditioning. There are two other vacant rooms on the first floor. They have air-conditioning but they are double rooms. Which would you prefer?

WANG: Strange! The room I reserved was an air-conditioned single room.

DESK CLERK: We're truly sorry. There have been so many tourists for the last couple of weeks. Every hotel in Beijing is completely full.

WANG: Then, how much is it for a double room?

DESK CLERK: It's thirty dollars extra per day. Sorry!

WANG: That's too bad! Fine, fine. Summer in Beijing is very hot so I'll take a double room.

DESK CLERK: Okay. Your room number is 116. Here's your key.

WANG: Thanks.

B. YǓFǍ HÉ YÒNGFǍ

1. THE MODAL YÀO INDICATING THE FUTURE

When _yào_ (to want) is used as a modal verb, it can be translated as "to want to do something," but it can also indicate a future action depending on the context.

110

Compare the following two examples.

Wǒ yào mǎi nèi tiáo kùzi.
  I want to buy that pair of pants.

Wǒ míngtiān yào mǎi nèi tiáo kùzi.
  Tomorrow I am going to buy that pair of pants.

Here are more examples of *yào* indicating the future.

Wǒ míngtiān yào qù Yǒuyí Shāngdiàn.
  I am going to go to the Friendship Store tomorrow.

Xuéxiào xiàge xīngqī yào jiéshù.
  School finishes up next week.

Many sentences with *yào* used in this way contain time words, but if the context of a sentence makes the future implication clear, a time word isn't necessary.

Wǒ yào qù.
  I want to go [but will not necessarily go in the near future].

Wǒ yào qù.
  I will go [this, perhaps, in response to the question "are you going?" the speaker plans to go at a specific time in the future].

2. "OR": *HÁISHÌ* VS. *HUÒZHĚ*

Háishì (or) is used to connect two clauses in a question where the response must be a choice between the two options. In this type of construction, if the subject is the same in both clauses it need not be repeated, but there must be a verb in both clauses even if it is the same verb.

Yào dānrén fáng háishì yào shuāngrén fáng?
  Do you want a single room or a double room?

Nǐ xiǎng mǎi nèi shuāng wàzi háishì wǒ mǎi?
  Do you want to buy that pair of socks or shall I?

Huòzhě (or) is used to connect phrases or clauses in a statement, not in a question.

Wǒ xiǎng xiě Zhōngwén zì huòzhě kànshū.
  I want to write Chinese characters or read a book.

111

Wǒ yào qǐng wǒ māma huòzhě wǒ jiějie.
I want to invite my mom or my older sister.

3. THE QUESTION WORD *DUŌJIǓ*

Duōjiǔ (how long) is used similarly to the other question words you have learned, which are placed at the end of a sentence.

Nǐ yào zhù duōjiǔ?
How long do you want to stay?

Nǐ kàn diànshì kàn duōjiǔ?
How long do you watch TV?

Duōjiǔ is found in conjunction with *yào* (to want to) when it implies a future or continuous action.

Nǐ kàn diànshì yào kàn duōjiǔ?
How long are you going to watch TV?

The question word *jǐ* with a specific time word can be used in place of *duōjiǔ*. Remember that *jǐ* does not come at the end of a sentence but is put in place of a number before the measure word.

Nǐ kàn diànshì yào kàn jǐ ge zhōngtóu?
How many hours are you going to watch TV?

Nǐ zhù jǐ tiān.
How many days are you staying?

4. THE PARTICLE *LE* USED WITH VERBS TO SIGNIFY COMPLETION

When the particle *le* is attached to a verb, the implication is that the action of the verb is already completed. Sentences with *le* attached to the verb are generally translated in a past tense in English; it depends on the context whether the sentence implies the simple past tense, the present perfect, or the past continuous.

Nǐ kànle shū ma?
Did you read books? or Have your read books?

Tā yǎngle háizi.
He has raised children.

112

Tā mǎile sān jiàn máoyī.
He bought three sweaters.

Wǒ xuéle sānbǎi ge Hànzì.
I learned three hundred characters.

Use the question word *duōjiǔ* or the question word *jǐ* with the particle *le* to ask how long an activity lasted in the past.

Nǐ xuéle duōjiǔ?
How long did you study?

Wǒ xuéle sān nián.
I studied for three years.

Nǐ zuòle jǐ ge zhōngtóu?
For how many hours did you do it?

Nǐ Zhōngwén xuéle jǐ nián?
How many years have you studied Chinese?

5. RELATIVE CLAUSES

Relative clauses are short phrases that give more information about an element in a sentence. For example, in the sentence "The room that I reserved is too noisy," the relative clause is "that I reserved," and it modifies the noun "room." In Chinese, relative clauses come before the nouns they modify, unlike in English. The particle *de* is used before the modified noun; it can mean "that," "which," "whom" or "where."

Wǒ dìng de fángjiān tài lěng le.
The room that I reserved is too cold.

Tāmen ná de xínglǐ hěn zhòng.
The luggage they are carrying is quite heavy.

Nǐ zhù de fángjiān hěn xiǎo.
The room in which you live is very small.

No matter how long the modifying clause, the modified noun always follows the clause.

Wǒ māma zuótiān wǎnshàng kàn de shū méiyǒu yìsi.
The book that my mother read last night is boring.

Relative clauses can modify nouns that function as the subject or the object of a sentence.

Wǒ māma zuótiān wǎnshàng kàn de shū hěn yǒu yìsi.
    The book that my mother read last night is very interesting. (subject=book)

Wǒ xǐhuan nǐ zhù de fángjiān.
    I like the room that you are living in. (object=room)

6. WORDS WITH *KĚ*

As you know, some Chinese syllables are used in conjunction with different words to impart a certain meaning. For example, you learned in lesson four that *guó* is used with many country names. The syllable *kě* (very) can be added to many adjectival verbs to imply that something is "completely" or "totally" or "very" the verb.

Běijīng měi ge lǚguǎn kěmǎn le.
    Every hotel in Beijing is completely full.

Nǐ de fángzi kěhǎo.
    Your house is really great.

C. HÀNZÌ

Practice the following characters and sentences.

旅馆   *lǚguǎn* (hotel)

丶　　丶　　亠　　方　　方　　斻　　斺　　斿　　斿　　旅

丿　　𠂆　　𠂢　　𰀀　　饣　　饣　　饣　　馆

馆　　馆

楼   *lóu* (floor)

一　　十　　才　　木　　术　　杉　　材　　杉　　杉

样　　楼　　楼　　楼

住   *zhù* (to live, to stay)

丿　　亻　　亻　　住　　住　　住　　住

114

我住在一楼。
Wǒ zhù zài yī lóu.
   I live on the first floor.

我住两个星期。
Wǒ zhù liǎng ge xīngqī.
   I'm staying for two weeks.

他住楼上。
Tā zhù lóushàng
   He lives upstairs.

我们住在旅馆。
Wǒmen zhù zài lǚguǎn.
   We are staying at a hotel.

D. SHĒNGCÍ

bàoqiàn	sorry
dānrén fáng	single room
dǎoméi	to be unfortunate
dìng	to reserve (a room or a table)
háizi	children
jiā	to add
jiàn	[measure word for suitcases and garments]
jiān	[measure words for rooms]
jiàqián	price
kànshū	to read a book
kōng	empty
kōngtiáo	air conditioner
lěngqìjī	air conditioner
lóu	floor
lóushàng	upstairs
lóuxià	downstairs
lǚkè	guest, traveler
ná	to take
qíguài	strange
rè	to be hot
shèngxia	to remain, to be left
shū	book
shuāngrén fáng	double room
suàn	to calculate, to count

xiàtiān	summer
yǎng	to raise
yàoshi	key (door)
zhǒng	kind, type, sort
zhù	to stay (in a hotel, for a set period)

LIÀNXÍ

A. In *pīnyīn*, write the following things that Mr. Wang did yesterday using the particle *le*.

1. Mr. Wang ate a jin of dumplings.
2. Mr. Wang wrote thirty-four Chinese characters.
3. Mr. Wang bought three ties and one shirt.
4. Mr. Wang reserved a room.
5. Mr. Wang bought a watermelon.

B. Combine the following sentences through the use of relative clauses.

EXAMPLE: *Wáng xiānsheng xǐhuan kànshū.*
　　　　　Wáng xiānsheng shì Xiǎoyīng de lǎoshī.
ANSWER: *Xǐhuan kànshū de Wáng xiānsheng shì Xiǎoyīng de lǎoshī.*

1. *Zhāng xiǎojie zài Běijīng tán shēngyi. Tā hěn máng.*
2. *Wáng tàitai dìngle yí ge shuāngrén fángjiān. Shuāngrén fáng yǒu kōngtiáo.*
3. *Lǐ xiānsheng xǐhuan nà jiàn chènshān. Nà jiàn chènshān shí kuài qián.*
4. *Nàge Měiguórén xìng Shí. Tā huì shuō Zhōngguóhuà.*
5. *Wénlín mǎile yì tiáo lǐngdài. Zhè tiáo lǐngdài cóng Zhōngguó lái de.*

C. Fill in the blanks using the following words:

dìng   suàn   zhǒng   bàoqiàn   qíguài   le

1. *Qǐng nǐ bāng wǒ zài nàge lǚguǎn _____ yí ge fángjiān.*
2. *Hěn _____, wǒ bù néng qù jīchǎng jiē nǐ.*
3. *Wǒ dìngle yì jiān dānrén fáng, kěshì lǚguǎn shuō wǒ dìng yì jiān shuāngrén fáng. Zhēn _____!*
4. *Nǐ xǐhuan nǎ _____ fángjiān? Dānrén háishì shuāngrén fáng?*
5. *Wǒ jīnnián mǎi _____ yí ge xīn fángzi.*
6. *Xiǎojie, zhè tào shāfā de jiàqián zěnme _____?*

D. Write the English equivalents.

1. 男厕所在三楼。
2. 他住四个星期。
3. 你房间是二二六。
4. 我们住楼下。
5. 你们旅馆很好。

WÉNHUÀ ZHÙJIĚ

Major Western-style hotels in China operate similarly to major hotels all over the world. You make a reservation and hopefully get the room that you want. In large cities like Beijing and Shanghai, you will find Western hotel chains offering the accommodations that you might be used to, but also at Western prices. The less expensive options—large Chinese hotels, small Chinese hotels or student dormitories—can be difficult to come by, as some hotels don't allow foreigners to stay. Sometimes it is a matter of persistence. If you hear "We don't have any rooms," keep asking and asking until a room "suddenly" opens up. It is possible at some Chinese hotels that the owner might get in trouble if you stay there. Use your best judgment and don't persist in this case. Foreign student or foreign teacher dorms at major universities might offer rooms when the students are away—you just need to go and take your chances.

DÁÀN

A. 1. *Wáng xiānsheng chīle yì jīn jiǎozi.* 2. *Wáng xiānsheng xiěle sānshísì ge Zhōngwén zì.* 3. *Wáng xiānsheng mǎile sān tiáo lǐngdài hé yí jiàn chènshān.* 4. *Wáng xiānsheng dìngle yì jiān fángjiān.* 5. *Wáng xiānsheng mǎile yí ge xīguā.*

B. 1. *Zài Běijīng tán shēngyi de Zhāng xiǎojie hěn máng.* 2. *Wáng tàitai dìng le yǒu kōngtiáo de shuāngrén fáng.* 3. *Lǐ xiānsheng xǐhuan nà jiàn shí kuài qián de chènshān.* 4. *Huì shuō Zhōngguóhuà de Měiguórén xìng Shí.* 5. *Wénlín mǎi le yì tiáo cóng Zhōngguó lái de lǐngdài.*

C. 1. *dìng* 2. *bàoqiàn* 3. *qíguài* 4. *zhǒng* 5. *le* 6. *suàn*

D. 1. The men's room is on the third floor. 2. He's staying for four weeks. 3. Your room is number 226. 4. We are staying downstairs. 5. Your hotel is great.

DÌ SHÍSĀN KÈ
Lesson 13
YÓULĂN. Sight-Seeing.

A. DUÌHUÀ

ZHŬNBÈI DÀO DÀTÓNG QÙ.

Ye Ling and Huang Yanfang plan to take a trip to Datong, in the north of
Shaanxi province.

YÈ LÍNG: **Yànfāng, nǐ qùguò Dàtóng méiyǒu?**

YÀNFĀNG: **Wǒ méi qùguò. Zhè shì nǐ dì jǐ cì zhǔnbèi dào Dàtóng
qù?**

YÈ LÍNG: **Dì sān cì. Dàtóng de dìfāng yǒu wénhuà yǒu lìshǐ.
Fēicháng yǒu yìsi. Wǒ xiǎng xiàtiān de shíhòu kěnéng yǒu hěn
duō de yóukè. Wǒmen yīnggāi dìng yí ge fángjiān.**

YÀNFĀNG: **Hǎo. Xiànzài wǒ de qián bù duō. Wǒmen kě bù kěyi zài
yí ge xuéshēng sùshè zhù? Nǐ zhīdào ma?**

YÈ LÍNG: **Dāngrán kěyǐ. Dàtóng yǒu Yúngǎng Shíkū. Dìzhì Dàxué lí
nèibiānr hěn jìn. Wǒmen zài nàr zhù dàgài méiyǒu wèntí.
Zhèyàng wǒmen kěyǐ yì tiān qù kàn yì kàn Yúngǎng Shíkū
ránhòu yì tiān zuò gōnggòng qìchē dào Xuánkōng Sì qù.**

YÀNFĀNG: **Yúngǎng Shíkū shì nǎge niándài de?**

YÈ LÍNG: **Shì dì wǔ shìjì de. Jiùshì wèile bài fó jiàn de.**

YÀNFĀNG: **Tǐng yǒu yìsi.**

PREPARING TO GO TO DATONG.

YE LING: Yanfang, have you ever been to Datong?

YANFANG: I've never been. How many times have you been?

YE LING: This is the third time. The places in Datong are full of culture and history. Very interesting. I bet in the summer there are a lot of tourists. We should reserve a room.

YANFANG: Okay. I don't have a whole lot of money right now. Do you think we could stay in a student dorm? Do you know?

YE LING: I'm sure we can. Datong has the Yungang Caves, and nearby there's a geology college. We probably can stay there. That way we could spend a day at the Yungang Caves and then take the bus another day to see the Hanging Temple.

YANFANG: What century are the caves from?

YE LING: They're from the fifth century. They were built for worshiping Buddha.

YANFANG: How interesting!

B. YǓFǍ HÉ YÒNGFǍ

1. THE QUESTION WORD *JǏ* AND ORDINAL NUMBERS

You learned about ordinal numbers in lesson 4. It is much easier in Chinese than in English to ask about a number in a sequence. In Chinese, you simply say *dì jǐ ge*. Of course, any measure word can replace *ge*.

Zhè shì dì jǐ kè?
Which lesson is this?

Zhè shì nǐ dì jǐ cì lái?
How many times have you been here? (Literally, which number time is this for you to come here?)

2. NEGATING SENTENCES WITH *LE* ATTACHED TO THE VERB

Sentences with the particle *le* used with the verb are negated with *méiyǒu*. *Méiyǒu* implies that an action has not been completed in the past, so *le* is deleted.

Wǒ chīfàn le.
I ate./I have eaten.

Wǒ méi(yǒu) chīfàn.

I have not eaten.

Wǒ xuéle sān nián.

I studied for three years.

Wǒ méiyǒu xué sān nián.

I didn't study for three years.

3. ASKING QUESTIONS WITH *LE* ATTACHED TO THE VERB

The sentence final particle *ma* can be added to sentences containing *le* to form questions. Alternative questions are formed using *méiyǒu* which is placed at the end of the sentence after the object.

Nǐ chī le méiyǒu?

Did you eat / have you eaten?

Tā xué le ma?

Has she studied?

4. *GUÒ* ATTACHED TO THE VERB EXPRESSING COMPLETED ACTION

When *guò* is used with a verb, the implication is that the verb has been experienced in a general way, similar to saying "I have done that" in English. This differs from the specific completed action that a verb used with *le* expresses.

Tā qùguò Dàtóng.

She has been to Datong.

Tà qù Dàtóng le.

She went to Datong [and is there now].

Wǒ chīle hěn duō cì Zhōngguó fàn.

I've eaten Chinese food many times.

Wǒ chīguò Zhōngguó fàn.

I have eaten Chinese food.

To negate sentences with *guò*, place *méiyǒu* before the verb.

Tā méi (yǒu) qùguò Dàtóng.

He has never been to Datong.

120

Wǒ māma méi(yǒu) láiguò wǒ de jiā.
My mother has never been to my house.

Questions with *guò* can be formed either with the sentence final particle *ma* or with question words or as alternative questions with *méiyǒu*.

Tā láiguò nǐ jiā jǐ cì?
How many times has she been to your house?

Tā láiguò nǐ jiā ma?
Has she ever been to your house?

Tā chīguò Zhōngguó fàn méi(yǒu)?
Has she ever eaten Chinese food?

5. THE CONJUNCTION *RÁNHÒU*

The conjunction *ránhòu* (and then) is used to connect phrases or clauses that follow each other sequentially. The subject of each phrase or clause need not be the same.

Wǒ qù shuìjiào ránhòu nǐ kěyǐ kànshū.
I'll go to sleep then you can read.

Wǒmen kěyǐ yì tiān qù kàn Yúngǎng Shíkū ránhòu yì tiān dào Xuánkōng Sì qù.
We can go to the Yungang Caves one day and then another day go to the Hanging Temple.

6. MORE ABOUT USING *LÍ* TO EXPRESS DISTANCE

In lesson 8, you learned about using *lí* (between) to express distance between two places.

Dìzhì Dàxué lí nèibiān hěn jìn.
Near there is the Geology College.

You can also begin a sentence with *lí* in conjunction with *yǒu* (to have) used in the passive sense (you will learn more about this in lesson 15).

Lí lǚguǎn yì lǐ yǒu bǎihuò shāngdiàn.
One mile from the hotel is the department store.

7. JIÙSHÌ

Jiùshì (literally, "just is") is an expression that means "the one and only" or "precisely."

Nǐ shì Huáng lǎoshī ma?
Wǒ jiùshì.
    Are you Teacher Huang?
    The one and only.

When *jiùshì* is used in stating a fact, it implies that the fact is quite interesting.

Yúngǎng Shíkū jiùshì wèile bài fó jiàn de.
    The Yungang Caves were built to worship Buddha.

C. HÀNZÌ

Read these new characters.

从（從）   *cóng* (from)

到   *dào* (to)

去   *qù* (to go)

来（來）   *lái* (to come)

有   *yǒu* (to have)

没有   *méiyǒu* (do not have)

122

意思   *yìsi* (interesting)

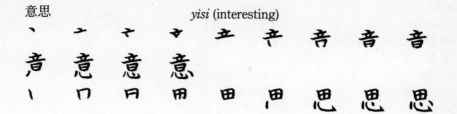

Read the following sentences.

你很有意思。

Nǐ hěn yǒu yìsi.

　　You are quite interesting.

我没有钱。

Wǒ méiyǒu qián.

　　I don't have any money.

他从美国到中国来。

Tā cóng Měiguó dào Zhōngguó lái.

　　He is coming to China from America.

他从北京到美国去。

Tā cóng Běijīng dào Měiguó qù.

　　He went to America from Beijing.

D. SHĒNGCÍ

bài	to worship
cháo	dynasty
dàgài	probably
Dàtóng	a town in northen Shanxi province
dìfāng	place
dìzhì	geology
dòng	cave
fēicháng	very
Fó	Buddha
Fójiào	Buddhism
gài	to build
guò	[particle implying "ever" or "never"]
jiào	belief system
kěnéng	possibly

lìshǐ	history
niándài	era
ránhòu	then
sùshè	dormitory
wèile	for the purpose of
wénhuà	culture
wèntí	problem
xuéshēng	student
yīnggāi	should
yìsi	meaning
yǒu yìsi	to be interesting
yóukè	tourists
yóulǎn	to go sight-seeing
zhǔnbèi	to prepare

LIÀNXÍ

A. Translate the following sentences into *pīnyīn*.

1. How many times have you stayed in the student dormitory?
2. I've been to Datong twice.
3. This is my third time to China.
4. What number shirt is this for you?

B. Ask questions to ellicit the following responses.

1. *Wǒ chīguò Zhōngguófàn.*
2. *Tāmen qùle Yǒuyí Shāngdiàn.*
3. *Wǒ xuéguò Rìyǔ.*
4. *Wǒmen kànle shū.*

C. Place either *le* or *guò* in the spaces provided.

1. *Nǐ chī zǎofàn _____ méiyǒu?*
2. *Tā jīntiān dào Yǒuyí Shāngdiàn qù _____ ma?*
3. *Tā cónglái méi qù _____ Yǒuyí Shāngdiàn.*
4. *Tā jīntiān chī _____ hěn duō fàn.*
5. *Tā chī _____ hěn duō cì Zhōngguófàn.*

D. Match the chinese character to the English.

1. 从
2. 去
3. 来
4. 有
5. 有意思

a. interesting
b. to go
c. to have
d. to come
e. from

E. Write the following in Chinese characters and then translate into English.

1. *Wǒ xiàge xīngqī cóng Měiguó dào Zhōngguó qù.*
2. *Běijīng hěn yǒu yìsi.*
3. *Tā zuò dìtiě cóng shāngdiàn lái.*

WÉNHUÀ ZHÙJIĚ

Buddhism developed in China in the 3rd to 6th centuries A.D., probably brought there by Indian merchants along the Silk Road. Today, although the Chinese government professes atheism, there still exists a significant Buddhist population that worships in temples all over the country. Taoist worship, involving spirits and faith healing, is one of the oldest of the world's religions and still has its adherents in China. Confucianism has a stronger presence, although it is more of a philosophy than a religion. It stresses filial piety and love of government—both strong forces throughout the course of China's history.

The Christian population in China is also steadily growing. The government provides authorized churches, both Protestant and Catholic, and in many cities their congregations are growing into the thousands.

DÁÀN

A. 1. *Nǐ zài xuéshēng sùshè zhùle jǐ cì?* 2. *Wǒ qùle Dàtóng liǎng cì.* 3. *Zhè shì wǒ dì sān cì lái Zhōngguó.* 4. *Zhè shì nǐ dì jǐ jiàn chènshān?*

B. 1. *Nǐ chīguò Zhōngguó fàn méiyǒu?* 2. *Tāmen qù le Yǒuyí Shāngdiàn ma?* 3. *Nǐ xuéguò Rìyǔ ma?* 4. *Nǐmen zuòle shénme?*

C. 1. *le* 2. *le* 3. *guò* 4. *le* 5. *guò*

D. 1.e 2.b 3.d 4.c 5.a

E. 1. 我下个星期从美国到中国去。I'm going from America to China next week. 2. 北京很有意思。Beijing is very interesting. 3. 他坐地铁从商店来。He is taking the subway here from the department store.

DÌ SHÍSÌ KÈ
Lesson 14
ZÀI FÀNGUǍN. At a Restaurant.

A. DUÌHUÀ

CHĪ BĚIJĪNG KǍOYĀ.

To welcome Mr. Stone to Beijing, his friend Mr. Li invites him to a local restaurant.

LǏ: Shí, nǐ zuótiān wǎnshàng shuì de zěnmeyàng? Shuì de hǎo ma? Xiànzài yǒu méiyǒu shíchā?

SHÍ: Wǒ shuì de hěn hǎo. Zuówǎn yí jìn fángjiān, wǒ jiù shuìjiào le. Suǒyǐ méi shíchā.

LǏ: Tài hǎo le! Wǒ qǐng nǐ qù chī Běijīng kǎoyā, gěi nǐ jiēfēng. Zěnmeyàng?

SHÍ: Hǎo a! Wǒ xiànzài è le.

_____

ZÀI FÀNGUǍN.

FÚWÙ YUÁN: Xiānsheng, zhè shì wǒmen de càidān. Nǐmen xiǎng diǎn shénme?

SHÍ: Wǒ bú tài shúxi càimíng. Lǐ, nǐ bāng wǒ jiào ba.

LǏ: Hǎo. Wǒmen lái yí ge Běijīng kǎoyā. Shí, nǐ chī bù chī là de?

SHÍ: Tián de, suān de, là de, wǒ dōu chī; wǒ jiùshì bù chī kǔ de.

LǏ: Hǎo. Wǒmen yào yí ge Gōngbǎo jī dīng, yí ge hóngshāo dòufu, zài chǎo yì pán qīngcài.

FÚWÙ YUÁN: Liǎng wèi xiānsheng yào mǐfàn háishì yào jiǎozi?

LǏ: Lái yìdiǎn mǐfàn ba.

FÚWÙ YUÁN: Nǐmen hē shénme yǐnliào?

LǏ: Shí, nǐ xiǎng hē píjiǔ háishì guǒzhī? Wǒmen lái liǎng píng Qīngdǎo píjiǔ, zěnmeyàng?

SHÍ: Hǎo!

_____

EATING BEIJING DUCK.

LI: Stone! How did you sleep last night? Did you sleep well? Do you have jet lag?

STONE: I slept well last night. As soon as I got into the room, I went to bed right away. So I don't have jet lag at all.

LI: Great! How about I treat you to Beijing duck to welcome you?

STONE: Okay! I am hungry.

_____

AT THE RESTAURANT.

WAITER: Gentlemen, this is our menu. What would you like to order?

STONE: I'm not familiar with the dishes. Li, why don't you order?

LI: Okay. Let's have Beijing duck. Stone, do you like spicy food?

STONE: I like sweet, sour and spicy food, but nothing bitter.

LI: Fine. We'll also have Gongbao chicken, tofu with brown sauce, and stir-fried vegetables.

WAITER: Would you gentlemen like steamed rice or dumplings?

LI: How about some rice?

WAITER: What would you like to drink?

LI: Stone, do you want beer or juice? How about a couple of bottles of Qingdao beer?

STONE: Great!

B. YǓFǍ HÉ YÒNGFǍ

1. ORDERING FOOD IN A RESTAURANT

Diǎn cài means "to order food" and the verb *lái* (to come) is used to mean "please bring" a dish.

Wǒmen lái yí ge Běijīng kǎoyā.
  Bring us a Beijing duck.

Lái yìdiǎn mǐfàn.
  Bring some rice.

Wǒmen lái liǎng píng píjiǔ.
  Bring us two bottles of beer.

2. DELETING A MODIFIED NOUN

The modified noun in a relative clause may be deleted if the context makes it clear.

Zhè shì wǒ de shū.
  This is my book.

Zhè shì wǒ de.
  This is mine. [While pointing to a book.]

Zhège fángjiān shì wǒ dìng de fángjiān.
  This room is the room that I reserved.

Zhè jiān fángjiān shì wǒ dìng de.
  This room is the one that I reserved.

Tián de cài, suān de cài, là de cài wǒ dōu xǐhuan.
  Sweet food, sour food, spicy food—I like it all.

Tián de, suān de, là de wǒ dōu xǐhuan.
  Sweet, sour, spicy—I like it all.

3. SENTENCE FINAL PARTICLE *LE*

The particle *le* is used at the end of sentences to stress that what is being said is important or relevant to the situation at hand or the situation under discussion. It is one of the most commonly used sentence final particles and can imply several different meanings depending on the context. Most often, sentence final *le* is used to indicate that what is being said is a change which will effect the

129

current situation in an important way, what in English might be expressed by "now" or "just."

Wǒ è le.
   I just got hungry. [So I want to eat soon.]

Tā zhīdào nèige xiāoxi le.
   He knows that piece of news now. [So you don't have to tell him.]

Tā shì wǒ de péngyou le.
   She is my friend now. [Which is why I'm suddenly being nice to her.]

Le is similarly used to indicate that something has happened, or is about to happen, that will determine how a situation progresses.

Huǒchē kuài yào kāi le.
   The train is about to leave. [So you'd better get on.]

Wǒ zuòwán gōngkè le.
   I finished my homework. [So we can go to the movies soon.]

Sentence final *le* is also used to indicate that the listener is being brought up to date on a situation, where "finally" or "to this point" or "still" might be used in English.

Wǒ zuótiān dào Zhāng jiā chīfàn le.
   I finally went to the Zhang's house for dinner yesterday.

Shí xiānsheng xiàge yuè yào huí Měiguó le.
   Mr. Stone is still going back to America next month.

Nǐ jǐ suì le?
   How old are you now?

Le can be used when a wrong assumption is being corrected, what in English might be stated with "on the contrary" or "but."

[To the accusation that the speaker has spent the afternoon sleeping:]
Wǒ kànle sān běn shū le!
   [On the contrary!] I have read three books!

[To the suggestion that the speaker go to the movies.]
Wǒ yào qù shàngbān le!
   But I have to go to work!

Much like "all I have to say" in English, *le* is used to indicate that the speaker has nothing more to add to the subject.

Tā yǐjīng líkāi Zhōngguó le.
   All I have to say is that he already left China. [I don't know what has happened since then.]

Hǎo le!
   Fine! [I am done discussing this with you!]

Compare sentences containing the verb suffix *le* to those with the sentence final *le*.

Wǒ kànle diànshì.
   I watched TV [at some unspecified point in the past].

Wǒ kàn diànshì le.
   But I've watched TV [so I don't want to watch it anymore today].

Wǒ chīle tài duō.
   I ate too much [that day in the past].

Wǒ chī tài duō le.
   I ate too much [so please don't give me anymore food now].

4. RESULTATIVE VERBS OF COMPLETION

You have already learned about several different types of compound verbs. Resultative verbs are verbs which have a second syllable attached to the main verb. This syllable can indicate a direction or degree of completion. You will learn more about resultative verbs of direction in a later lesson. The resultative verb ending *wán* indicates completion and can be attached to almost any verb.

Wǒ chīwán le.
   I am finished eating.

Wǒ de gōngkè zuòwán le.
   My homework is finished.

Nǐ shénme shíhòu yào zuòwán nǐ de gōngkè?
   When are you planning on finishing your homework?

5. THE CONJUNCTION *YĪ . . . JIÙ*

The conjunction *yī . . . jiù* connects two phrases or clauses to mean "as soon as . . . then . . . " The subjects of the two parts may or may not be the same.

Wǒ yí jìn fángjiān, jiù shuìjiào le.

As soon as I got into the room, I fell asleep.

Tā yì lái Běijīng, wǒ jiù qǐng tā chīfàn.

As soon as she comes to Beijing, I will invite her to dinner.

6. MORE ABOUT THE ADVERB *DŌU*

You already know that *dōu* is used with plural subjects to mean "all." *Dōu* can also be used to refer to a series of phrases, all of which the subject of the sentence acts upon in the same way. If someone is offering an opinion, as in the last example, the phrases themselves form the subject.

Tián de, suān de, là de, wǒ dōu chī.

Sweet, sour, spicy—I eat them all.

Jīdīng, doùfu, qīngcài, tā dōu xǐhuan.

Diced chicken, tofu, vegetables, she likes them all.

Běijīng, Niǔyuē, Bōshìdùn dōu yǒu yìsi.

Beijing, New York and Boston are all interesting.

C. HÀNZÌ

Practice writing these characters.

吃   *chī* (to eat)

丶   冂   口   叮   吒   吃

吃饭（吃飯）   *chīfàn* (to eat a meal)

丿   人   饣   饣   饣   饭   饭

饭店（飯店）   *fàndiàn* (restaurant)

Being able to recognize these characters will help you look at restaurant menus in China. The names of dishes can be complicated, but if you see one of these general food characters in a name you can be fairly sure of what type of meat or tofu you will be served.

牛肉   *niúròu* (beef)

羊肉   *yángròu* (lamb)

鸡肉   *jīròu* (chicken)

鱼   *yú* (fish)

烤鸭	*kǎoyā* (roasted duck)
蔬菜	*shūcài* (vegetables)
豆腐	*dòufu* (tofu)
猪肉	*zhūròu* (pork)
米饭	*mǐfàn* (rice)
啤酒	*píjiǔ* (beer)
辣	*là* (spicy)
甜酸	*tiánsuān* (sweet and sour)

D. SHĒNGCÍ

càidān	menu
chǎo	to stir-fry
diǎn (cài)	to order food
fànguǎn(r)	restaurant
fúwù	service, to serve
fúwùyuán	waiter, waitress
Gōngbǎo jīdīng	Kongpao chicken
hǎixiān	seafood
hóngshāo	cooked in soy sauce
jī	chicken
jīròu	chicken (meat)
jīdīng	chunks of chicken
jiēfēng	to treat a guest to a welcoming dinner
kǎo	to roast, to barbeque
kǔ	to be bitter
kuàizi	chopsticks
là	to be spicy
mǐfàn	rice
pán	plate [measure word]
qīngcài	vegetables
ròu	meat, flesh
shíchā	jet lag, time difference
shūcài	green vegetables
shúxi	to be familiar with someone or something
suān	to be sour
tāng	soup
tián	to be sweet
tiánsuān	sweet and sour
yā	duck

yángròu	lamb
yǐnliào	drink
yú	fish
zhūròu	pork

SUPPLEMENTARY VOCABULARY 3: FOOD

niúròu	beef
niúpái	steak
zhūròu	pork
jīròu	chicken
yángròu	lamb
yāròu	duck
hǎixiān	seafood
hǎidài	seaweed
yú	fish
xiā	shrimp
xiè	crab
xièròu	crabmeat
lóngxiā	lobster
yóuyú	squid
dòufu	tofu
báicài	bok choy
huācài	cauliflower
yùmǐ	corn
zhúsuěn	bamboo shoot
lúsǔn	asparagus
dòuyá	bean sprout
mógu	mushroom
qíncài	celery
húluóbo	carrot
xīhóngshì	tomato
huángguā	cucumber
yángcōng	onion
tǔdòu	potato
shuǐguǒ	fruit
shūcài, qīngcài	vegetable
júzi	tangerine
píngguǒ	apple
lǐzi	lychee

cǎoméi	strawberry
níngméng	lemon
xiāngjiāo	banana
yīngtao	cherry
méizi	plum
táo	peach
lí	pear
zhīma	sesame seed
zhīmayóu	sesame oil
xìngrén	almond
huāshēng	peanut
tiáowèipǐn	seasoning, spices
dàsuàn	garlic
jiāng	ginger
hēihújiāo	black pepper
làjiāo	chili pepper
jiàngyóu	soy sauce
yán	salt
yóu	oil
huāshēngyóu	peanut oil
yǐnliào	beverage
shuǐ	water
chá	tea
kāfēi	coffee
guǒzhī	juice
qìshuǐ	soda
niúnǎi	milk
rǔlào	cheese
huángyóu	butter
jīdàn	egg
dànbái	egg white
dànhuáng	egg yolk
dòu	bean
mǐfàn	rice
miànbāo	bread
dàngāo	cake
bǐng	cookie
tángguǒ	candy
bīngqílín	ice cream

LIÀNXÍ

A. Translate the following sentences in English.

1. *Jī, yā, yú, wǒ dōu chī le.*
2. *Nǐmen xiǎng diǎn shènme?*
3. *Gōngbǎo jīdīng shì là de.*
4. *Wǒ shùi de hěn hǎo, méiyǒu shíchā.*

B. Answer the following questions using the appropriate negative form.

1. *Nǐ chī qīngcài ma?*
2. *Nǐ hēle píjiǔ méiyǒu?*
3. *Nǐ qùguò Rìběn ma?*
4. *Nǐ kànle diànshì ma?*
5. *Nǐ chīguò Zhōngguó cài méiyǒu?*
6. *Nǐ de mǔqīn qù fànguǎnr ma?*

C. Fill in the blanks according to the English.

1. *Wǒ de gōngkè zuò _____ le.*
   My homework is finished.
2. *Tā zhīdào nèige xiāoxi _____.*
   Now he knows that bit of news.
3. *Nǐ _____ suì le?*
   How old are you now?
4. *Nǐ chīguò _____ méiyǒu?*
   Have you ever eaten roast duck?

D. Translate into Chinese *pīnyīn*.

1. I have finished ordering the food.
2. As soon as I finish eating, I go to sleep.
3. Subways, buses, I take them all.
4. Yesterday I went to the Li's to eat.

136

E. Write the English for these characters.

1. 牛肉
2. 羊肉
3. 鸡肉
4. 鱼
5. 烤鸭
6. 蔬菜
7. 豆腐
8. 猪肉
9. 米饭
10. 啤酒

WÉNHUÀ ZHÙJIĚ

Ordering food in restaurants in China is something of a rushed ritual. The *fúwù yuán* (waiter) allows very little time for you to peruse the menu and will stand over you while you decide. If a Chinese host has invited you to the meal, he or she will make quite a show of ordering the food—choosing mostly exotic dishes and usually far too many of them. The custom is to show the guest how much he or she is appreciated and honored. The dishes arrive in a particular order. First, the "stir-fries" of various kinds, then *tāng* (soups), then a whole fish (the guest of honor is often given the eyes and the brain of the fish, so beware!), then dumplings or rice and finally fruit. Rice is rarely eaten with the rest of the meal, as it is in Chinese restaurants here, and in some cases it is rude to ask for rice at the end of the meal because you imply that the dishes weren't plentiful or delicious enough. Desserts, with the exception of fruit, are rarely offered, but beer, fruit juice and tea are abundantly offered in restaurants.

DÁÀN

A. 1. Chicken, duck, fish, I've had them all. 2. What would you like to order? 3. Gongbao chicken is spicy. 4. I slept well and have no jet lag.

B. 1. *Wǒ bù chī qīngcài.* 2. *Wǒ méi hē píjiǔ.* 3. *Wǒ méiyǒu qùguò Rìběn.* 4. *Wǒ méi kàn diànshì.* 5. *Wǒ méi chīguò Zhōngguó cài.* 6. *Tā bù qù.*

C. 1. *wán* 2. *le* 3. *jǐ* 4. *kǎoyā*

D. 1. *Wǒ diǎnwán le cài.* 2. *Wǒ yì chīwán fàn, wǒ jiù shuìjiào.* 3. *Dìtiě, gōnggòng qìchē, wǒ dōu zuò.* 4. *Wǒ zuótiān qù Lǐ jiā chīfàn le.*

E. 1. beef 2. lamb 3. chicken 4. fish 5. roast duck 6. vegetables 7. tofu 8. pork 9. rice 10. beer

DÌ SHÍWǓ KÈ
Lesson 15
BÈI DÀO LE! There's Been a Robbery!

A. DUÌHUÀ

Zài Qīngyuè hé Hǎixīng de jiā.

Qingyue and Haixing arrived home to find that their house had been robbed.

QĪNGYUÈ: **Hǎixīng, mén zěnme kāizhe? Nǐ chūmén yǐqián méiyǒu suǒ mén ma?**

HǍIXĪNG: **Bú huì ba! Wǒ jìde chūmén de shíhòu, wǒ suǒhǎo mén le.**

QĪNGYUÈ: **Zhēn qíguài! Chuānghù yě shì kāizhe.**

HǍIXĪNG: **Āiyā! Bú shì zéi jìn lái tōu dōngxi? Nǐ gǎnkuài qù kànkan, yǒu méiyǒu dōngxi diū le?**

QĪNGYUÈ: **Zāogāo! Wòshì de chōutì dōu kāizhe. Yīguì lǐ de yīfu yě bú jiàn le.**

HǍIXĪNG: **Qīngyuè, wǒmen de diànshì, shōuyīnjī yě dōu bú jiàn le.**

QĪNGYUÈ: **Nǐ gǎnkuài dǎ diànhuà gěi jǐngchá a!**

HǍIXĪNG: **Kěshì diànhuà yě bú jiàn le. Zhèyàng ba! Wǒ zǒulù qù qiánmiàn de pàichūsuǒ bàoàn. Nǐ dào gébì wènwen Wáng tàitai. Yěxǔ tā kàndào zéi le.**

QĪNGYUÈ: **Wǒ xiànzài jiù qù.**

At Qingyue and Haixing's house.

QINGYUE: Haixing, how come the door is open? Didn't you lock the door before you left?

HAIXING: No way! I remember I locked the door when I left.

QINGYUE: Strange! The windows are also open.

HAIXING: Oh no! Did a burglar come in and steal something? Go check to see if anything is missing.

QINGYUE: Damn! All of the drawers in the bedroom are open. The clothes in the closets are gone.

HAIXING: Qingyue, our TV and radio have disappeared, too.

QINGYUE: Call the police right away!

HAIXING: But the telephone is gone, too. How about this: I'll walk to the police station down the road to report the case and you go next door and talk to Mrs. Wang. Maybe she saw the burglar.

QINGYUE: I'll go right now.

B. YŬFĂ HÉ YÒNGFĂ

1. RESULTATIVE VERBS OF DIRECTION

You already know that the resultative verb endings *hǎo* or *wán* indicate that the action of the verb has been completed. Directional verb endings are added to verbs of motion to show whether the motion is toward the speaker (*lái*) or away from the speaker (*qù*).

jìn lái	come in
chū lái	come out
zǒu lái	walk over here
jìn qù	go in
chū qù	go out
zǒu qù	walk over there

Zéi jìn lái tōu dōngxi le.
  The thief came in and stole things.

Háizi pǎo chū qù le.
  The kids ran outside.

With verb-object compound verbs, the object is placed in between the verb and the directional ending.

Tā shàng shān qù le.
  He went up the mountain.

Wǒ zǒu dào fànguǎn qù le.
  I walked to the restaurant.

140

2. RESULTATIVE VERBS OF PERCEPTION

The resultative verb endings *dào* (to arrive) and *jiàn* (to perceive) are added to verbs of perception like *kàn* (to see), *tīng* (to hear) and *wén* (to smell) to indicate that something has been successfully perceived. Note that *dào* is more often used with singular events and *jiàn* is used for a more general perception. *Jiàn* is not used with *wén* (to smell).

Wǒ xiǎng kàn nàge diànyǐng; kěshì rén tài duō le, méiyǒu kàndào.
I wanted to see that movie, but there are too many people there so I didn't see it.

Wǒ tīngdào tā shuō de hùa le.
I heard what he said.

Tā méiyǒu wéndào huā xiāng.
He didn't smell the flowers.

Wǒ kànjiàn nǐ le!
I see you!

Wǒ tīng de jiàn nǐ shuō de huà le.
I can hear what you are saying.

3. THE PARTICLE *ZHE* USED FOR A PRESENT CONTINUOUS ACTION

When the particle *zhe* is attached to a verb, it means that the action of the verb is continuously happening in the present. This can be expressed in English with the "-ing" ending or in the simple present with the implication that the action has been going on and will continue to go on. *Zhe* appears with verbs whose action is often prolonged, like *kāi* (to open), *zuò* (to sit) and *suǒ* (to lock).

Chuānghù kāizhe.
The window is open.

Mén suǒzhe.
The door is locked.

Tā zuòzhe.
He is sitting.

The negative of this verb form is made by adding *méiyǒu* before the verb.

Chuānghù méiyǒu kāizhe.
The window isn't open.

Mén méiyŏu suŏzhe.
   The door is not locked.

Tā méiyŏu zuòzhe.
   He is not sitting.

4. THE EXPRESSION *SHÌ BÚ SHÌ*

When *shì bú shì* is used at the beginning of a sentence, it serves to question the truth of the sentence, what we might say in English "did . . . really happen?"

Shì bú shì zéi jìn lái le?
   Did the thieves really come in?

Shì bú shì tā méi suŏ mén?
   Did he really not lock the door?

Shì bú shì tā huílái le?
   Is he really coming back?

C. HÀNZÌ

Here are the characters for "entrance" and "exit" that you will see on signs in China.

入口   *rùkŏu* (entrance)

丿 入   丶 冂 口

出口   *chūkŏu* (exit)

凵 屮 出 出 出

Read these additional characters and sentences.

了	*le* (particle)
门（門）	*mén* (door)
开（開）	*kāi* (to open)
锁（鎖）	*suŏ* (to lock)
着	*zhe* (particle)
见（見）	*jiàn* (to see)

出口锁着。

Chūkŏu suŏzhe.
   The exit is locked.

142

钱不见了！

Qián bú jiàn le!
  The money is missing!

D. SHĒNGCÍ

aīyā	oh no! oh dear!
bàoàn	to report a crime
bú jiàn	to have disappeared
chōutì	drawer
chūkǒu	exit
chūmén	to exit, to go out
diànshì	TV
diū	to lose
gǎnkuài	quickly, at once
gébì	neighboring
jìde	to remember
jìn lái	to come in
jǐngchá	policeman
línjū	neighbor
mén	door
pàichūsuǒ	local police station
rùkǒu	entrance
shīqiè	to have something stolen
shōuyīnjī	radio
suǒ	to lock
suǒmén	to lock a door
tōu	to steal
xiǎotōu	thief
yěxǔ	perhaps
yīguì	closet
zāogāo	damn
zéi	thief

LIÀNXÍ

A. Fill in the directional ending according to the clues in parentheses.

1. *Jīnglǐ zài bàngōngshì děng nǐ, qǐng jìn _____ ba.* (to go in)
2. *Nǐ kàn. Wáng lǎoshī zǒu _____ le.* (to walk here)
3. *Mén kāizhe. Nǐ zìjǐ jìn _____ ba.* (to come in)
4. *Wǒ qù jīchǎng jiē bàba _____ mèimei jiā.* (to go to)

B. Rearrange the individual elements to make a sentence.

1. *yǐqián chūmén suǒmén jìde*
2. *lǎoshī tā bàba jiāoshū jìnlái de shíhòu*
3. *kāizhè diànshì zěnme*
4. *dǎ wán nǐ chīfàn qù diànhuà jiù*

C. Translate the following sentences into *pīnyīn*.

1. The door is open.
2. Why is the window open?
3. Please come in.
4. Did you see anything?
5. Did you finish reading this book?
6. Did you really see the thief?

D. Write the English equivalents.

1. 出口在哪儿?
2. 我的老师出去了。
3. 请进来。
4. 是不是他回来了?

E. Write the Chinese characters.

1. restaurant
2. exit
3. entrance
4. to see
5. to lock

WÉNHUÀ ZHÙJIĚ

Chinese people believe deeply in destiny (*mìngyùn*). Fortunes and misfortunes in life are generally believed to be predestined (*huò fú yǒu mìng*, "fortune and misfortune are governed by fate"). This belief in an unavoidable fate allows people to deal with hardships—when something bad happens, *méiyǒu bànfǎ*, "there is nothing to be done" but wait for the misfortune to be replaced by good fortune. People feel better when they are robbed or injured because they have checked off another of life's inevitable misfortunes.

DÁÀN

A. 1. *qù* 2. *lái* 3. *lái* 4. *qù*

B. 1. *Chūmén yǐqián jìde suǒmén.* 2. *Lǎoshī jiāoshū de shíhòu, tā bàba jìn lái.* 3. *Diànshì zěnme kāizhe?* 4. *Nǐ dǎwán diànhuà jiù qù chīfàn.*

C. 1. *Mén kāizhe.* 2. *Chuānghù zěnme kāizhe?* 3. *Qǐng jìn lái.* 4. *Nǐ jiàndào shénme?* 5. *Nǐ kànwán zhè běn shū ma?* 6. *Shì bú shì nǐ kàndào zéi le?*

D. 1. Where is the exit? 2. My teacher went out. 3. Please come in. 4. Did he really come back?

E. 1. 饭店 2. 出口 3. 入口 4. 看见 5. 锁

A. Answer the questions according to the clues in parentheses.

1. *Lǐngdào duōshǎo qián? (3 yuán 15)*
2. *Nà jiàn chènshān zěnme mài (25 yuán each)*
3. *Xīguā duōshǎo qián yì jīn (3 máo per jīn)*

B. Write the *pīnyīn* equivalents.

1. This is the first time I've bargained.
2. How many times have you been to China?
3. That is his third room.

C. Add *le* to these sentences in the appropriate position to match the English equivalents.

1. *Tā mǎi sān jiàn máoyī.*
   He bought three sweaters.
2. *Tā zhīdào nèige xiāoxi.*
   He knows that bit of news now.
3. *Nǐ chīfàn ma?*
   Have you eaten dinner today?

D. Combine the pairs of sentences using relative clauses to match the English equivalents.

1. *Wǒ chī jiǎozi. Jiǎozi hěn hǎo chī.*
   The dumplings that I ate are delicious.
2. *Wǒ de lǎoshī shì Wáng xiānsheng. Wáng xiānsheng hěn gāo.*
   My teacher is the tall Mr. Wang.

E. Fill in the blanks with either *le* or *guò*.

1. *Tā qù _____ Zhōngguó.*
2. *Tā méiyǒu qù _____ Zhōngguó.*
3. *Wǒ zuótiān chī _____ Gōngbǎo jīdīng.*
4. *Wǒ chī _____ Gōngbǎo jīdīng hěn duō cì.*

146

F. Write the following in Chinese characters.

1. *Tā yào mǎi dōngxi.*
2. *Zhège lǚguǎn hěn hǎo.*
3. *Nǐmen méiyǒu qián.*
4. *Wǒ xǐhuan kǎoyā hé píjiǔ.*

DÁÀN

A. 1. *Lǐngdào sān yuán shíwǔ.* 2. *Zhè jiàn chènshān èrshí wǔ yuán yī jiàn.* 3. *Xīguā sān máo yì jīn.*

B. 1. *Zhè shì wǒ dì yí cì jiǎngjià.* 2. *Nǐ qùguò Zhōngúo jǐ cì?* 3. *Nà shì tā dì sān ge fángjiān.*

C. 1. *Tā mǎile sān jiàn máoyī.* 2. *Tā zhīdaò nèige xiāoxi le.* 3. *Nǐ chīfàn le méiyǒu?*

D. 1. *Wǒ chī de jiǎozi hěn hǎo chī.* 2. *Hěn gāo de Wáng xiānsheng shì wǒ de lǎoshī.*

E. 1. *guò* 2. *guò* 3. *le* 4. *guò*

F. 1.他要买东西。 2.这个旅馆很好。 3.你们没有钱。 4.我喜欢烤鸭和啤酒。

DÌ SHÍLIÙ KÈ
Lesson 16

HŪNLǏ. A Wedding.

A. DUÌHUÀ

TǍOLÙN ZĚNME ZHǓNBÈI HŪNLǏ.

Mingfen is discussing her wedding plans with her friend Yuzhu.

YÙZHŪ: **Míngfēn, nǐ de hūnlǐ zhǔnbèi de zěnmeyàng?**

MÍNGFĒN: **Shì tài duō le. Hǎoxiàng shénme shì dōu méi zuò.**

YÙZHŪ: **Nǐ xǐtiē jì le méiyǒu?**

MÍNGFĒN: **Hái méiyǒu ne. Wǒ hái méiyǒu qù ná wǒ de xǐtiē.**

YÙZHŪ: **Wénlín ne? Tā shì nǐ de wèihūnfū, yīnggāi bāng nǐ a!**

MÍNGFĒN: **Tā yǐjīng zuòle hěn duō shì le. Kěshì, tā děi qù shàngbān, bù néng tiāntian qǐngjià.**

YÙZHŪ: **Wǒ jīntiān yǒu kòng, kěyǐ bāng nǐ. Yǒu méiyǒu shénme shì yào wǒ bāngmáng?**

MÍNGFĒN: **Wǒ yào qù ná xǐtiē, zài qù lǐfú diàn kànkan lǐfú.**

YÙZHŪ: **Shénme? Nǐ hái méiyǒu dìng jiéhūn lǐfú a?**

MÍNGFĒN: **Wǒ yǐjīng xuǎnle wǒ de jiéhūn lǐfú. Kěshì, wǒ hái méi juédìng jìngjiǔ hé sòngkè de yīfu. Nǐ péi wǒ qù kànkan hǎo ma?**

YÙZHŪ: **Hǎo. Nǐ xuǎn de jiéhūn lǐfú shì hóngsè de ma?**

MÍNGFĒN: **Bù, báisè. Wénlín hé wǒ dōu juéde hóngsè de lǐfú tài tǔ le. Wǒmen juéde xīfāng de lǐfú yòu diǎnyǎ yòu dàfāng. Wǒmen de fùmǔ dōu hěn xǐhuan. Kěshì, wǒmen xiǎng jìngjiǔ hé sòngkè de yīfu yīnggāi hěn jiǎndān. Wǒmen xiànzài qù tiāo lǐfú ba!**

YÙZHŪ: **Hǎo.**

TALKING ABOUT WEDDING PREPARATIONS.

YUZHU: Mingfen, how are your wedding preparations going?

MINGFEN: Oh, there's so much to do! I feel like nothing is getting done!

YUZHU: Have you mailed out your wedding invitations?

MINGFEN: Not yet. I haven't even picked them up yet.

YUZHU: What about Wenlin? He's your fiance. He should help you!

MINGFEN: He's already done a lot, but he has to go to work and can't take every day off.

YUZHU: Well, I've got nothing to do today so I can help you. What do you need?

MINGFEN: I'm going to pick up the wedding invitations and then look at gowns at the store.

YUZHU: What? You haven't reserved your wedding gown?

MINGFEN: I've already chosen the wedding gown, but haven't decided what to wear for proposing toasts to the guests and seeing off the guests. Can you go with me to pick them out?

YUZHU: Sure! Is the wedding dress you chose red?

MINGFEN: No, it's white. Wenlin and I both feel that red wedding dresses are too old-fashioned. We think that Western dresses are classic and elegant. Both our parents like that also. But we think that the other dresses should be very simple. Let's go now and pick them out!

YUZHU: Okay.

B. YǓFǍ HÉ YÒNGFǍ

1. QUESTION WORDS USED IN STATEMENTS

Question words such as *shénme* (what), *shéi* (who) and *nǎr* (where) can function as the subject or object of a sentence. Followed with the adverb *dōu* or the adverb *yě*, they imply "every 'thing,' 'person' or 'place'" respectively. Question words used in statements can stand on their own or modify a noun.

Shénme dōngxi dōu guì.
Everything is expensive.

Shéi yào chī, jiù yào fù wǔ kuài qián.
Whoever wants to eat has to pay 5 dollars.

Tā nǎr dōu qùguò.
He has gone everywhere.

2. THE ADVERBS *YǏJĪNG* AND *HÁI*

The adverb *yǐjīng* (already) often occurs in sentences containing *le* attached to a verb.

Wǒ yǐjīng chīle wǎnfàn.
I have already eaten dinner.

Tāmen yǐjīng qùle Dàtóng.
They have already gone to Datong.

The negative of *yǐjīng* is *hái méiyǒu* (still haven't; not yet).

Wǒ hái méiyǒu chī wǎnfàn.
I still haven't eaten dinner.

Tāmen hái méiyǒu qù Dàtóng.
They haven't gone to Datong yet.

3. THE CONJUNCTION *YÒU . . . YÒU*

Yòu . . . yòu is used with two adjectival verbs to express the meaning "both . . . and."

Wǒmen juéde xīfāng de lǐfú yòu diǎnyǎ yòu dàfang.
We think that Western wedding gowns are both classic and elegant.

Nǐ zuò de cài yòu tián yòu suān.
The food that you cook is both sweet and sour.

4. REDUPLICATION OF MEASURE WORDS

When a measure word is reduplicated, it means "every one" of the measured noun. Just as with question words operating as subjects or objects, reduplicated measure words and their nouns are usually followed by *dōu*.

Tā jiànjian shì dōu zuò de hěn hǎo.
She does everything well.

150

Tiáotiao lǐngdài dōu hěn guì.
Every tie is very expensive.

5. THE MODAL *YĪNGGĀI*

The modal verb *yīnggāi* (ought to/should) is commonly used. It is placed in a sentence before the main verb.

Tā yīnggāi bāng nǐ.
He should help you.

Nǐ yīnggāi chīfàn.
You ought to eat.

6. MORE ABOUT THE PREPOSITION *BǍ* AND RESULTATIVE VERBS

The preposition *bǎ* that you learned about in lesson 10 is often used in combination with resultative verbs of completion (lesson 14) and resultative verbs of perception (lesson 15). Remember that the preposition *bǎ* must be used in conjunction with the direct object of a sentence and the combination is placed after the subject. This conveys that something is being done to the direct object by the subject. When *bǎ* is used in sentences with resultative verbs, then, the meaning is that the direct object is being completed or perceived by the subject. If a modal verb appears in the sentence in addition to the main verb, it is placed before *bǎ*.

Tā bǎ jīdīng chīwán le.
He finished eating the diced chicken.

Wǒ yào bǎ Hànzì xuéhǎo.
I want to finish studying the Chinese characters.

C. HÀNZÌ

Learn to recognize these characters for colors.

黄   *huáng* (yellow)

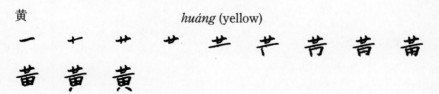

151

红（紅）　　　　　　　　　*hóng* (red)

蓝（藍）　　　　　　　　　*lán* (blue)

青　　　　　　　　　　　　*qīng* (green)

白　　　　　　　　　　　　*bái* (white)

黑　　　　　　　　　　　　*hēi* (black)

Yánsè is the general word for "color."
颜色（顏色）

De is the possessive particle
的

When you refer to a specific color by name, use the second half of *yánsè* after the color word.

蓝色　　　　　　　　　　the color blue
红色　　　　　　　　　　the color red
黄色　　　　　　　　　　the color yellow

你的房间是白色的。

Nǐ de fángjiān shì báisè de.
　　Your room is white.

152

D. SHĒNGCÍ

bái	white
bàn	to do, to manage
bāngmáng	to help
bāngzhù	to help
bùtóng	different from, distinct from
dàfāng	with grace and ease
diǎnyǎ	elegant and classic
dìnghūn	to get engaged
fěnhóngsè	pink
hǎoxiàng	to look like
hēi	black
hóng	red
huáng	yellow
hūnlǐ	wedding ceremony
jì	to mail, to send
jiéhūn	to get married
jìngjiǔ	to propose a toast
juédìng	to decide
lán	blue
lǐfú	evening gown
lǜ	green
péi	to accompany
qǐngjià	to ask for a day off, to ask for leave
shídài	times, era, epoch
sòngkè	to see guests to the door
tiāntian	everyday
tiāo	to pick, to choose
tǔ	old-fashioned, not stylish
wèihūnfū	fiancé (m)
wèihūnqī	fiancé (f)
xīfāng	western
xǐshì	happy events (usually a wedding)
xǐtiē	wedding invitation
xuǎn	to choose
yánsè	color
yòu . . . yòu	both . . . and
zhǔnbèi	to prepare
zǐsè	purple
zōngsè	brown

A. Fill in the blanks with a question word used as a nonquestion according to the English equivalents.

    1. *Tā hěn xǐhuan lǚxíng.* _____ *dōu qùguò le.*
       She really likes to travel. She has been everywhere.
    2. *Nèige diànyǐng tǐng yǒu yìsi.* _____ *dōu yào qù kànkan.*
       That movie is quite interesting. Everyone wants to see it.
    3. _____ *dōngxi dōu guì.*
       Everything is expensive.

B. Use simple answers based on the cues in parentheses to respond to the following questions.

    1. *Nǐ jīntiān chīle wǎnfàn méiyǒu?* (yes)
    2. *Nǐ mǎi le zhè tào lǐfú ma?* (yes)
    3. *Nǐ tiāole nǐ de jiéhūn lǐfú ma?* (not yet)
    4. *Nǐ péi wǒ qù xuǎn lǐfú, hǎo bù hǎo?* (no)

C. Translate the following sentences into English.

    1. *Zhè jiàn lǐfú yòu tǔ yòu guì.*
    2. *Shénme shì dōu méi zuò.*
    3. *Wǒ tiāntian dōu shàngbān.*
    4. *Zhè fèn xǐtiē shì wǒ bàba zhǔnbèi de.*

D. Translate into Chinese characters.

    1. My room is yellow.
    2. Your food is delicious.
    3. I love Beijing!

WÉNHUÀ ZHÙJIĚ

The traditional color for weddings in China is red, and white is reserved for funerals. However, Chinese women are increasingly wearing elaborate white dresses in the Western style for their wedding ceremonies. The ceremony itself is quite an affair. Since religion doesn't play a big part in China, weddings are often officiated by local disc jockeys or wedding announcers who guide the couple through a series of rituals—vows are exchanged, many toasts are offered and guests are cajoled onto the dance floor even as they enjoy an excessive feast. The couple must also go around to each table of guests and drink a toast as well as light a cigarette for everyone for good luck. Often the bride will change into another dress for this ordeal and then will change again to see the guests off and then to head to her new home. It is during these rituals that the bride might choose to wear red to appease her more traditional relatives.

DÁÀN

A. 1. *Năr* 2. *Shéi* 3. *Shénme*

B. 1. *chī le* 2. *măi le* 3. *hái méiyŏu* 4. *bù hăo*

C. 1. This gown is both old-fashioned and expensive. 2. I haven't done a single thing. 3. I go to work everyday. 4. These invitations were prepared by my father.

D. 1.我的房间是黄色的。 2.你的饭好吃。 3.我爱北京！

DÌ SHÍQĪ KÈ
Lesson 17
DIÀNHUÀ. The Telephone.

A. DUÌHUÀ

DĂ DIÀNHUÀ

Mr. Wang is a businessman from Hong Kong who calls the Dacheng Corporation to reschedule an appointment.

WÁNG: **Wéi, shì Dáchéng gōngsī ma?**

MÌSHŪ: **Shì a. Nǐ zhǎo shéi?**

WÁNG: **Qǐngwèn, Zhāng jīnglǐ zài ma?**

MÌSHŪ: **Zhāng jīnglǐ xiànzài zhèngzài dǎ diànhuà. Qǐngwèn, nǐ yǒu shénme shì?**

WÁNG: **Wǒ jiào Wáng Bīng, shì Měiguó Shāngyè Gùwèn Gōngsī de jīnglǐ. Zuótiān gāng cóng Měiguó lái. Wǒ gēn Zhāng Jīnglǐ yuē le, yào qù gōngsī bàifǎng tā.**

MÌSHŪ: **A! Nín hǎo, Wáng Jīnglǐ. Zhāng Jīnglǐ yìzhí zài děng nín ne. Nín xiànzài lái wǒmen gōngsī ma?**

WÁNG: **Zhēn bù hǎo yìsi. Wǒ xiànzài děi bàn biéde shì, xiǎng gǎi shíjiān gēn Zhāng Jīnglǐ jiànmiàn. Míngtiān zǎoshàng jiǔdiǎn Zhāng Jīnglǐ fāngbiàn bù fāngbiàn?**

MÌSHŪ: **Míngtiān shàngwǔ shídiǎn bàn xíng bù xíng? Zhāng Jīnglǐ jiǔdiǎn yào kāihuì.**

WÁNG: **Xíng. Míngtiān jiàn.**

MÌSHŪ: **Míngtiān jiàn.**

MAKING A PHONE CALL.

WANG: Hello, is this the Dacheng Corporation?

SECRETARY: Yes, who are you looking for?

WANG: Is Manager Zhang there, please?

SECRETARY: Manager Zhang is on the phone right now. May I ask what this is concerning?

WANG: My name is Wang Bing. I am the manager of the American Business Consulting Corporation. I just came from the United States yesterday. I made an appointment with Manager Zhang and would like to pay him a visit.

SECRETARY: Oh, Manager Wang, how are you? Manager Zhang has been waiting for you. Are you coming to our company now?

WANG: I'm so sorry but I need to take care of some other things now and would like to reschedule my appointment with Manager Zhang. Do you know if he is free at 9:00 A.M. tomorrow?

SECRETARY: Is tomorrow morning at 10:30 all right? Manager Zhang has a meeting at 9:00.

WANG: That's fine. See you tomorrow.

SECRETARY: See you tomorrow.

B. YǓFǍ HÉ YÒNGFǍ

1. NORMS FOR TELEPHONE CONVERSATIONS

The word *wéi* (hello) is only used in Chinese when answering the phone. You might hear *wéi, shì shéi a?* (hello, who is this?) or *wéi, nǐ zhǎo shéi a?* (hello, who are you looking for?). There are no formalities for hanging up the phone; in fact, people quite often hang up without saying good-bye when the business at hand is taken care of.

Dǎ (to hit) when used with *diànhuà* (phone) means "to make a phone call."

Wǒ dǎ diànhuà.
    I make phone calls.

This expression is often used with *gěi* (to give) in two ways.

Wǒ dǎ diànhuà gěi nǐ.
    I'll call you.

Wǒ gěi nǐ dǎ diànhuà.
I'll call you.

2. USING *ZHÈNGZÀI* OR *ZÀI* TO INDICATE THAT AN ACTION IS CURRENTLY TAKING PLACE

Zhèngzài (right now) or the abbreviated *zài* (now) is added to a sentence just before the verb to indicate that the action is currently taking place.

Wǒmen zhèngzài kàn diànshì.
We are watching TV right now.

Zhāng jīnglǐ xiànzài zhèngzài dǎ diànhuà.
Manager Zhang is on the phone right now.

Tā zài zuò gōngkè.
He is doing homework.

The sentence final particle *ne*, when added to these sentences, serves to emphasize that a person is busy and not available to do anything else.

Wǒ māma xiànzài zài shuìjiào ne.
My mom is sleeping [so she can't come to the phone].

Tā zài kāihuì ne.
He is in a meeting [so he can't see you now].

These sentences are negated with *méiyǒu*, which comes before *zài*. In negative sentences, *zhèng* is not used.

Tā xiànzài méiyǒu zài chīfàn.
He is not eating dinner now.

Nǐ háizi méiyǒu zài zuò gōngkè.
Your kid is not doing her/his homework now.

Questions involving an action currently taking place usually receive abbreviated answers: *shì (de)* for "yes" or *méiyǒu* for "no."

Nǐ xiànzài zhèngzài dǎ diànhuà ma?
Are you making a phone call right now?

Shì.
Yes.

Méiyǒu.
No.

158

3. *YĪZHÍ ZÀI* WITH AN ACTION CURRENTLY TAKING PLACE

When *yīzhí* (all along) is used in place of *zhèng*, the implication is that not only is an action currently taking place, but it has been going on for quite some time. *Yīzhí zài* is often used to correct a wrong assumption.

Tā yīzhí zài děng nǐ ne.
He has been waiting for you all along.

Wǒ yīzhí zài shàngkè.
I've been in class all along.

4. THE ADVERB *GĀNG*

Gāng is used before a verb to indicate that the action of the verb just happened recently. It is often reduplicated. It can be translated as "have/has just."

Wǒ zuótiān gāng cóng Měiguó lái.
I just came from America yesterday.

Wǒ gānggang dàxué bìyè.
I just graduated college.

The adverb *gāngcái* (just) is used when the action of the verb has happened in the immediate past.

Tā gāngcái xiàkè.
She's just gotten out of class.

5. *HĚN YǑU YÌSI* VS. *BÙ HǍO YÌSI*

Yìsi (meaning) is an interesting little word that means different things in different contexts.
You have seen *yìsi* used with *yǒu* (to have) to mean "interesting."

Nèi běn shū hěn yǒu yìsi.
That book is very interesting.

In this lesson, *yìsi* is used with *bù hǎo* to mean "embarrassing."

Wǒ zhēn bù hǎo yìsi.
I'm really embarrassed.

6. OTHER WAYS TO SAY GOOD-BYE

You already know that *zàijiàn* (good-bye) literally means "see you again." You can add *jiàn* to many time words to say "see you (at that time)."

Míngtiān jiàn.
  See you tomorrow.

Wǒmen xīngqīwǔ jiàn.
  See you Friday.

C. HÀNZÌ

Read these new characters.

给（給）   *gěi* (to give)

乡　乡　纟　纟　纟　纟　纟　给　给

打   *dǎ* (to make, as in a phone call)

一　十　扌　扩　打

电话（電話）   *diànhuà* (phone)

丶　冂　曰　日　电
丶　讠　讠　讠　讠　讠　话　话

公司   *gōngsī* (company)

丿　八　公　公
𠃌　𠃌　司　司　司

明天   *míngtiān* (tomorrow)

丶　冂　日　日　日　明　明　明
一　二　于　天

昨天   *zuótiān* (yesterday)

丶　冂　日　日　日　日　昨　昨　昨
一　二　于　天

160

我打电话给你。
Wǒ dǎ diànhuà gěi nǐ.
   I'll call you.

我们明天见！
Wǒmen míngtiān jiàn!
   See you tomorrow!

D. SHĒNGCÍ

ānpái	to arrange
bàifǎng	to pay a visit
biànhuà	a change
děi	to need to, to have to
dìzhǐ	an address
fāngbiàn	to be convenient
gǎi	to change
gǎibiàn	to change, a change
gāng	just
gùwèn	consultation, consultant
jiànmiàn	to have a meeting with someone
jīnglǐ	manager
kāihuì	to hold a meeting
mìshū	secretary
qiāotán	to discuss, to talk
shāngyè	business
shíjiān	time
yuē (huì)	appointment, to make arrangements for
yìsi	meaning
yìzhí	continuously
zhèngzài	[occurs before a verb to indicate an action in progress]
zìjǐ	self

LIÀNXÍ

A. Complete the following exchanges according to the cues in parentheses and using *zhèngzài* or *zài*.

1. A: *Zhāng jīnglǐ zài gōngsī ma?*
   B: *Zài. Tā* _____ *ne.* (is making a phone call)
2. A: *Liú xiǎojie xiànzài máng bù máng?*
   B: *Tā hěn máng. Tā* _____. (is attending a meeting)
3. A: *Wǒ de shū ne?*
   B: *Wǒ xiànzài* _____. (am reading it)
4. A: *Nǐ bàba ne?*
   B: *Tā* _____. (is drinking beer)
5. A: *Píngguǒ yígòng duōshǎo qián?*
   B: *Qǐng děng yíxià. Wǒ* _____ *ne.* (am figuring it out)

B. Construct sentences with *zhèngzài . . . ne*, using the words below.

1. *Zhāng tàitai, děng*
2. *Nǐ de māma, zhǎo*
3. *Wǒ de bàba, shàngbān*
4. *Wáng xiǎojie, mǎi cài*

C. Answer the following questions negatively, in *pīnyīn*, using complete sentences.

1. *Nǐ xiànzài zài kàn diànshì ma?*
2. *Nǐ zài děng wǒ ma?*
3. *Nǐ yǐqián chīguò Zhōngguó cài ma?*
4. *Nǐ qùguò Běijīng ma?*
5. *Nǐ kànguò Zhōngguó diànyǐng ma?*
6. *Nǐ xuéguò Zhōngguóhuà ma?*

D. Fill in the blanks with the correct Chinese character according to the English translation.

1. 他 ___ 给我。
   He is giving me a call.
2. 我 ___ 你二十五块钱。
   I'll give you twenty-five kuai.

3. ＿＿ 见！

See you tomorrow!

4. 他 ＿＿ 从美国来。

He came from America yesterday.

Telephones are a relatively new technology in Mainland China, so they don't have as visible a presence as they do in other countries. In China, it is still common for visitors to show up at friends' houses without calling first, or for plans to be made in person, even days in advance without subsequent phone confirmation. For an American in China, it can seem odd or intrusive when a Chinese friend shows up at the door saying "It's time for a visit!" or "Are you ready to go?" It is also uncommon for people in China to make a phone call just to chat. Long-distance phone charges are added every three minutes, so don't be surprised if a Chinese friend abruptly hangs up the phone after two minues and fifty-nine seconds.

In Taiwan, Hong Kong and major Chinese cities, pay phones are easily found on the street. In smaller towns, local and international calls can be made with a phone card at a Post and Telecommunications Office. You might also find small shops consisting of a person and a phone where you can make local and international calls—but be careful of being overcharged.

Finally, cell phones are now visible in China as well, and e-mail is of course popular. Cyber-cafés are found, especially in large cities.

DÁÀN

A. 1. *zhèngzài dǎ diànhuà* 2. *zài kāihuì* 3. *zài kàn* 4. *zhèngzài hē píjiǔ* 5. *zài suàn*

B. 1. *Zhāng tàitai zhèngzài děng nǐ ne.* 2. *Nǐ de māma zhèngzài zhǎo nǐ ne.* 3. *Wǒ de bàba zhèngzài shàngbān ne.* 4. *Wáng xiǎojie zhèngzài mǎi cài ne.*

C. 1. *Wǒ xiànzài bú zài kàn diànshì.* 2. *Wǒ bú zài děng nǐ.* 3. *Wǒ yǐqián méi chīguò Zhōngguó cài.* 4. *Wǒ méi qùguò Běijīng.* 5. *Wǒ méi kànguò Zhōngguó diànyǐng.* 6. *Wǒ méi xuéguò Zhōngguóhuà.*

D. 1. 打电话 2. 给 3. 明天 4. 昨天

DÌ SHÍBĀ KÈ
Lesson 18
ZÀI YÍNHÁNG. At the Bank.

A. DUÌHUÀ

HUÀN QIÁN.

Mr. Stone wants to change American dollars into Chinese currency.

Zài lǚguǎn guìtái qián.

SHÍ: **Nǐmen duìhuàn bú duìhuàn wàibì?**

GUÌTÁI: **Duìbùqǐ. Wǒmen lǚguǎn bù néng duìhuàn wàibì. Nǐ kěyǐ qù Zhōngguó Rénmín Yínháng duìhàn.**

SHÍ: **Zhōngguó Rénmín Yínháng zài nǎr?**

GUÌTÁI: **Zài wǒmen lǚguǎn duìmiàn. Bú tài yuǎn.**

SHÍ: **Xièxie.**

ZÀI ZHŌNGGUÓ YÍNHÁNG.

SHÍ: **Nǐ hǎo, wǒ xiǎng huàn rénmín bì.**

CHŪNÀYUÁN: **Nǐ yǒu xiànjīn háishì lǚxíng zhīpiào?**

SHÍ: **Lǚxíng zhīpiào.**

CHŪNÀYUÁN: **Hǎo. Nǐ xiān tián zhè zhāng duìhuàndān ránhòu gěi wǒ kàn nǐ de hùzhào.**

SHÍ: **Qǐngwèn, jīntiān měijīn hé rénmínbì de duìhuànlǜ shì duōshǎo?**

CHŪNÀYUÁN: **Yī bǐ bā. Nǐ dǎsuàn huàn duōshǎo?**

SHÍ: **Qībǎi kuài měijīn. Qián zài zhèr.**

CHŪNÀYUÁN: **Hǎo. Yígòng shì wǔqiān liùbǎi kuài.**

SHÍ: **Qǐng gěi wǒ bā zhāng yìbǎi kuài, qíyú shì shí yuán de, hǎo ma?**

CHŪNÀYUÁN: **Méi wèntí. Qǐng nǐ diǎn yì diǎn.**

SHÍ: **Méi cuò. Xièxie nǐ.**

CHŪNÀYUÁN: **Bú kèqi.**

_____

CHANGING MONEY.

STONE: Do you exchange foreign currency?

DESK CLERK: Sorry. This hotel can't change foreign currency. Try the People's Bank of China.

STONE: Where is that?

DESK CLERK: There's one across the street from our hotel. It's not too far.

STONE: Thank you.

_____

INSIDE THE BANK OF CHINA.

STONE: Excuse me, I'd like to exchange dollars for Chinese currency.

TELLER: Do you have cash or traveler's checks?

STONE: Traveler's checks.

TELLER: Okay. Please fill out this exchange form and then show me your passport.

STONE: Could you please tell me what the exchange rate is between U.S. dollars and renminbi today?

TELLER: One to eight. How much do you want to exchange?

STONE: Seven hundred dollars. Here you go.

TELLER: Okay. That comes to 5,600 yuan altogether.

STONE: I'd like eight one-hundred-yuan bills and the rest in ten-yuan bills. All right?

TELLER: No problem. Please count them.

STONE: It's all here. Thank you.

TELLER: You're welcome.

B. YǓFǍ HÉ YÒNGFǍ

1. RATIOS AND DECIMALS

Ratios are expressed with the comparison particle *bǐ,* which you learned about in lesson 7.

Duìhuànlǜ shì yī bǐ bā diǎn yī.
The exchange rate is one to eight point one.

The multipurpose word *diǎn* (o'clock, a little) also stands for a decimal point and is translated as "point."
liǎng bǎi wǔ shí jiǔ diǎn yī sān èr
259.132

2. THE CONJUNCTION *XIĀN . . . RÁNHÒU*

You learned in lesson 13 that *ránhòu* means "and then." The conjunction pair *xiān . . . ránhòu* means "first . . . then" and is used to connect two verb phrases which share the same subject.

Nǐ xiān tián zhè zhāng duìhuàndān ránhòu gěi wǒ kàn nǐ de hùzhào.
First fill out this exchange form and then show me your passport.

Háizi yīnggāi xiān zuò gōngkè ránhòu kàn diànshì.
Children should first do their homework and then watch TV.

3. THE CONJUNCTION *XIĀN . . . ZÀI*

Xiān . . . zài also means "first . . . then" but is used to connect verb phrases with different subjects.

Nǐ xiān tián zhè zhāng duìhuàndān wǒ zài gěi nǐ huàn qián.
First you fill out this exchange form and then I'll change money for you.

Nǐ xiān zǒu wǒ zài zǒu.
First you go and then I'll go.

4. USES OF *CUÒ* (TO BE WRONG)

You have already learned the idiom *búcuò* (not bad), which really means that something is "pretty good."

Nǐ zuò de cài búcuò.
Your cooking is not bad.

The real meaning of *cuò* is "to be wrong or incorrect."

Nǐ bǎ zhège zì xiě cuò le.
  You wrote this character incorrectly.

The opposite of *cuò* is *duì* (correct); most sentences with *cuò* are not negated due to the confusion with the idiom *bú cuò*.

Nǐ bǎ zhège zì xiě duì le.
  You wrote this character correctly.

Cuò can be negated with *méi* in short answers.
Qǐng nǐ diǎn yì diǎn.
Méi cuò. Xièxie nǐ.
  Please count it.
  There's no mistake. Thank you.

5. MORE ABOUT *GĚI* (TO GIVE)

You learned in lesson 17 that *gěi* (to give) is used in the expression *dǎ diànhuà gěi wǒ* (give me a phone call). *Gěi* can also be used before another verb to show that one person is doing that action for another person.

Wǒ gěi nǐ kāi mén.
  I'll open the door for you.

Gěi wǒ kàn nǐ de hùzhào.
  Show me your passport.

Qǐng nǐ gěi wǒ huàn qián.
  Please change my money.

C. HÀNZÌ

Here are some characters that will help you find a bank and the right window for changing money.

银行   *yínháng* (bank)

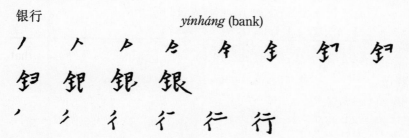

人民   *rénmín* (the people)

人民币   *rénmínbì* (Chinese currency)

外币   *wàibì* (foreign currency)

护照   *hùzhào* (passport)

兑换   *duìhuàn* (to exchange)

外   *wài* (outside, foreign)

外国人   *wàiguórén* (foreigner)

D. SHĒNGCÍ

chūnàyuán	bank teller
diǎn	point (as in decimal point)
diǎn	to check (a number)
duìhuàn	to exchange
duìhuàndān	currency exchange form
duìhuànlǜ	exchange rate
duìmiàn	opposite
huàn	to exchange
lǚxíng zhīpiào	traveler's checks

měijīn	U.S. currency
qíyú	the rest, the remainder
rénmínbì	the currency of the PRC
tián	to fill out a form
wàibì	foreign currency
xiànjīn	cash
yígòng	all together
yínháng	bank

LIÀNXÍ

A. Fill in the blanks according to the English translation.

1. *Qǐng _____ yíxià nǐ huàn de qián.*
   Please count the money you've exchanged.
2. *Yígòng shì sān ____ wǔ ____ bā ____ liù kuài ____.*
   The total is 3,586 U.S. dollars.
3. *Jīntiān de duìhuànlǜ shì yī ____ èr diǎn ____.*
   Today's exchange rate is one to two point six.
4. *Nǐ xiǎng _____ duōshǎo qián?*
   How much money are you going to exchange?
5. *Huàn wàibì yǐqián, qǐng _____ tián duìhuàn dān.*
   Please fill out the exchange form first before exchanging any foreign currency.

B. Connect the following pairs of phrases using *xiān . . . ránhòu* or *xiān . . . zài*. Remember that *xiān . . . ránhòu* connects two phrases with the same subject while *xiān . . . zài* connects phrases with different subjects.

1. *Wǒ zǒu. Nǐ zǒu.*
2. *Wǒ chīfàn. Wǒ zǒu.*
3. *Nǐ tián yìzhāng duìhuàndān. Nǐ gěi wǒ kàn nǐ de hùzhào.*
4. *Nǐ tián yìzhāng duìhuàndān. Wǒ gěi nǐ huàn qián.*

C. Translate the following sentences into *pīnyīn*.

1. I want to exchange it for renminbi.
2. What is today's exchange rate between U.S. currency and renminbi?
3. 8.675
4. 1:1.92

169

D. Write the English equivalents.

1. 银行

    2. 兑换

         人民币

4. 外币

   5. 中国银行

      6.   我是外国人。

WÉNHUÀ ZHÙJIĚ

Cash is the payment method of choice in China. While it is no trouble changing or using traveler's checks in most cities, credit cards are accepted only in the larger cities at hotels or department stores. You can only use cash to pay for any means of domestic travel including planes, trains and buses. Checking accounts are rare in China. Foreigners are able to cash personal checks from their home country using the American Express card and foreigners can open up a bank account in China—but basically there is no such thing as a checking account there at all. Chinese receive their pay in cash, and if they have bills to pay that aren't covered by their *dānwèi* they pay in person, in cash.

DÁÀN

A. 1. *diǎn* 2. *qiān, bǎi, shí, měijīn.* 3. *bǐ, liù* 4. *(duì)huàn* 5. *xiān*

B. 1. *Wǒ xiān zǒu nǐ zài zǒu.* 2. *Wǒ xiān chīfàn, ránhòu zǒu.* 3. *Nǐ xiān tián duìhuàndān ránhòu gěi wǒ kàn nǐ de hùzhào.* 4. *Nǐ xiān tián yì zhāng duìhuàn dān wǒ zài gěi nǐ huànqián.*

C. 1. *Wǒ xiǎng huàn rénmínbì.* 2. *Jīntiān měijīn hé rénmínbì de duìhuànlǜ shì duōshǎo?* 3. *Bā diǎn liù qī wǔ.* 4. *yī bǐ yī diǎn jiǔ èr.*

D. 1. bank 2. to exchange 3. renminbi 4. foreign currency 5. the Bank of China 6. I am a foreigner.

DÌ SHÍJIǓ KÈ
Lesson 19
ZÀI YÓUJÚ. At the Post Office.

A. DUÌHUÀ

Mǎi yóupiào.

Mr. Liu needs to buy stamps.

LIÚ: Wǒ yào jì zhè fēng hángkōng xìn dào Měiguó, yào tiē duōshǎo qián de yóupiào?

RÉNYUÁN: Nǐ jì píngxìn háishì guàhào xìn?

LIÚ: Guàhào xìn bǐ píngxìn kuài ma?

RÉNYUÁN: Bù yídìng. Yǒu shíhòu guàhào xìn bǐ píngxìn màn.

LIÚ: Nàme, wǒ jì píngxìn.

RÉNYUÁN: Zhè fēng xìn chāozhòng le, yào tiē liù kuài sì de yóupiào.

LIÚ: Hǎo. Wǒ hái yào jì yí ge bāoguǒ dào Rìběn. Wǒ yào jì guàhào.

RÉNYUÁN: Zhège bāoguǒ lǐ yǒu shénme?

LIÚ: Liǎng jiàn chènshān hé yì tiáo kùzi.

RÉNYUÁN: Nǐ tián le bāoguǒ dān méiyǒu?

LIÚ: Tián le. Bāoguǒ dān zài zhèr.

RÉNYUÁN: Zhège bāoguǒ yào èrshí yī kuài bā.

LIÚ: Zhège bāoguǒ duōjiǔ néng dào Rìběn?

RÉNYUÁN: Chàbùduō yí ge xīngqī ba. Hái yào biéde ma?

LIÚ: Wǒ hái yào mǎi shí zhāng wǔ kuài de yóupiào hé wǔ zhāng liǎngmáo de yóupiào.

RÉNYUÁN: **Zhè shì nǐ de yóupiào. Yígòng shì qīshíjiǔ kuài liǎng máo.**

LIÚ: **Hǎo. Zhè shì bāshí kuài.**

RÉNYUÁN: **Zhǎo nǐ bā máo.**

BUYING STAMPS.

LIU: I want to send this by air to the United States. What's the rate?

CLERK: Will it be regular mail or registered?

LIU: Is registered mail faster than regular?

CLERK: Not necessarily. Sometimes registered mail can be slower.

LIU: Then I'll use regular mail.

CLERK: This letter is overweight. The postage comes to 6 yuan 40.

LIU: Fine. I also want to send a package to Japan registered mail.

CLERK: What's in it?

LIU: Two shirts and one pair of pants.

CLERK: Have you filled out a parcel form?

LIU: Yes, I have, and here it is.

CLERK: That will be 21 yuan 80.

LIU: How long will it take to get to Japan?

CLERK: About a week. Anything else?

LIU: I also want to buy 10 five-yuan and 5 two-mao stamps.

CLERK: Here are your stamps. That will be 79 yuan 20 all together.

LIU: All right. Here is 80 yuan.

CLERK: Eight mao is your change.

B. YǓFǍ HÉ YÒNGFǍ

1. METHODS OF MAILING

To express how you would like a letter sent, use *jì* (to send) followed by the way you want your letter sent.

jì guàhào
  to send by certified mail

jì kuàidì or jì kuàiyóu
  to send by express mail

jì hángkōng
  to send by airmail

jì kōngyùn
  to send by air

jì píngxìn
  to send by regular mail

jì shuǐyùn
  to send by sea

jì lùyùn
  to send by land

Zhège bāoguǒ, wǒ yào jì hángkōng.
  I want to send this package by air.

Qǐng nǐ bǎ zhè fēng xìn jì kuàidì.
  Please send this letter by express mail.

To indicate where you want the letter or package sent, use *dào* (to go) followed by the destination.

Wǒ xiǎng jì zhège bāoguǒ dào Zhōngguó.
  I want to send this package to China.

2. SENDING AND RECEIVING

You can talk about sending letters using some of the ways that you can talk about making a phone call.

Wǒ dǎ diànhuà gěi tā.
Wǒ gěi tā dǎ diànhuà.
  I'll call her.

Wǒ jì gěi tā yì fēng xìn.
Wǒ gěi tā jì yì fēng xìn.
   I'm sending her a letter.

Wǒ xiě gěi tā yì fēng xìn.
Wǒ gěi tā xiě yì fēng xìn.
   I am writing her a letter.

The resultative verb *shōudào* means "to receive."

Wǒ shōudàole yì fēng hángkōng xìn.
   I received an airmail letter.

3. MORE ABOUT COMPARATIVE PARTICLE *BǏ*

Remember that *bǐ* is used to compare a certain quality of two nouns. *Bǐ* is placed in between the two nouns and the verb follows.

Guàhào xìn bǐ píngxìn kuài.
   Registered mail is faster than regular mail.

Xiě xìn bǐ dǎ diànhuà màn.
   Writing a letter is slower than making a phone call.

4. "TO BE ABLE TO": *NÉNG, KĚYǏ* AND *HUÌ*

In lesson 6, you learned that *kěyǐ* implies that a person "is able to" do something because they have the time or the inclination and *huì* means that a person "is able to" do something because of a natural or learned talent. *Néng* also means "to be able to" but implies that a person or thing is able to do something because there are no *external* elements to stop them, or that they do it despite adverse external elements.

Wǒ bù máng, wǒ kěyǐ chīfàn.
   I'm not busy, I can eat.

Wǒ huì xiě Hànzì.
   I can write Chinese characters.

Wǒ bù lǎo, wǒ néng zǒu.
   I'm not old, I can walk.

Wǒ néng chīfàn.
   I can eat [even though I have a toothache].

174

External elements often have to do with time.

Zhège bāoguǒ duōjiǔ néng dào Rìběn?
How long before this package is able to get to Japan?

5. *BIÉDE*

Biéde (other, another) is used to modify a noun. If the noun is understood, it can be deleted.

Nǐ yào jì biéde xìn ma?
Do you want to send other letters?

Wǒ yào mǎi biéde chènshān.
I want to buy a different shirt.

Hái yào biéde ma?
Would you like anything else?

C. HÀNZÌ

Here are some new characters. You should write *hángkōng* (airmail) on letters you want to send overseas from China.

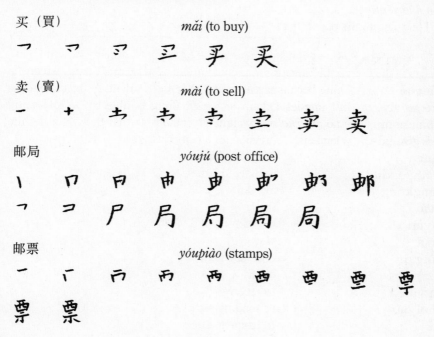

买（買）　　　　　　*mǎi* (to buy)

卖（賣）　　　　　　*mài* (to sell)

邮局　　　　　　*yóujú* (post office)

邮票　　　　　　*yóupiào* (stamps)

航空   *hángkōng* (airmail)

´   丿   几   舟   舟   舟   舟   舟   航   航

丶   丷   宀   宀   穴   空   空   空

要   *yào* (to want)

一   一   一   两   西   西   亜   要   要

Review these sentences.

我要买邮票。

Wǒ yào mǎi yóupiào.

    I want to buy stamps.

他没有空。

Tā méiyǒu kòng.

    He has no free time.

我到邮局去。

Wǒ dào yóujú qù.

    I'm going to the post office.

D. SHĒNGCÍ

bāoguǒ	parcel
biéde	other
chāozhòng	overweight
fēn gōngsī	division (of a company)
fēng	classifier for letters
guàhào xìn	registered letter
hángkōng	airmail
kuài	fast
lùyùn	to send by land
màn	slow
píngxìn	ordinary mail
rényuán	clerk
shōudào	to receive
shuǐyùn	to send by sea
tiē	to paste, to stick
xìn	letter

xìnfēng	envelope
xīnxiān	fresh
yóupiào	a stamp

LIÀNXÍ

A. Combine the following sentences using *bǐ*.

1. *Guàhào xìn guì. Píngxìn piányí.*
2. *Zhè tiáo yú xīnxiān. Nà tiáo yú bù xīnxiān.*
3. *Wáng lǎoshī de jiā xīn. Zhāng jīnglǐ de jiā jiù.*
4. *Zhèr de huánjìng hǎo. Nàr de huánjìng chà.*
5. *Běijīng de Měiguó fēn gōngsī dūo. Xī ān de Měiguó fēn gōngsī shǎo.*

B. Create grammatically and logically correct sentences with *bǐ* using the words given.

1. *píngguǒ, júzi, dà*
2. *guàhào xìn, píngxìn, guì*
3. *hóngshāo yú, suānlà tāng, hǎochī*
4. *chūzūchē, gōnggòng qìchē, màn*

C. Put the following words in the correct order to form a sentence.

EXAMPLE: mǎi/wǒ/yóupiào/le/shízhāng
  wǒ mǎi le shí zhāng yóupiào

1. *duōshǎo/tiē/wǒ/qián/de/yóupiào*
2. *zuò/gōnggòng/qìchē/zuò/chūzūchē/bǐ/kuài/yìdiǎnr*
3. *Nǐ/zhǎo/qián/yíkuài/bāmáo*
4. *hái/qǐngwèn/biéde/yào/nǐ/ma*
5. *xiǎng/wǒ/hángkōng/jì/guàhào/bāoguǒ*

D. Write the following in Chinese characters.

1. post office
2. bank
3. postage stamp
4. airmail
5. to want

WÉNHUÀ ZHÙJIĚ

In China, as in most of the U.S., you have to take your mail to the post office to mail it or drop it into the mailbox (*yóutǒng*). Stamps can also only be purchased at the post office. Unfortunately, stamps and envelopes in China are not self-sticking, and there are large vats of messy glue for you to use with wooden sticks to apply stamps or close envelopes. It is worth bringing a glue stick with you to China to avoid this mess! If you address envelopes in red ink in China, the letter will not be sent; use only black or blue ink. Red ink in any situation is considered rude or unlucky, so avoid using it even when writing a simple note to a friend.

DÁÀN

A. 1. *Guàhào xìn bǐ píngxìn guì.* 2. *Zhè tiáo yú bǐ nà tiáo yú xīnxiān.* 3. *Wáng lǎoshì de jiā bǐ Zhāng jīnglǐ de jiā xīn.* 4. *Zhèr de huánjìng bǐ nàr de huánjìng hǎo.* 5. *Xī'ān de Měiguó fēn gōngsī bǐ Běijīng de Měiguó fēn gōngsī shǎo.*

B. 1. *Píngguǒ bǐ júzi dà.* 2. *Guàhào xìn bǐ píngxìn guì.* 3. *Hóngshāo yú bǐ suānlà tāng hǎochī.* 4. *Gōnggòng qìchē bǐ chūzūchē màn.*

C. 1. *Wǒ tiē duōshǎo qián de yóupiaò?* 2. *Zuò chūzūchē bǐ zuò gōnggòng qìchē kuài yìdiǎnr.* 3. *Zhǎo nǐ yí kuài bā máo qián.* 4. *Qǐngwèn, nǐ hái yào biéde ma?* 5. *Wǒ xiǎng jì hángkōng guàhào bāoguǒ.*

D. 1.邮局 2.银行 3.邮票 4.航空 5.要

DÌ ÈRSHÍ KÈ
Lesson 20
YÙNDÒNG. Sports.

A. DUÌHUÀ

QÙ KÀN LÁNQIÚ SÀI.

Mr. Li is a basketball fan. Today, Mr. Li's wife finds Mr. Li waiting for someone outside of their house.

LǏ TÀITAI: **Nǐ zài děng shéi?**

LǏ XIĀNSHENG: **Wǒ zài děng Lǎo Chén lái jiē wǒ. Wǒmen yào qù kàn lánqiúsài.**

LǏ TÀITAI: **Nǐ zěnme měitiān dōu qù kàn lánqiúsài? Jīntiān bié qù le ba.**

LǏ XIĀNSHENG: **Bù xíng, bù xíng! Jīntiān shì zuìhòu yì chǎng guàn yǎ jūn juésài. Bǐsài yídìng fēicháng jīngcǎi. Wǒ bù néng cuòguò.**

LǏ TÀITAI: **Kěshì, nǐ shàngge xīngqī dāyìng gēn wǒ qù xué tàijíquán.**

LǏ XIĀNSHENG: **Tàitai, zhè liǎng duì de shílì xiāngdāng. Wǒ yào qù kàn nǎ yí duì yíng, nǎ yí duì shū. Wǒmen míngtiān zài qù dǎ tàijíquán, hǎo bù hǎo?**

LǏ TÀITAI: **Lánqiú bǐsài yì jiéshù, nǐ yòu yào kāishǐ kàn bàngqiú bǐsài le.**

LǏ XIĀNSHENG: **Bú huì. Wǒ kěyǐ zǎoshàng dǎ tàijíquán, wǎnshàng kàn diànshì guǎngbō.**

LǏ TÀITAI: **Nǐ tiāntiān dōu shuō yùndòng hěn zhòngyào. Kěshì nǐ zǒng kàn qiúsài, cónglái bú qù duànliàn.**

LǏ XIĀNSHENG: **Hǎo, hǎo! Wǒ míngtiān kāishǐ. Nǐ kàn, Lǎo Chén lái le. Wǒmen zǒu ba.**

GOING TO A BASKETBALL GAME.

MRS. LI: Who are you waiting for?

MR. LI: I'm waiting for Old Chen to pick me up. We're going to a basketball game.

MRS. LI: Why do you need to go every day? Don't go today.

MR. LI: I can't! Today is the finals—the championship competition. It's going to be an exciting game. I can't miss it.

MRS. LI: But, last week, you agreed to study *taiqi* with me!

MR. LI: Darling, these two teams are well matched; I want to see which one wins and which one loses. Let's do *taiqi* tomorrow, okay?

MRS. LI: Once the basketball teams finish, you'll start watching baseball again.

MR. LI: I won't. I'll do *taiqi* in the morning and watch the television broadcast at night.

MRS. LI: You always say it's important to work out, but you always watch the games and never exercise.

MR. LI: Fine, I'll start tomorrow. Oh look! Here's Old Chen now. We're leaving.

B. YǓFǍ HÉ YÒNGFǍ

1. "AGAIN": *YÒU* VS. *ZÀI*

The adverb *yòu* means that something has already happened again. It is used in a sentence before the main verb and is often used with the particle *le* to show that the event already happened.

Tā zuótiān lái, jīntiān yòu lái le.
    He came yesterday and came again today.

Zài can also mean again but is used with an auxiliary verb indicating future, such as *yào* or *huì*, to say that an event will happen again. *Zài* also occurs in the sentence before the main verb.

Tā zuótiān lái, míngtiān huì zài lái.
    He came yesterday and will come again tomorrow.

Yòu can also be used with *yào* used as a modal verb of desire if the planning is currently happening. *Le* is used here in the sense that something is about to happen. *Yòu* is placed after the subject.

Tāmen yòu yào kàn qiúsài le!
   They are planning to watch the ball games again!

Contrast the previous sentence with the following where *zài* is used to simply say that the event will happen.

Tāmen yào zài kàn qiúsài.
   They will watch the ball games again.

2. *CÓNGLÁI BÙ/CÓNGLÁI MÉIYǑU*

Cónglái (never) must be used in a negative sentence. Use it with *bù* if something never happens in the present. Use it with *méiyǒu* or *méi* if something has never happened in the past. Like other adverbs, *cónglái* comes directly after the subject of a sentence.

Nǐ cónglái bù liànxí tàijíquán.
   You never practice taichi.

Nǐ cónglái méiyǒu liànxí.
   You have never practiced.

In sentences in the past that contain a direct object, the verb suffix *guò* must come after the verb and before the object.

Tā cónglái bù lái wǒ jiā.
   He never comes to my house.

Tā cónglái méi láiguò wǒ jiā.
   He has never been to my house.

3. THE PARTICLE *LE* USED FOR SOMETHING ABOUT TO HAPPEN

You have learned many uses for the particle *le*; most of them imply a "change of state." The sentence final particle *le* can also be used if a state is *about* to change.

Qiúsài yào kāishǐ le.
   The ball game is about to begin.

Wǒ yào qù kàn diànyǐng le.
  I am going to see a movie.

4. THE ADVERB *ZHǏ* (ONLY)

The adverb *zhǐ* (only) is placed in a sentence after the subject. *Zhǐ* implies that only one thing is being done.

Wǒ zhǐ huì shuō Yīngwén.
  I can only speak English.

Nǐ zhǐ kàn qiúsài, cónglái bú qù duànliàn.
  You only watch sports competitions, you never exercise.

5. MORE USES OF THE QUESTION WORD *ZĚNME*

You learned in lesson 6 that *zěnme* is used when asking how to do something or how someone is. It can also be used to express surprise at the condition of something. In English, we might express this with "How can that be!"

Nǐ zěnme měitiān dōu qù kàn lánqiúsài?
  How can you go to a basketball game every day?

Wǒ zěnme huì shuō Zhōngwén!
  How can I possibly speak Chinese!

When expressing the notion of surprise using an adjectival verb or other verb describing a person, the expression *zěnme nàme* is used.

Nǐ zěnme nàme méiyǒu yìsi!
  How can you be so boring!

Tā zěnme nàme è!
  How can he be so hungry!

C. HÀNZÌ

Read these characters.

运动（運動）　　　　　*yùndòng* (sports)

一　二　云　云　云　运　运

一　二　云　云　动　动

182

想   *xiǎng* (to think)

一　十　才　木　木　相　相　相　相　相

相　想　想　想

可以   *kěyǐ* (to be able to)

一　丁　丌　口　可

丶　丷　丷　以　以

会（會）   *huì* (to be able to)

丿　人　人　会　会　会

能   *néng* (to be able to)

厶　厶　广　介　介　育　能　能　能　能

D. SHĒNGCÍ

bàngqiú	baseball
bǐsài	match, game, competition
bùxíng	it's not possible/allowable
chǎng	a sports field
cónglái	always have (been) + negative
cuòguò	to miss an opportunity
dǎ	to play a sport
dāyìng	to promise, to agree
duànliàn	exercise
duì	a team
huì	to be likely to
guànjūn	champion
guǎngbō	to broadcast, broadcast
jiéshù	to end, to finish
jīngcǎi	brilliant, wonderful
juésài	the final competition
lánqiú	basketball
lánqiúduì	basketball team
lánqiúsài	basketball game

qiúduì	sports team
shílì	strength, ability
shū	to lose
tàijíquán	taichi
xiāngdāng	equal to, relative to
yǎjūn	second place finisher
yíng	to win
yòu	again
yùndòng	sports
zài	again
zhuǎnbō	to transmit a live broadcast, live relay
zhòngyào	to be important
zuìhòu	the last, the final

SUPPLEMENTARY VOCABULARY 4: SPORTS

zúqiú	soccer
gǎnlǎnqiú	American football
pǎobù	to run
gōngfu	kungfu
wǎngqiú	tennis
gāo'ěrfūqiú	golf
tǐcāo	gymnastics
bīngqiú	ice hockey
huábīng	skating (ice)
qí zìxíngchē	ride a bike
páshān	climb a mountain
mànpǎo	jog
yěyíng	camp
yóuyǒng	swim
qímǎ	ride a horse
fàng fēngzhēng	fly a kite
dǎqiú	throw a ball
liànxí yújiā	practice yoga
dǎ qìgōng	practice chi gong
dǎ tàijíchuán	practice taichi
dǎzuò	sit in meditation

LIÀNXÍ

A. Put either *yòu* or *zài* in the following sentences according to whether the event is past or future.

1. *Wǒ zuótiān chī yú, jīntiān _____ chī yú.*
2. *Zuótiān Wáng xiānsheng kàn le yì chǎng lánqiúsài, míngtiān tā yào _____ kàn yì chǎng.*
3. *Wǒ jì le yì fēng píngxìn. Xiàwǔ xiǎng _____ jì yì fēng guàhào xìn.*
4. *Wǒ qùnián qù le Zhōngguó, míngnián xiǎng _____ qù.*
5. *Zhège lǚguǎn wǒ zhùguò, yǐhòu bù xiǎng _____ zhù.*

B. Fill in the blanks using the words below.

cuòguò jīngcǎi cónglái zhòngyào dǎ duànliàn dāyìng

1. *Wǒmen míngtiān qù _____ tàijíquán, hǎo ma?*
2. *Wáng xiānsheng tiāntiān _____, suǒyǐ tā de shēntǐ hěn hǎo.*
3. *Jīntiān de kǎoshì hěn _____, suǒyǐ, wǒ xiànzài yào hǎohao yònggōng.*
4. *Māma _____ ràng wǒ qù dǎ bàngqiú.*
5. *Jīntiān bā diǎn de diànshì hěn _____, wǒ bú yào _____.*
6. *Lǎo Zhāng _____ méi xuéguò Yīngyǔ, suǒyǐ tā bú huì shuō.*

C. Translate the following sentences into *pīnyīn*.

1. Today's baseball game is the championship.
2. These two teams are well matched.
3. I never watch TV.
4. It is very important to exercise every day.
5. China's basketball team beat Japan 113 to 98.

D. Write the Chinese character for the underlined word and then translate each sentence into English.

1. *Wǒ fēicháng xǐhuan <u>yùndòng</u>.*
2. *Wǒ bú<u>huì</u> dǎ tàijíquán.*
3. *Tā bù <u>kěyǐ</u> lái kàn bàngqiú bǐsài.*
4. *Nǐ <u>xiǎng</u> dǎ gǎnlánqiú ma?*

185

WÉNHUÀ ZHÙJIĚ

If you get out of bed early (before 6 A.M.!) in China and go to any park, you will see a good number of people engaged in the slow and steady movements of taichi. As a form of *gōngfu*, a Chinese martial art, taichi mimics the movements of fighting, but in slow motion. Many Chinese, particularly the elderly, swear by taichi as a way toward good health and long life. The types of exercise that are ubiquitous in the United States such as jogging or pick-up basketball games are basically unheard of in China. Considering that people there ride their bicycles everywhere and otherwise are engaged in basic survival, this is not surprising. If you jog in China or exercise at any time except in the early morning, expect to get comments and stares from the people on the street.

DÁÀN

A. 1. *yòu* 2. *zài* 3. *zài* 4. *zài* 5. *zài*

B. 1. *dǎ* 2. *duànliàn* 3. *zhòngyào* 4. *dāyìng* 5. *jīngcǎi, cuòguò* 6. *cónglái*

C. 1. *Jīntiān de bàngqiúsài shì juésài.* 2. *Zhè liǎng ge qiúduì de shílì xiāngdāng.*
   3. *Wǒ cónglái bú kàn diànshì.* 4. *Tiāntiān yùndòng hěn zhòngyào.*
   5. *Zhōngguó lánqiúduì yíngle Rìběn duì: yībǎi yīshí sān bǐ jiǔshí bā.*

D. 1. 运动 I like to exercise very much. 2. 会 I can't do taichi. 3. 可以 He is not allowed to come see the baseball game. 4. 想 Do you want to play football?

186

FÙXÍ 4

A. Complete the dialogue using the words below to fill in the blanks.

shéi	*jiàn*
zhǎo	*wéi*
cuò	*zhèr*

1. Wáng: _____! Nǐ zhǎo _____?
2. Lín: *Wǒ* _____ *Wáng tàitai.*
3. Wáng: *Duìbùqǐ, nǐ dǎ* _____ *le.* _____ *méiyǒu Wáng tàitai.*
4. Lín: *Duìbùqǐ, zài* _____.

B. Combine the two sentences using the conjunction pairs in parentheses.

1. *Nǐ tián yìzhāng duìhuàn dān. Nǐ gěi wǒ kàn nǐ de hùzhào. (xiān . . . ránhòu)*
2. *Wǒ shuìjiào. Wǒ shūfu le. (yī . . . jiù)*
3. *Tā gǎnmào le. Tā bú shàngbān. (yīnwèi . . . suǒyǐ)*
4. *Nèi bù diànyǐng yǒu yìsi. Nèi bù diànyǐng hěn yǒumíng (yòu . . . yòu)*

C. Translate into English.

1. *Tā yìzhí zài děng nǐ ne.*
2. *Nǐ zhèngzài dǎ diànhuà ma?*
3. *Nǐ háizi méiyǒu zài zuò gōngkè.*
4. *Wǒmen zhèngzài kàn diànshì.*

D. Choose the best response to the questions from the responses below.

1. *Nǐ de lǚguǎn duìhuàn bú duìhuàn wàibì?*
2. *Nǐ yào jì kuàixìn háishì píngxìn?*
3. *Nǐ de lǎobǎn zhèngzài dǎ diànhuà ma?*
4. *Nǐ yǒu méiyǒu jìsuànjī?*

a. *Wǒ yào jì kuàixìn.*
b. *Wǒ yǒu jìsuànjī.*
c. *Wǒmen zhèr bú duìhuàn wàibì.*
d. *Tā bú zài dǎ diànhuà.*

E. Match the characters with the English.

1. office		a.	工作
2. bank		b.	家人
3. welcome		c.	中国
4. work		d.	饭馆
5. beer		e.	出口
6. family		f.	啤酒
7. restaurant		g.	银行
8. post office		h.	办公室
9. China		i.	邮局
10. exit		j.	欢迎

F. Answer these questions using Chinese characters.

1. 中国银行兑换外币吗？
2. 你的老板喜欢不喜欢开会？
3. 你会不会用计算机？

DÁÀN

A. 1. *wéi, shéi* 2. *zhǎo* 3. *cùo, Zhèr* 4. *jiàn*

B. 1. *Nǐ xiān tián yì zhāng duìhuàndān ránhòu gěi wǒ kàn nǐ de hùzhào.* 2. *Wǒ yī shuìjiào jiù shūfu le.* 3. *Tā yīnwèi gǎnmàole suǒyǐ tā bú shàngbān.* 4. *Nèi bù diànyǐng yòu yǒu yìsi yòu yǒumíng.*

C. 1. He's been waiting for you all along. 2. Are you on the phone? 3. Your child is not doing his/her homework. 4. We are watching TV.

D. 1. C 2. A 3. D 4. B

E. 1. H. 2. G 3. J 4. A 5. F 6. B 7. D 8. I 9. C. 10. E

F. 1. 中国银行不兑换外币 2. 我的老板喜欢开会 3. 我会用计算机。

YUÈDÚ LIÀNXÍ 2

Jīntiān wǒ mǎile shū. Wáng xiānsheng yě mǎile shū. Tā hái mǎile qiānbǐ, máobǐ, lán běnzi. Wǒ mǎi yì běn zìdiǎn, yì zhāng dìtú. Yígòng sì kuài jiǔ máo qián. Wǒmen liǎng ge rén hūrán hěn è. Nèige shíhòu shì shíèr diǎn zhōng. Wǒ qǐng Wáng xiānsheng chī wǔfàn. Wǒmen zuò gōnggòng qìchē dào xiǎo fàndiàn qù chī jiǎozi. Jiǎozi hěn hǎochī. Wǒmen chīfàn yǐhòu lèi le. Wǒ huíjiā xiūxi.

qiānbǐ	pencil
máobǐ	calligraphy brush
běnzi	notebook
dìtú	map
hūrán	suddenly
xiūxi	to rest

DÌ ÈRSHÍYĪ KÈ
Lesson 21

YUĒHUÌ. An Appointment.

A. DUÌHUÀ

ZÀI CHÁGUǍN.

Min wants to set her cousin up on a date with Lin.

MÍN: Xiǎo Lín, Nǐ xiànzài yǒu méiyǒu nánpéngyou?

LÍN: Méiyǒu. Zěnme? Nǐ dǎsuàn gěi wǒ jièshào ma?

MÍN: Shì a! Wǒ yǒu yí ge biǎogē, rén hěn lǎoshí. Wǒ xiǎng ràng
nǐmen rènshi rènshi, jiāo jiāo péngyou.

LÍN: Tā jīnnián duō dà? Shì zuò shénme de?

MÍN: Tā jīnnián èrshíwǔ suì. Qiánnián cóng Kējì Dàxué bìyè, shì
niàn gōngchéng de. Xiànzài zài jìsuànjī gōngsī gōngzuò.

LÍN: Tā zhǎng de zěnmeyàng?

MÍN: Hái búcuò. Tā de liǎn yuányuan de, yǎnjīng hěn dà. Tā tǐng
huì shuōhùa de.

LÍN: Hái yǒu shénme yōudiǎn a?

MÍN: Tā bù hē jiǔ, yě bù xīyān. Yǒu kòng jiù xǐhɪan kàn diànyǐng,
gēn nǐ yíyàng.

LÍN: Tīng qǐlái hěn yōuxiù. Wèishénme hái méiyǒu nǚpéngyou ne?

MÍN: Tā shàng dàxué de nà jǐ nián mángzhe niànshū, xiànzài yòu
mángzhe shìyè, gēnběn méi shíjiān. Tā māma hěn dānxīn,
yào wǒ bāng tā liúyì yíxià. Zěnmeyàng?

LÍN: Hǎo a! Nǐ yuē tā chū lái yī xià jiàn jian miàn ba!

AT THE TEAHOUSE.

MIN: Lin, do you have a boyfriend right now?

190

LIN: No. Why? Are you planning to set me up with someone?

MIN: Absolutely. I have an older cousin who is very sincere and honest who I'd like to introduce you to. Maybe you two will get along.

LIN: How old is he? What does he do?

MIN: He's twenty-five years old. He graduated from the University of Science and Technology two years ago. He majored in Engineering and works for a computer company now.

LIN: What does he look like?

MIN: Not bad. He has a round face and big eyes and a nice way of speaking.

LIN: What other strong points does he have?

MIN: He doesn't drink or smoke. When he has free time, he likes to watch movies, just like you.

LIN: He sounds wonderful. Why doesn't he have a girlfriend yet?

MIN: He was busy with his studies when he was in school. Now he pursues his career seriously. He doesn't have a lot of time and his mother is worried about him. She asked me to look around for someone for him. What do you think?

LIN: Hey sure, go ahead and arrange for him to come one time and meet me.

B. YǓFǍ HÉ YÒNGFǍ

1. REDUPLICATION OF TWO-SYLLABLE VERBS AND ADJECTIVES

When two-syllable verbs are reduplicated to imply "a little bit" or to express tentativeness in commands, the verb can be simply repeated twice.

Nǐ xuéxí xuéxí ba.
   Why don't you study?

Wǒ tài máng le. Nǐ bāngmáng bāngmáng ba.
   I'm so busy. Why don't you give me a hand?

For verb-object compound verbs and resultative verbs only the first syllable can be reduplicated.

Nǐ bāng bang máng ba!
    Why don't you give me a hand?

Nǐ yuē tā chū lái jiàn jian miàn ba!
    Why don't you ask him to come out so we can meet?

Wǒ qù zuò zuo shì.
    I'm going to do a few things.

When two-syllable adjectives are reduplicated, each syllable is repeated in turn. This can only occur in a clause that modifies a noun or a verb (see lesson 10, complement of degree).

Wǒ hěn xiǎng mǎi yí jiàn piàopiaoliàngliang de qúnzi.
    I would really like to buy a pretty skirt.

Tā tiāntian dōu shì kuàikuailèle de.
    He is happy every day.

Wǒ xǐhuan gānganjìngjing de fángzi.
    I like houses that are clean.

Tāmen gāogaoxìngxing de lái le.
    They came happily.

Tā shūshufúfu de shuì le.
    He slept comfortably.

2. THE *SHÌ* . . . *DE* CONSTRUCTION

Shì (to be) . . . *de* (modifying particle) is used to highlight the action or state of the subject.

Tà shì niàn gōngchéng de.
    He is a student of engineering.

Tā shì tíng huì shuōhuà de.
    He is quite good with words.

Tā shì zuò shénme de?
    What does he do?

Wáng Bīng shì zúotiān lái de.
    Wang Bing came yesterday.

Compare the *shì . . . de* construction to the other types of descriptive phrases you have learned.

Tā hěn huì shuōhuà.
Tā shuōhuà shuō de hěn hǎo.
Tā shì hěn huì shuōhuà de.
  He speaks very well.

3. RESULTATIVE VERBS WITH *QǏLÁI*

The ending *qǐlái* (which literally means "to get up") when used with a verb implies that the action of the verb is in fact happening and is just being noticed or realized. *Qǐlái* is only used with verbs of perception and reflection.

Tā kàn qǐlái bù shūfu.
  He doesn't look comfortable.

Tā tīng qǐlái hěn yōuxiù.
  He sounds outstanding.

To negate this type of verb, place *bù* between the main verb and *qǐlái*. The negative implies that a person is currently trying to perceive or think of something, but cannot.

Zhège zì wǒ xiǎng bù qǐlái.
  I can't recall this word.

4. MORE ABOUT THE PARTICLE *ZHE*

You learned in lesson 15 how to use the particle *zhe* to express a present continuous act. *Zhe* can also be attached to a verb to indicate that the action or quality of the verb was going on continuously in the past. In this case, a time expression is usually placed before the verb.

Tā shàng dàxué de nà jǐ nián mángzhe niànshū.
  He was busy with his studies when he was in school.

C. HÀNZÌ

朋友   *péngyou* (friend)

丿 几 月 月 刖 朋 朋 朋

一 十 方 友

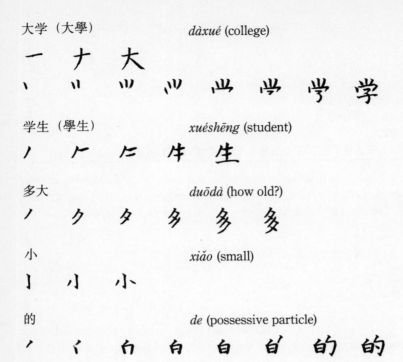

大学（大學）　　　　　*dàxué* (college)

学生（學生）　　　　　*xuéshēng* (student)

多大　　　　　　　　　*duōdà* (how old?)

小　　　　　　　　　　*xiǎo* (small)

的　　　　　　　　　　*de* (possessive particle)

Sentence examples:

我的朋友是大学生。
Wǒ de péngyou shì dàxuéshēng.
　My friend is a college student.

你多大了？
Nǐ duōdà le?
　How old are you?

我没有男朋友。
Wǒ méiyǒu nánpéngyou.
　I don't have a boyfriend.

D. SHĒNGCÍ

āyí	auntie
bìyè	to graduate
dānxīn	to worry
dàxuéshēng	college student
gēnběn	fundamental

hējiǔ	to drink alcohol
jìsuànjī	computer
kējì	science and technology
lǎoshí	honest, sincere
liúyì	to keep an eye on
nánpéngyou	boyfriend
nǚpéngyou	girlfriend
tǐng	very
xīyān	to smoke (cigarettes)
yǎnjīng	eye
yōudiǎn	strong point
yōuxiù	outstanding
yuán	round
zhuàng	strong, healthy
zuǒyòu	about, more or less

LIÀNXÍ

A. Fill in the blanks using the words below.

lǎoshí shuōhuà yōuxiù dānxīn yíyàng yōudiǎn

1. *Lǐ xiānsheng mǎi de gǔdiǎn yīnyùe gēn nǐ mǎi de _____.*
2. *Wǒ dìdi shì yí ge hěn _____ de rén, tā yǒu hěn duō yōudiǎn.*
3. *Wǒ de nánpéngyou yǒu hěnduō _____. Tā bù xīyān, yě bù hē jiǔ.*
4. *Wáng xiānsheng shì yí ge hěn _____ de jīnglǐ.*
5. *Tā zuótiān wǎnshàng méi huíjiā. Tā māma hěn _____.*
6. *Wǒ de lǎoshī hěn huì _____.*

B. Fill in the blanks using the reduplicated form of the verb or adjective in parentheses.

1. *Wǒ gěi nǐmen _____. (jièshào)*
2. *Nǐ yīnggāi duō _____ zhōngwén. (xuéxí)*
3. *Wáng xiǎojie jīntiān chuān de _____ de. (piàoliàng)*
4. *Lín lǎoshī _____ huíjiā le. (gāoxìng)*
5. *Qǐng bāng wǒ mèimei _____ yǒu méiyǒu hǎo de duìxiàng. (liúyì)*

C. Rewrite the following sentences using the *shì . . . de* construction.

1. *Tā de nǚpéngyou hěn piàoliang.*
2. *Tā shì lǎoshī.*
3. *Nèige fángjiān hěn xīn.*
4. *Běijīng de yóukè hěn duō.*

D. Translate the following sentences into *pīnyīn*.

1. He sounds very busy.
2. It appears that your relative is outstanding.
3. You look extremely tired.
4. It sounds like that guy isn't sincere.

E. Write the Chinese characters.

1. I am a college student.
2. How old are you?
3. My college is very good.
4. Is your friend a teacher?

WÉNHUÀ ZHÙJIĚ

Although there are no longer arranged marriages in China, friends are always trying to fix up friends with each other, especially at an older age. Dating in all but the biggest cities is practically Victorian. Generally, the first boyfriend or girlfriend is the last—it is considered immoral to be seen dating more than one member of the opposite sex, and when a girl is jilted she is thereafter considered flawed. If a person is not married by the age of twenty-five, others, especially of the older generation, wonder what is wrong with him or her. Things are certainly changing in China, but more slowly on the dating front than anywhere else. Kissing in public, even among married couples, is uncommon, and premarital sex is frowned upon. Same-sex relationships, as well, are still generally frowned upon, although some progress has been made in big cities, such as Shanghai, where attitudes are more open.

DÁ ÀN

A. 1. *yíyàng* 2. *yōuxiù* 3. *yōudiǎn* 4. *lǎoshí* 5. *dānxīn* 6. *shuōhuà*

B. 1. *jièshào jièshào* 2. *xuéxí xuéxí* 3. *piàopiaoliàngliang* 4. *gāogaoxìngxing*
5. *liúyì liúyì*

C. 1. *Tā de nǚpéngyou shì hěn piàoliang de.* 2. *Tā shì jiāoshū de.* 3. *Nèige fángjiān shì hěn xīn de.* 4. *Běijīng de yóukè shì hěn duō de.*

D. 1. *Tā tīng qǐlái hěn máng.* 2. *Nǐ de qīnqi kàn qǐlái hěn yōuxiù.* 3. *Nǐ kàn qǐlái hěn lèi.* 4. *Tīng qǐlái tā bú tài lǎoshí.*

E. 1. 我是大学生 2. 你多大了？ 3. 我的大学很好。 4. 你的朋友是不是老师？

DÌ ÈRSHÍÈR KÈ
Lesson 22
XÍGUÀN. Habits.

A. DUÌHUÀ

ZÀI SÙSHÈ FÁNGJIĀN.

Sally, an American student, is talking about life in China with her roommate, Xiaoying.

XIĀOYĪNG: **Shālì, nǐ lái Zhōngguó hǎo jǐ ge yuè le. Yíqiè dōu xíguàn ma?**

SHĀLÌ: **Shénme dōu hǎo, jiù shì yòng kuàizi bú tài xíguàn.**

XIĀOYĪNG: **Zěnme huí shì?**

SHĀLÌ: **Zài Měiguó, wǒmen dōu yòng chāzi hé dāozi chīfàn. Kěshì, Zhōngguó rén dōu yòng kuàizi. Zhēn bù xíguàn. Wǒmen chīfàn de shíhòu, xíguàn hē bīng shuǐ. Kěshì Zhōngguó rén bù hē bīngshuǐ.**

XIĀOYĪNG: **Duì. Wǒmen xǐhuan hē rè chá huòzhě kāishuǐ.**

SHĀLÌ: **Lìngwài, zài Měiguó wǒmen dōu xíguàn zǎoshàng xǐzǎo. Wǒmen dàxué zǎoshàng de shíhòu méiyǒu rè shuǐ.**

XIĀOYĪNG: **Shì ma? Wǒmen Zhōngguórén dōu zài wǎnshàng xǐzǎo.**

SHĀLÌ: **Xuéxiào zìzhù xǐyījī hé hōnggānjī tài shǎo le. Wǒ děi yòng shǒu xǐ yīfu, yě bú tài xíguàn. Suàn le! Wǒ yào xuézhe shìyìng dāngdì de xíguàn.**

IN A DORM ROOM.

XIAOYING: Sally, you've been in China for several months. Are you used to everything?

SALLY: I can deal with everything except for using chopsticks.

XIAOYING: What's wrong?

SALLY: In the United States, we all use a knife and fork to eat, but Chinese people all use chopsticks. I'm really not used to it. Also, we're used to drinking ice water with meals. Chinese people don't drink ice water.

XIAOYING: Right. We like to drink hot tea or boiled water.

SALLY: Also, in America we like to take showers in the morning. At the university, we don't even have hot water in the morning.

XIAOYING: Really? We Chinese are used to taking showers at night.

SALLY: There are not enough self-service washing machines and dryers in the school, so I need to hand-wash my clothes—I'm really not used to that! Forget it. I'm going to try to adjust my habits according to the local customs.

B. YǓFǍ HÉ YÒNGFǍ

1. *XÍGUÀN* AS A NOUN AND A VERB

The noun *xíguàn* means habit, and when it is used as a verb is translated as "to be used to."

Wǒ xíguàn yòng kuàizi chīfàn.
   I am used to using chopsticks to eat.

Tā bù xíguàn Zhōngguó de shēnghuó.
   He is not used to life in China.

Tā hái méiyǒu xíguàn Zhōngguó de shēnghuó.
   He is still not used to life in China.

2. THE EXPRESSION *DUÌ . . . LÁI SHUŌ*

Duì . . . lái shuō means "according to . . . " or "as far as . . . is concerned" with a pronoun or noun placed between the two elements. Look at the following examples and their translations.

Duì xīfāngrén lái shuō, zhè xūyào mànman shìyìng.
   For a Westerner, this requires a gradual adjustment.

Duì wǒ lái shuō, zhè jiàn shìqing kàn qǐlái xiāngdāng nán.
   This looks quite difficult to me.

Duì gōngsī lái shuō, nǐ shì bù néng zǒu de.
   As far as the company is concerned, you can't go.

3. SUMMARY OF THE MULTIPURPOSE WORDS *DĚI, XŪYÀO* AND *YĪNGGĀI*

Děi, xūyào and *yīnggāi* are similar in meaning and in usage, but can only be used interchangeably in certain cases. *Xūyào* (to need) can be a noun, a main verb or a modal verb. *Děi* (to need) and *yīnggāi* (should) can only be used as modal verbs and can usually be used interchangeably with each other as well as with *xūyào* as a modal verb. Note that although these three modal verbs can be used interchangeably, there are subtle differences in meaning.

Wǒ xūyào yìdiǎnr qián.
  I need some money.

Tā bù xūyào zhège gōngzuò.
  He doesn't need this job.

Wǒ méiyǒu zhège xūyào.
  I don't have this need.

Nǐ xūyào mǎshàng xiūxi.
  You need to rest immediately.

Nǐ děi mǎshàng xiūxi.
  You have to rest immediately.

Nǐ yīnggāi mǎshàng xiūxi.
  You should rest immediately.

Wǒmen xūyào zhǎo shíjiān liáoliao.
  We need to find some time to chat.

Wǒmen děi zhǎo shíjiān liáoliao.
  We have to find time to chat.

Wǒmen yīnggāi zhǎo shíjiān liáoliao.
  We should find time to chat.

4. *HǍO* WITH EXPRESSIONS OF TIME OR QUANTITY

Hǎo (to be good) can be paired with a time word or an amount to mean "a good."

Nǐ lái Zhōngguó hǎo jǐ ge yuè le.
  You've been in China for a good many months.

Tā gěi wǒ hǎo duō qián.
  He gave me a good deal of money.

5. *CHÉNGYǓ*, A TYPE OF IDIOMATIC EXPRESSION

Chinese is full of idiomatic expressions known as *chéngyǔ*. These are four character expressions that usually come from a traditional tale or observation of life. In this lesson, you saw *rùjìng suísú*, which literally means "when you enter a country, follow their customs," but as an idiom it is better translated "when in Rome, do as the Romans do." Here are a few more examples of *chéngyǔ*.

zhēngxiān kǒnghòu
Push ahead for fear of lagging behind.

huàlóng diǎnjīng
A few well chosen words can speak volumes (literally, "to describe a dragon, paint its eye").

yǎněr dàolíng
To be in deep denial (literally, "cover your ears to steal a bell").

C. HÀNZÌ

用   *yòng* (to use)

手   *shǒu* (hand)

水   *shuǐ* (water)

热   *rè* (hot)

洗   *xǐ* (to wash)

201

衣服   *yīfu* (clothes)

丶 一 亠 亠 衣 衣 衣
丿 几 月 月 月 朋 服 服

Sentence practice:

我们大学没有热水。

Wǒmen dàxué méiyǒu rè shuǐ.

Our college has no hot water.

你要用手洗衣服。

Nǐ yào yòng shǒu xǐ yīfu.

You should wash your clothes by hand.

D. SHĒNGCÍ

bīng shuǐ	ice water
chāzi	fork
dāozi	knife
dāngdì	local
hōnggānjī	clothes dryer
kāishuǐ	boiled water, potable water
kuàizi	chopsticks
lěng	cold
liáng shuǐ	cool water
lìngwài	in addition
rè shuǐ	hot water
rìcháng shēnghuó	daily life, routine
rùjìng suísú	when in Rome, do as Romans do
shìyìng	to adapt, to fit
xīfāngrén	Westerners
xíguàn	habit, to be used to
xǐyīdiàn	dry cleaner
xǐyīfáng	laundry room
xǐyījī	clothes washing machine
xūyào	to need, to require
Zěnme huíshì?	What's up? What happened?
zìzhù	self-service

LIÀNXÍ

A. Fill in the blanks according to the English equivalents.

1. *Shālì bù* _____ *yòng kuàizi chīfàn.*
   Sally isn't used to using chopsticks to eat.
2. *Měiguórén xíguàn hē* ____ *shuǐ. Zhōngguórén xíguàn hē* _____ *shuǐ.*
   Americans are used to drinking ice water. Chinese people are used to drinking boiled water.
3. *Zhōngguórén xíguàn* _____ *xǐzǎo. Měiguórén xíguàn zǎoshàng* ____.
   Chinese people are used to taking showers in the evening. Americans are used to taking showers in the morning.

B. You want to give advice to a Chinese friend coming to the United States. Describe in *pīnyīn* what she might encounter.

1. You will need to take showers in the morning.
2. You will need to drink ice water.
3. You will need to wash clothes by using washers and dryers in the United States.
4. In Rome, do as the Romans do!

C. Translate the following sentences into *pīnyīn* using the phrases in parentheses.

1. For me, I'm not used to this. (*duì . . . lái shuō*)
2. I need your help. (*xūyào*)
3. We need to hand-wash our clothes today. (*děi*)
4. We should find time to chat. (*yīnggāi*)

D. Write the English equivalents.

1. 我不要热水。
2. 他的朋友用手洗衣服。
3. 你要不要到邮局去？
4. 北京大学很好！

There are elements of life in China that foreigners have a hard time getting used to — water in particular seems to be the source of frustration in various ways. In many buildings, especially universities, the bathrooms only have hot water during certain hours of the day, usually at night, so showers need to be planned. Of course, foreign students and other foreign guests are fortunate in that they are given a bathroom with a shower—many Chinese have to wait in line at a public shower for hours and pay to get clean. This is changing quickly; many city dwellers in China can now afford private showers with an electric heater that provides hot water when desired. Drinking water can also be a source of stress. Don't drink out of the tap anywhere in China. Cold bottled water is easy to find and cheap. Chinese people prefer to drink *kāishuǐ* (boiled hot water) and in every hotel or guest room you will always find a flask of freshly boiled water that you can let cool and drink or use to make instant coffee, the only kind available in most places in China.

DÁÀN

A. 1. *xíguàn* 2. *bīng, kāi* 3. *wǎnshàng, xǐzǎo*

B. 1. *Nǐ yào zǎoshàng xǐzǎo.* 2. *Nǐ yào hē bīng shuǐ.* 3. *Nǐ zài Měiguó yào yòng xǐyījī xǐ yīfu.* 4. *rùjìng suísú*

C. 1. *Duì wǒ lái shuō, wǒ bù xíguàn.* 2. *Wǒ xūyào nǐ de bāngzhù.* 3. *Wǒmen jīntiān děi yòng shǒu xǐ yīfu.* 4. *Wǒmen yīnggāi zhǎo shíjiān tán.*

D. 1. I don't want hot water. 2. His friend washes clothes by hand. 3. Do you want to go to the post office? 4. Beijing University is great!

DÌ ÈRSHÍSĀN KÈ
Lesson 23

YĪNYUÈ. Music.

A. DUÌHUÀ

TÁN JĪNGJÙ.

Ms. Ma and Mr. Zhang are discussing traditional versus modern music.

MǍ: Xiǎo Zhāng, xiàge xīngqīrì shìlì jùyuàn yǒu yí ge Běijīng jīngjùyuán yǎnchū. Nǐ xiǎng bù xiǎng qù kàn.

ZHĀNG: Wǒ bú qù. Wǒ tīng bù dǒng tāmen chàng de. Nǐ tīng de dǒng ma?

MǍ: Wǒ dǒng yìdiǎnr. Xiǎo shíhòu, wǒ bàba cháng dài wǒ qù kàn jīngjù. Nǐ xǐhuan shénme yīnyuè?

ZHĀNG: Wǒ bǐjiaò xǐhuan tīng xīfāng de gǔdiǎn yīnyuè. Wǒ xiǎo shíhòu lāguò xiǎotíqín.

MǍ: Nǐ xiànzài hái lā ma? Biǎoyǎn yíxià ba.

ZHĀNG: Hěn jiǔ méi lā, dōu wàng le! Nǐ ne? Nǐ xuéguò jīngjù ma?

MǍ: Xiǎo shíhòu wǒ bàba sòng wǒ qù jùxiào xuéle jǐnián.

ZHĀNG: Jīngjù nánxué ma?

MǍ: Yào tiāntian liàn, cái xué de hǎo. Hòulái, wǒ shàngle zhōngxué, gōngkè tài duō, jiù bú zài qù le.

ZHĀNG: Zhè gēn liàn xiǎotíqín yíyàng. Wǒ jìde xiǎo shíhòu měitiān xiàwú dōu yào lā liǎng, sān ge zhōngtóu. Tài lèi le.

MǍ: Duì, kěshì yīnyuè shì wénhuà de yí ge zhòngyào bùfèn.

TALKING ABOUT BEIJING OPERA.

MA: Little Zhang, there is a Beijing opera group performing in the city theater next Sunday. Do you want to go?

ZHANG: No thanks, I don't understand what they are singing about. Do you understand?

MA: I understand a little. When I was a kid, my father often took me to see Beijing operas. What style of music do you listen to?

ZHANG: I prefer to listen to Western classical music. I studied the violin when I was younger.

MA: Do you still play? Perform something for me.

ZHANG: I haven't played for a long time and have forgotten everything. How about you? Have you ever studied Beijing opera?

MA: My dad sent me to opera school when I was a kid.

ZHANG: Is Beijing opera difficult to learn?

MA: If you practiced everyday, you would do well. But I quit when I went to middle school because I had too much work.

ZHANG: It's the same thing with the violin. I remember when I was a kid, I used to play violin for two or three hours every afternoon. It was exhausting.

MA: That's true, but music is such an important part of culture.

B. YǓFǍ HÉ YÒNGFǍ

1. POTENTIAL RESULTATIVE VERBS

You have already learned about resultative verbs where the second syllable indicates to what extent the first syllable is realized. When *de* or *bù* is inserted in between the two syllables, this means that the subject is able or unable respectively to do the action of the verb. For example, *chī wán* means "to finish eating," while *chī de wán* means "able to finish eating" and *chī bù wán* means "unable to finish eating." Any type of resultative verb—those of degree, completion or direction—can be used in this way.

Wǒ kànwán diànyǐng le.
I am finished watching the movie.

Wǒ kàn de wán diànyǐng.
I am able to finish watching the movie. [I have time.]

Wǒ kàn bù wán diànyǐng.
   I am unable to finish watching the movie. [I don't have time.]

Wǒ tīng de dǒng jīngjù.
   I am able to understand Beijing opera.

Wǒ tīng bù dǒng jīngjù.
   I can't understand Beijing opera.

Questions using this construction can be asked by placing *ma* at the end of a sentence or alternative questions can be used as follows.

Nǐ tīng de dǒng tīng bù dǒng Zhōngguóhuà?
   Are you able to understand Chinese?

Míngtiān nǐ kàn de jiàn kàn bú jiàn Xiǎo Zhāng?
   Can you see Xiao Zhang tomorrow?

2. THE CONJUNCTION *CÁI*

The conjunction *cái* (and then) is used to connect cause-and-effect clauses, especially if the effect takes place later or with more difficulty than expected. *Cái* is placed after the subject of a clause. Of course, if the subject is understood it can be deleted.

Yào tiāntiān liàn, cái xué de hǎo.
   One has to practice every day, and then one will learn.

Wǒ xuéxí Zhōngwén, cái zhīdào Zhōngwén hěn nánxué.
   It was not until I studied Chinese that I realized how difficult it is.

Verbs with *cái* already imply "not" so they cannot be negated with *bù* or *méi*. These types of sentences also don't take the particle *le* because verbs with *cái* imply that the action is not or will not be completed. *Cái* should not be confused with another cause and effect conjunction *yī . . . jiù . . .* (as soon as) that you learned about in lesson 14. *Yī . . . jiù . . .* is used when the effect comes sooner or more easily than expected.

Wǒ yì xué Zhōngwén, jiù zhīdào Zhōngwén hǎo xué le.
   As soon as I studied Chinese, I realized how easy it is.

3. EASY AND DIFFICULT

You can put *nán* (difficult) or *hǎo* (good) before a verb to indicate that this verb is difficult or easy to do.

Zhōngwén hěn nánxué.
Chinese is difficult to learn.

Zhōngwén hěn hǎoxué.
Chinese is easy to learn.

Jīngjù nánxué ma?
Is Beijing opera difficult to learn?

Jīngjù hǎoxué ma?
Is Beijing opera easy to learn?

4. *YǏHÒU* VS. *HÒULÁI*

You learned in lesson 5 that *yǐhòu* means "after." *Hòulái* also means "after, afterwards," but where *yǐhòu* is used with short term or specific times or events *hòulái* is used with larger chunks of time or nonspecific events. *Hòulái* is placed in a sentence directly before or after the subject.

Wǒ xiàbān yǐhòu qù chīfàn.
After I get out of work, I'll eat.

Hòulái, wǒ shàngle zhōngxué, wǒ bú zài qù le.
Afterwards, when I started middle school, I didn't go back.

5. THE CONSTRUCTION *HĚN JIǓ MÉI* . . .

In lesson 1, you learned that *hǎo jiǔ bú (jiàn)* means "long time no (see)." *Hěn jiǔ méi* . . . is a similar expression meaning that someone hasn't done something for a long time. It is placed in a sentence between the subject and the verb.

Wǒ hěn jiǔ méi lā.
I haven't played it in a long time.

Tā hěn jiǔ méi shuō Yīngwén.
He hasn't spoken English in a long time.

C. HÀNZÌ

In lesson 21, you learned how to write the character for the possessive particle *de* (的). The *de* that is used in potential resultative verb constructions is pronounced the same, but the character is different.

得   *de* (resultative verb particle)

ノ　ノ　彳　彳　彳コ　彳ユ　彳　彳　彳
得　得

Here are some other characters and sentences that show potential resultative verb structures.

看   *kàn* (to see)

ノ　二　三　手　手　看　看　看　看

听（聽）   *tīng* (to hear)

丨　口　口　口'　叮　叮　听

懂   *dǒng* (to understand)

丶　丬　十　忄　忄　忄　忄　忄　忄
忄　忄　忄　忄　懂　懂

完   *wán* (to finish)

丶　宀　宀　宀　宁　宁　完

Sentence practice:

你想不想去看？
Nǐ xiǎng bù xiǎng qù kàn?
　Do you want to go to watch?

你想来运动吗？
Nǐ xiǎng lái yùndòng ma?
　Do you want to come exercise?

你听得懂听不懂？
Nǐ tīng de dǒng tīng bù dǒng?
　Do you understand [what you hear]?

我看得完。

Wǒ kàn de wán.

I am able to finish reading.

D. SHĒNGCÍ

biǎoyǎn	to perform
dǒng	to understand
gōngkè	homework
gǔdiǎn	classical
hǎoxué	easy to learn
hùxiāng	mutually, each other
jīngjù	Chinese opera, Beijing Opera
jīngjùyuàn	opera theater
jùtuán	theater company
jùxiào	drama school
jùyuàn	theater
lā	to pull, to play (stringed instruments)
liàn	to practice
nán	difficult
nánxué	difficult to learn
shìlì	municipal
tīng	to listen to
xīfāng	the West
xiǎotíqín	violin
xīnshǎng	to appreciate, to enjoy
xuéxí	to study
yíyàng	the same
yīnyuè	music

LIÀNXÍ

A. Fill in the blanks with the appropriate resultative verb ending (*dǒng, hùi, hǎo* or *sǐ*).

1. *Jīntiān de xiǎotíqín nǐ liàn _____ le ma?*
2. *Jīntiān de gōngkè wǒ zuò _____ le.*
3. *Xiǎoyīng bú jiàn, tā māma jí _____ le.*
4. *Nǐ tīng _____ lǎoshī shuō de ma?*

210

B. Fill in the blanks with the appropriate question form for resultative verbs and the appropriate answer.

1. *Nǐ _____ Zhōngwén ma?*
   Wǒ méi xué Zhōngwén. Wǒ tīng _____ dǒng.
2. *Nǐ _____ qiánmiàn de bǎihuò gōngsī ma?*
   Tài yuǎn le. Wǒ kàn _____ dào.

C. Fill in the blanks with *yǐhòu* or *hòulái*.

1. *Nǐ _____ qù Zhōngguó le ma?*
2. *Wǒ xiàbān _____ qù kàn diànyǐng.*
3. *Shídiǎn _____, wǒ zài zhèr děng nǐ.*
4. *_____, wǒ mǎile yì dǐng màozi.*

D. Translate the following sentences into *pīnyīn*.

1. Studying Chinese is the same as studying violin.
2. We didn't go to the Peking opera afterwards.
3. You need to practice every day and then you'll learn well.
4. I can't understand this Chinese character. Can you?
5. Chinese is not difficult to learn.

E. Translate into English.

1. 我听不懂你说的话。
2. 我想去看。
3. 他的大学早上的时候没有热水。

WÉNHUÀ ZHÙJIĚ

Beijing opera was prominent in China during the dynastic system as the main form of entertainment for the emperor and high officials. The performances were rich in colors and sounds—opera singers wore elaborate costumes and makeup and the stage sets would rival what you see today at Lincoln Center. A small band of instruments accompanied the singers as they acted and sang traditional tales. During this century, the Beijing opera almost disappeared—considered as it was to be a symbol of the aristocracy. As a result, few people in China study opera, and those who do are seen mainly in performances geared specifically to tourists. The new generation in China especially is drawn toward Western pop music and doesn't understand the appeal of the high-pitched and arcane sounds of Beijing opera. When you are in China, it is worth catching a performance, simply to catch a glimpse of China as it once was. Be prepared, Chinese opera can be surprising to the ears and the story line difficult to follow, even with subtitles if they are provided. Just sit back and marvel at the intricacies of China's history.

DÁÀN

A. 1. *huì or hǎo* 2. *hǎo* 3. *sǐ* 4. *dǒng*

B. 1. *xué, bù* 2. *kàn de jiàn kàn de dào, bù*

C. 1. *hòulái* 2. *yǐhòu* 3. *yǐhòu* 4. *Hòulái*

D. 1. *Xué Zhōngwén hé xué xiǎotíqín yíyàng.* 2. *Wǒmen hòulái méiyǒu qù kàn jīngjù.* 3. *Nǐ yào tiāntian liànxí, cái xué de hǎo.* 4. *Wǒ kàn bù dǒng zhège Zhōngwén zì. Nǐ ne?* 5. *Zhōngwén bù nánxué.*

E. 1. I don't understand what you are saying. 2. I want to go and see. 3. Her university doesn't have hot water in the morning.

DÌ ÈRSHÍSÌ KÈ
Lesson 24
CHŪNJIÉ. Spring Festival.

A. DUÌHUÀ

Zài sùshè.

Chen and Lin are roommates in college and are discussing their plans for the Spring festival.

CHÉN: Jīnnián chūnjià, xuéxiào bú shàngkè. Nǐ dǎsuàn zěnme guò?

LÍN: Wǒ xiǎng yí ge rén qù Hángzhōu fùjìn wánr wānr.

CHÉN: Wǒ qùnián gāng qùguò Hángzhōu. Nàr de fēngjǐng měi, gǔjī yě duō. Fēicháng zhíde qù.

LÍN: Tài hǎo le. Nǐ kěyi gàosù wǒ nǎr hǎo wánr ma?

CHÉN: Dāngrán! Míngtiān wǒ bǎ qùnián shōují de zīliào dōu gěi nǐ. Xiàng Xīhú, Língyǐn Sì zhèxiē dìfāng, nǐ dōu yīnggāi yào qù kànkan.

LÍN: Fēicháng gǎnxiè. Nǐ dǎsuàn zuò shénme?

CHÉN: Wǒ yào dào wǒ de lǎojiā qù, kànkan qīnqì. Wǒ de bàba, māma, xiōngdì jiěmèi dōu yào qù nàr. Wǒmen jiā de chuántǒng shì měinián tuánjù chī hěn duō dōngxī, dǎ májiàng.

LÍN: Jiā hěn zhòngyào. Nǐ de lǎojiā zài nǎr?

CHÉN: Wǒ de jiā zài Hāěrbīn. Chūnjià de tiānqì hái huì tèbié lěng, kěshì wǒmen dōu bù zàihu, dōu zài fángzi lǐmiàn wánr.

LÍN: Májiàng wǒ yě huì dǎ. Kěshì zài dōngběi, májiàng bǐjiào fùzá. Nǐmen dǔ qián ma?

CHÉN: Wǒmen zhǐ yòng pái wánr. Bú yòng qián.

LÍN: Gēn wǒmen zài xuéxiào de shíhòu bù yíyàng! Yǒu hǎo jǐ cì wǒ de qián dōu shū le! Tài dǎoméi le!

AT THE DORMITORY.

CHEN: There are no classes this year during spring break. What do you plan to do?

LIN: I'm going to go to places near Hangzhou by myself.

CHEN: I went to Hangzhou last summer. It's really beautiful there, with a lot of historical sites. It's definitely worth visiting.

LIN: Great! Can you tell me where to go?

CHEN: Sure. I'll give you all of the information I found last year about places like Xihu Lake and Lingyin Temple, where you should definitely go.

LIN: Thanks a lot. What do you plan to do?

CHEN: I'm going back to my hometown to see my relatives. My dad, mom and brothers and sisters will all be there. Our tradition is to get together every year, eat a lot and play some mah-jongg.

LIN: Family is really important. Where is your hometown?

CHEN: It's in Harbin. The weather will probably still be really cold during spring break, but we don't care, we just stay inside and play.

LIN: I can play mah-jongg also, but the rules in northeast are much more complicated. Do you play for money?

CHEN: We use playing cards to gamble. We don't use money.

LIN: Not like when we are in school! There have been many times where I have lost all of my money. Very bad luck!

B. YŬFĂ HÉ YÒNGFĂ

1. PLACE + FÙJÌN

Fùjìn (neighborhood) comes after a place-name to indicate the area surrounding the place.

Hārbīn fùjìn de dìfāng hěn yǒu yìsi.
    The area around Harbin is quite interesting.

Wǒ fùmǔ jiā fùjìn yǒu hěn duō fànguǎnr.
    My parents' neighborhood has a lot of restaurants.

2. TALKING ABOUT YEARS

In lesson 6, you learned how to say "next week" and "last week" by using *xià* and *shàng*. To talk about "next year" and "last year," you need to use *míng* (bright) and *qù* (to go). This *míng* is the same *míng* used in *míngtiān* (tomorrow).

Wŏ qùnián dàxué bìyè le.
   I graduated from college last year.

Tā míngnián yào dào Zhōngguó qù.
   She wants to go to China next year.

"This year" is *jīnnián*.

Wŏ jīnnián bú yào shēngbìng.
   I don't want to get sick this year.

3. *MĚI* (EVERY) WITH TIME WORDS

Place *měi* (every) directly before a time word such as *xīngqī yī* (Monday) or *nián* (year) to indicate that something is done at every one of these times. The measure word *ge* needs to be placed between *měi* and the noun — except with *nián* (year).

Wŏ měinián xiūjià.
   I take a vacation every year.

Tā měi ge yuè chī Hánguófàn.
   He eats Korean food every month.

Wŏ de lăoshī měi ge xīngqīwŭ gĕi wŏmen kăoshì.
   Our teacher gives us a test every Friday.

4. SUMMARY OF RESULTATIVE VERBS

You have learned about several types of resultative verbs. The important thing to remember is that for each type, a specific resultative ending is attached to the verb to indicate the result of the action of the verb, or, in the case of potential resultative verbs, the possible result of the action of the verb. Here is a summary of resultative verb endings and what type of result they indicate.

dào
Tā méi xiăngdào Chūnjié yŏu zhème duō chuántŏng de cài.
   He didn't know Spring Festival had this many traditional dishes.

dǒng

Wǒmen tīng bù dǒng Zhōngguó diànshì jiémù.

We don't understand Chinese television programs.

jiàn

Wǒ méiyǒu kànjiàn nǐ de hóngbāo.

I haven't seen your red envelope.

lái

Chūnjié de shíhòu wǒ de qīnqi guò lái chī jiǎozi.

My relatives all come over to eat dumplings during Spring Festival.

liǎo

Là de cài wǒ chī bù liǎo.

I can't eat spicy food.

qǐlái

Wǒ xiǎng qǐlái Chūnjié wǎnhuì de dìfāng yīnggāi zěnme zǒu.

I remember how to go to the Spring Festival party.

qù

Qǐng nǐ huíqù.

Please go back.

wán

Nǐ chīwán fàn le ma?

Did you finish eating?

C. HÀNZÌ

今年   *jīnnián* (this year)

丿 人 仐 今

丿 𠂉 𠂉 𠂉 𠂉 年

每年   *měinián* (every year)

丿 𠂉 仁 每 每 每

妈妈   *māma* (mother)

一 大 女 女 妈 妈

爸爸   *bàba* (father)

丶 八 少 父 谷 谷 谷 爸

D. SHĒNGCÍ

běi	north
chūnjià	spring break
Chūnjié	the Spring Festival
dǎsuàn	to plan
dōng	east
fēngjǐng	natural environment
gǎnxiè	to be grateful
gǔjī	historic site
hú	lake
huàirén	bad person
jiàrì	vacation, holiday
jìhuà	a plan, to plan
jīnnián	this year
lǎojiā	hometown
májiàng	mah-jongg
míngnián	next year
nán	south
pái	card
pūkè pái	playing cards
qùnián	last year
shōují	to collect, to gather
sì	temple
tuánjù	to gather together
xī	west
yīnyuèhuì	concert
zàihu	to care
zhíde	to be worthwile
zīliào	data, information

SUPPLEMENTARY VOCABULARY 5: NATURE

cǎo	grass
fēng	wind
hǎi	ocean

hé	river
hú	lake
huā	flower
shān	mountain
shāngǔ	valley
shítou	rock
shù	tree
tàiyáng	sun
tiān	sky

LIÀNXÍ

A. Choose from the following words to fill in the blanks.

guò zhíde yídìng fùjìn kǒngpà zuìhǎo xiǎoxīn shǎo

1. *Cóng zhèr qù huǒchēzhàn hěn yuǎn. Nǐ _____ zuò Chūzūchē qù.*
2. *Zhège yīnyuèhuì hěn jīngcǎi, fēicháng _____ qù kàn.*
3. *Chūmén de shíhòu, nǐ yào _____ huàirén.*
4. *Xiànzài de fēijī piào hěn _____ Nǐ yào gǎnkuài qù mǎi.*
5. *Nǐ dǎsuàn zěnme _____ nǐ de chūnjià?*
6. *Jīntiān wǒ hěn máng, _____ méi shíjiān qù nǐ jiā.*
7. *Tā hěn yǒu shílì, _____ kěyǐ zhǎo dào gōngzuò.*
8. *Běijīng _____ yǒu hěn duō gǔjī.*

B. Change the following sentences into the passive form using the *bǎ* construction.

1. *Wǒ gěi lǎoshī gōngkè.*
2. *Xiǎotōu tōule diànshì.*
3. *Māma zuòhǎo fàn le.*

C. Answer the following questions using complete sentences and the *bǎ* construction.

1. *Shéi chīle zhège dàngāo? (dìdi)*
2. *Shéi kāizǒule wǒ de chē? (bàba)*
3. *Wǒ de qián zài nǎr? (gěi nǐ de àirén)*

218

D. Match the characters to the English.

1. 学生		a.	bank
2. 邮局		b.	post office
3. 每年		c.	student
4. 朋友		d.	this year
5. 妈妈		e.	mom
6. 今年		f.	every year
7. 银行		g.	dad
8. 爸爸		h.	friend

WÉNHUÀ ZHÙJIĚ

Spring Festival is an important holiday for Chinese families. It coincides with *xīnnián* (Chinese New Year) but lasts for about three weeks. Schools are closed and many people take off from work to enjoy a series of traditional activities, such as eating round cakes for good luck in the new year, as well as more informal family interaction. Playing mah-jongg can be a family activity in some parts of the country. Mah-jongg is similar to the card game rummy but is played with small plastic blocks. Betting is an integral part of the game and for this reason it is banned in schools and universities. When the game is played with family or friends, there is no betting, but playing cards are used to keep track of the overall score between hands.

DÁÀN

A. 1. *zuìhǎo* 2. *zhíde* 3. *xiǎoxīn* 4. *shǎo* 5. *guò* 6. *kǒngpà* 7. *yídìng* 8. *fùjìn*

B. 1. *Wǒ bǎ gōngkè gěi lǎoshī.* 2. *Xiǎotōu bǎ diànshì tōu le.* 3. *Māma bǎ fàn zuòhǎo le.*

C. 1. *Dìdi bǎ zhège dàngāo chīwán le.* 2. *Bàba bǎ wǒ de chē kāizǒu le.* 3. *Wǒ bǎ nǐ de qián gěi nǐ de àirén le.*

D. 1.c 2.b 3.f 4.h 5.e 6.d 7.a 8.g

DÌÉRSHÍWǓ KÈ
Lesson 25
JÌSUÀNJĪ. Computers.

A. DUÌHUÀ

RUǍNJIÀN DE WÈNTÍ.

Mr. Wang goes to visit Mr. Zhang at his office to discuss computers.

ZHĀNG: Wáng jīnglǐ, huānyíng. Qǐng jìn, qǐng zuò. Nín zhè cì lái Běijīng shì chūchāi háishì bàn sīshì?

WÁNG: Wǒ zhè cì shì zhuānmén lái bàifǎng guì gōngsī de.

ZHĀNG: Bù gǎndāng! Yǒu shénme yàojǐn de shì ma?

WÁNG: Méi shénme. Yīnwèi guì gōngsī cóng qùnián kāishǐ jiù yìzhí shǐyòng wǒmen de jìsuànjī chǎnpǐn, suǒyǐ, wǒ xiān lái nín zhèr bàifǎng yíxià, yě liǎojiě nǐmen shǐyòng de qíngkuàng.

ZHĀNG: Nǐmen gōngsī de fúwù shízài tài zhōudào le. Mùqián gōngsī shàng shàng xià xià dàyuē yǒu liǎngbǎi duō tái jìsuànjī. Hǎoxiàng méi shénme bù mǎnyì de dìfāng. Wǒ kěyǐ qǐng jìshù chù Lín chùzhǎng gēn nǐ tán.

WÁNG: Tài hǎo le. Lìngwài, wǒmen gōngsī zuìjìn qǔdé Měiguó hǎo jǐ jiā ruǎnjiàn gōngsī de Zhōngguó dàilǐ quán, yě xiǎng kànkan nǐmen yǒu méiyou ruǎnjiàn de xūyào.

ZHĀNG: Ruǎnjiàn xūqiú shàng de wèntí, nǐ hái shì děi gēn Lín chùzhǎng tán. Kěshì, tā jīntiān zǎoshàng zhènghǎo wàichū bú zài. Wǒ kàn, wǒmen xiān qù chī wǔfàn, xiàwǔ wǒ ràng mìshū tōngzhī Lín chùzhǎng lái. Nǐmen zài shāngliang.

WÁNG: Hǎo, jiù zhènme bàn ba.

SOFTWARE PROBLEMS.

ZHANG: Hello, Manager Wang. Come in. Have a seat. Are you in Beijing for business or for a personal matter?

WANG: Actually, I came specifically to visit your company.

ZHANG: You flatter me. Are there any serious matters?

WANG: No. But because last year your company started using our computer products, I wanted to visit and see how the computers have been working.

ZHANG: That's thoughtful of your company. Of all the 200 computers we presently have, there have been no complaints. I can ask Mr. Lin, the Director of Technical Support, to talk to you about it.

WANG: That would be great. By the way, my company has authorization to represent several American software companies in China. I wanted to find out if your company needs software as well.

ZHANG: You also should talk to Mr. Lin about our software needs. Unfortuantely, he's out of the office all morning. Why don't we go out to lunch first. I'll ask the secretary to tell Mr. Lin to meet with you in the afternoon so you can discuss this with him.

WANG: Good, let's do it that way.

B. YǓFǍ HÉ YÒNGFǍ

1. *WÈISHÉNME?* "WHY?"

The question word *shénme* is paired with *wèi* (why?) to form "why" questions. *Wèishénme* can stand on its own or can be placed in a longer sentence between the subject and the verb.

Nǐ wèishénme lái?
 Why have you come?

Tā wèishénme yào xiě nèi běn shū?
 Why does she want to write that book?

2. *YĪNWÈI* "BECAUSE"

When answering questions with *wèishénme*, place *yīnwèi* (because) at the beginning of the sentence.

Nǐ wèishénme yào zài wǒmen zhèr gōngzuò?
Yīnwèi wǒ xǐhuan nǐ de gōngsī.
 Why do you want to work here with us?
 Because I like your company.

221

Tā wèishénme méiyǒu hěn duō qián?
Yīnwèi tā shì lǎoshī.

    Why doesn't she have a lot of money?

    Because she is a teacher.

3. THE CONJUNCTION *YĪNWÈI . . . SUǑYǏ*

In lesson 4, you learned that the conjunction *suǒyǐ* means "therefore." *Yīnwèi . . . suǒyǐ* (because . . . therefore) connects two clauses or phrases of cause and effect. *Yīnwèi* is always paired with *suǒyǐ* unless *yīnwèi* is used as above, as a response to a question with *wèishénme*.

Tā yīnwèi bù shūfu, suǒyǐ bú shàngbān.

    He's not feeling well, so he's not going to work.

Yīnwèi wǒ bù xǐhuan tā, suǒyǐ tā bù xǐhuan wǒ.

    Because I don't like him, he doesn't like me.

4. THE VERB *TŌNGZHĪ*

Tōngzhī can be used as a verb (to inform) or a noun (notice). When used as a verb, it is only used among peers or from a senior person to a more junior person.

Tā gěile wǒmen yí ge kāihuì de tōngzhī.

    He gave us notice for a meeting.

Wǒ méiyǒu shōudào tōngzhī.

    I did not receive the notice.

Nǐ qù tōngzhī tā yào kāishǐ kāihuì le.

    Go inform him that the meeting is about to start.

Jīnglǐ tōngzhī nǐmen mǎshàng kāihuì.

    The manager is telling you to have a meeting right now.

5. *SHÀNG SHÀNG XIÀ XIÀ*

You already know that *shàng* means "above" and *xià* means "below." The idiom *shàng shàng xià xià* means "throughout" or "from top to bottom."

Wǒ de fángzi shàng shàng xià xià dōu hěn shūfu.

    My house is comfortable from top to bottom.

Wǒmen gōngsī shàng shàng xià xià yǒu wǔshí duō tái jìsuànjī.

    Our company has more than fifty computers throughout [the building].

C. HÀNZÌ

办公室   *bàngōngshì* (office)

ㄱ　力　劢　办

ノ　八　公　公

丶　宀　宀　宀　宀　宀　室　室

计算机   *jìsuànjī* (computer)

丶　讠　讠　计

ノ　ㅏ　ㅏ　日　日　竹　竹　竹

筒　筒　笪　算　算

一　十　才　木　机　机

软件   *ruǎnjiàn* (software)

一　ナ　た　车　车　车　轩　轩　软

ノ　亻　亻　仁　仁　件

欢迎   *huānyíng* (welcome)

フ　又　ヌ　欢　欢　欢

丶　乚　㇐　印　印　迎　迎

D. SHĒNGCÍ

bàifǎng	to pay a visit
chǎnpǐn	product
chūchāi	to be on a business trip
chù	division, department, office
chùzhǎng	division head
dàilǐ	to represent
dàilǐquán	the right to represent
dàyuē	approximately

diànnǎo	computer
jìshù	technology
jìsuànjī	computer
liǎojiě	to understand
mǎnyì	satisfied
mìshū	secretary
mùqián	presently
nǎo	brain
qíngkuàng	condition, situation
quán	authority
qǔdé	obtain
ruǎnjiàn	software
shāngliang	to discuss
shàng xià	up and down
shǐyòng	to make use of
sīshì	personal affairs
xūqiú	needs; requirements
yàojǐn	important, pressing
yíngjiē	to meet, greet
yuē	to make arrangements for
zhōudào	thoughtful, considerate
zhuānmén	specialized

SUPPLEMENTARY VOCABULARY 6: COMPUTERS

diànnǎo, jìsuànjī	computer
yíngmù	screen
dǎyìnjī	printer
jiànpán	keyboard
guāngpánjī	CD-ROM drive
guāngpán	CD-ROM
jiànzi	key
zìfú	character
kōngjiàn	space bar
kōnggé	single spaced
kōngwèi	space
ruǎnpán	floppy disk
ruǎnpánjī	floppy drive
yìngjiàn	hardware
yìngpán	hard drive
shuāngmìpán	double density diskette

wǎnglù	Internet
wǎngyè	Web page
shàng wǎng	to get on the Web
wénjiàn	file/document
wénjiànmíng	file name
wénshǒu	home/beginning of file
wénmò	end of file or document
diànyóu (diànzi yóujiàn)	e-mail
diànyóu dìzhǐ	e-mail address
jì diànxìn	send an e-mail
chǔcún	to save
shūrù	to enter
yìn	to print
kāiqǐ	to open
guānbì	to close
diǎn	to click
tuìchū	to exit
xiāochú	to delete
xiàzài	to download
kǎobèi	to copy
zhāntiē	to paste
guāngbiāo	cursor
cúnchǔ	memory
mùlù	directory
zhǔ mùlù	root directory
zǐ mùlù	subdirectory
zìjié	byte
zhàozìjié	megabyte
guāndiào	turn off/shut down
zhǐlìng	command
zháozhù	highlight
xuǎnmùdān	menu
shàngyè	page up
xiàyè	page down
shìchuāng	window
qǔxiāojiàn	ESC key
qǔxiāo	escape

LIÀNXÍ

A. Answer the following questions based on the dialogue.

1. *Wáng Bīng lái Běijīng shì chūchāi háishì bàn sīshì?*
2. *Wáng Bīng zhǎo Zhāng jīnglǐ zuò shénme?*
3. *Zhāng jīnglǐ de gōngsī mùqián yǒu duōshǎo jìsuànjī?*
4. *Zhāng jīnglǐ shuō shǐyòng ruǎnjiàn de shì yīnggāi wèn shéi?*
5. *Mùqián Zhāng jīnglǐ de gōngsī duì Wáng Bīng gōngsī de jìsuànjī mǎnyì ma?*

B. Fill in the blanks using the words below.

tōngzhī   qǐng   yíngjiē   yīnwèi   yìzhí

1. _____ *Lǐ jīnglǐ bú rènshì Xiǎo Lín, suǒyǐ tā yào mìshū gěi tā jièshào.*
2. *Mìshū* _____ *Xiǎo Lín qù jiàn Wáng jīnglǐ.*
3. *Xiǎo Lín* _____ *Lǐ jīnglǐ chīfàn.*
4. *Xiǎo Lín* _____ *zài yì jiā ruǎnjiàn gōngsī gōngzuò.*
5. *Wǒ péngyou cóng Měiguó lái. Wǒ qù* _____ *tā.*

C. Translate the following sentences into *pīnyīn*.

1. I have an appointment with my teacher today.
2. My father is expecting you.
3. This time I specifically came to visit you.
4. I will inform Mr. Wang to talk with you this afternoon.

D. Match the English to the Chinese character.

1. software	a. 计算机
2. computer	b. 三点钟
3. welcome	c. 软件
4. office	d. 欢迎
5. three o'clock	e. 办公室

WÉNHUÀ ZHÙJIĚ

China is a communal country. People live in crowded quarters and spend little time by themselves either at home or in the office. Friends and family consider the community to be more important than the individual—a notion that infiltrates how people think about visiting each other. It is very common in China for people to stop in and visit unannounced—at home or in the office. Appointments aren't always necessary and even if appointments are made, people don't always show up at the agreed upon time. This is all taken in stride, though. This lesson's dialogue may seem strange to Westerners, who wouldn't think of having a business meeting without previous arrangements. If you go to China on business or for pleasure, expect your hosts and acquaintances there to show up at your hotel without notice to take you to a meeting or to dinner or sight-seeing.

DÁÀN

A. 1. *chūchāi* 2. *Qù bàifǎng tā, yě liǎojiě tāmen gōngsī shǐyòng jìsuànjī de qíngkuàng.* 3. *liǎngbǎi duō tái.* 4. *yīnggāi zhǎo jìshùchù Lín chùzhǎng tán.* 5. *Méiyǒu shénme bù mǎnyì.*

B. 1. *Yīnwèi* 2. *tōngzhī* 3. *qǐng* 4. *yìzhí* 5. *yíngjiē*

C. 1. *Wǒ gēn wǒ de lǎoshī yuēle jīntiān lái jiàn tā.* 2. *Wǒ bàba zhèngzài děng nǐ.* 3. *Wǒ zhè cì shì zhuānmén lái bàifǎng nín de.* 4. *Wǒ tōngzhī Wáng xiānsheng xiàwǔ gēn nǐ tán.*

D. 1.c 2.a 3.d 4.e 5.b

FÙXÍ 5

A. Place *děi, xūyào* or *yīnggāi* in the blanks according to the English translations.

1. *Nǐ _____ mǎshàng shuìjiào.*
   You need to sleep immediately.
2. *Nǐ _____ mǎshàng shuìjiào.*
   You have to sleep immediately.
3. *Nǐ _____ mǎshàng shuìjiào.*
   You should sleep immediately.

B. Write the following in *pīnyīn* using the *shì . . . de* construction.

1. He is quite good with words.
2. He came this morning.
3. The teacher came from the United States.

C. Choose from the words in parentheses to complete the sentences.

1. *Tā _____ bù lái wǒ de jiā. (le, cónglái, qǐlái)*
2. *Wǒ qù shàngbān _____. (le, qǐlái, fùjìn)*
3. *Nǐ de _____ yǒu méiyǒu hǎo fàndiàn. (cónglái, fùjìn, zài)*
4. *Duì wǒ _____ shuō, zhè běn shū méiyǒu yìsi. (zài, lái, qǐlái)*

D. Write the following in English.

1. *Wǒ kànwán le zhè běn shū.*
2. *Wǒ kàn de dǒng zhè běn shū.*
3. *Tā kàn qǐlái hěn piàoliang.*
4. *Wǒ chīwánle wǎnfàn.*
5. *Xiǎo háizi tīng bù dǒng jīngjù.*
6. *Tā guò de qù guò bú qù?*

E. Write the simplified character for these traditional characters.

1. 鐘
2. 點
3. 説話
4. 中國

DÁÀN

A. 1. *xūyào* 2. *děi* 3. *yīnggāi*

B. 1. *Tā shì hěn huì shuōhuà de.* 2. *Tā shì jīntiān zǎoshàng lái de.* 3. *Lǎoshī shì cóng Měiguó lái de.*

C. 1. *cónglái* 2. *le* 3. *fùjìn* 4. *lái*

D. 1. I finished reading this book. 2. I understand this book. 3. She looks very pretty. 4. I finished eating dinner. 5. Small children don't understand Chinese opera. 6. Can he get by?

E. 1. 钟 2. 点 3. 说话 4. 中国

DÌ ÈRSHÍLIÙ KÈ
Lesson 26
BÓWÙGUǍN. Museums.

A. DUÌHUÀ

ZÀI CĀNTĪNG.

Amy Stone's sister is coming to Beijing for a visit, so Amy talks to Ye Ling, one of her students, to find out about the best museums to visit.

AÌMÉI: Yè Líng, qǐngwèn yíxià, Běijīng shénme bówùguǎn zuì yǒu yìsi? Wǒ de mèimei yào dào Běijīng lái, suǒyǐ wǒ yào dài tā kàn kan yǒu wénhuà de dìfāng.

YÈ LÍNG: Nǐ dāngrán zhīdào Běijīng GùGōng hé Zhōngguó Rénmín Bówùguǎn. Kěshì, Běijīng yě yǒu yīxiē bú tài yǒumíng dàn tǐng yǒu yìsi de xiǎo bówùguǎn.

AÌMÉI: Duì a. Běijīng GùGōng wǒ qùguò hǎo dūo cì. Wǒ de mèimei shì zuòjiā. Wǒ xiǎng dài tā qù kànkan gǔdài de huàr, diāoke, jiànzhù děng děng. Běijīng hái yǒu shénme dìfāng zhíde qù kànkan?

YÈ LÍNG: Lǔ Xùn Bówùguǎn hěn zhíde qù kàn. Nèige bówùguǎn lí zhèr bǐjiào jìn, zài Fǔchéngménnèi lù. Lǔ Xùn shì Zhōngguó yí wèi yǒumíng de zuòjiā. Xiànzài de bówùguǎn, shì tā yǐqián shēnghuó hé gōngzuò de dìfāng. Zài nàr, Lǔ Xùn xiěle hěn dūo tā de yǒumíng de zuòpǐn.

AÌMÉI: Tài hǎo le. Hǎo xiè xie nǐ bāng wǒ de máng.

YÈ LÍNG: Rúguǒ wǒ xiǎng dào biéde dìfāng de huà, wǒ zài gàosù nǐ.

AÌMÉI: Xièxie!

───────────

AMY: Ye Ling, I was wondering, what are the most interesting museums in Beijing? My little sister is coming to Beijing so I want to show her some cultural spots.

YE LING: You certainly know about the Forbidden City and the National People's Museum. But, Beijing also has some lesser known but very interesting small museums.

AMY: That's what I hear. I've been to the Forbidden City many times. My sister is a writer. I would like to take her to see ancient paintings, sculptures, architecture and the like. Where else is worth visiting in Beijing?

YE LING: The Lu Xun Museum is worth visiting. It's not too far from here on Fuchengmennei road. Lu Xun is a famous writer in China. The museum is the place where he used to live and work. Lu Xun wrote many of his famous works there.

AMY: Very good. Thanks for your help.

YE LING: If I think of any other places, I'll let you know.

AMY: Thanks.

B. YǓFǍ HÉ YÒNGFǍ

1. *DĚNG DĚNG*

Děng děng (and so on) can be placed at the end of a series of nouns or verb phrases.

Wǒ xǐhuan xué gǔdài huàr, diāokè, jiànzhù, děng děng.
  I like to study ancient paintings, sculptures, buildings and so on.

Zuòjiā měitiān kànshū, xiě xiǎoshuō, biānjí, děng děng.
  Every day writers read books, write novels, edit and so on.

2. "TO KNOW": *LIǍOJIĚ* AND *ZHĪDÀO*

You have already learned that *zhīdào* means "to know." *Liǎojiě* also means "to know" but in the sense of "to know something completely" or "to have an understanding of something." So *wǒ zhīdào Běijīng* means "I know of (or have heard of) Beijing" while *wǒ liǎojiě Běijīng* means "I know all about Beijing (all the streets, the best restaurants, etc.)." *Zhīdào* is used with single facts while *liǎojiě* is more often used for broader field of knowledge.

Wǒ zhīdào Lǔ Xùn xiě de shū.
I know which books Lu Xun wrote.

Wǒ liǎojiě Lǔ Xùn xiě de shū.
I know [because I have studied/read] Lu Xun's books well.

Nǐ zhīdào bù zhīdào Běijīng GùGōng?
Have you heard of the Forbidden City?

Nǐ liǎojiě bù liǎojiě Běijīng GùGōng?
Do you have a real understanding of the Forbidden City?

3. THE CONJUNCTION *RÚGUǑ . . . (DE HUÀ), JIÙ . . .*

In lesson 18, you learned that conjunctions in Chinese often occur in pairs. The conjunction pair *rúguǒ . . . (dehuà), jiù . . .* (if . . . then) is one way to express conditionally; that is, that the second phrase of a sentence is, or will be, true only if the first phrase is true. *De huà* (literally, "of speech") introduces the "if" clause. As with other conjunction pairs, the subject of the first and second parts of the sentence can be the same or different.

Rúguǒ wǒ xiǎng dào biéde dìfāng, wǒ jiù gàosù nǐ ba.
If I think of any other place, I'll tell you.

Rúguǒ tā qù de huà, wǒ jiù bú qù.
If he goes, then I'm not going.

4. THE VERBS *BĀNGMÁNG* AND *BĀNGZHÙ*

Bāngmáng and *bāngzhù* both mean "to help" but since *bāngmáng* is a verb-object compound verb (see lesson 5) and *bāngzhù* is not, they function differently in a sentence. The object comes between *bāng* and *máng* but after *bāngzhù*. Generally, *bāngmáng* is used with more serious situations.

Wǒ mèimei bìng le, suǒyǐ wǒ yào bāng tā de máng.
My little sister is sick so I want to help her.

Nǐ kě bu kěyǐ bāngmáng?
Can you help?

Nǐ kě bu kěyǐ bāng wǒ mǔqīn de máng?
Can you help my mother?

Lǎoshī bāngzhù xuéshēng zuò gōngkè.
The teacher helps the students with their homework.

5. *MÁFAN*

Máfan is an often-heard multipurpose word that can be translated as a verb (to bother) or as an adjective (annoying). When you approach a stranger on the street to ask the time or for directions, the most polite way to get their attention is to say *máfan nǐ* (excuse me). The following examples further illustrate the various uses of *máfan*.

Háizi bú yào máfan dàrén.
Children shouldn't annoy their elders.

Máfan can also be used with *gěi* (to give) as follows.

Wǒ bú yào gěi nǐ máfan.
I don't want to bother you.

Gěi rén máfan méi yǒu yìsi.
To annoy people is just not worth it [isn't interesting].

C. HÀNZÌ

Beginning with this lesson, you will no longer be shown the stroke order for each character you learn. Remember that characters are written from the top left corner to the bottom right corner and that horizontal lines are written before any vertical lines that may intersect. As you practice the characters that you learn from now on, bear in mind the others that you have practiced—many elements recur and you already have a good sense of how written characters flow.

Although many signs for tourist attractions in China are written in English as well as in characters, being able to recognize some common sign words might help you get around. First, review these characters that you learned in previous lessons which are also found on the streets and in the buildings of China.

房间	*fángjiān* (room)
厕所	*cèsuǒ* (bathroom)
地铁	*dìtiě* (subway)
路	*lù* (road)
商店	*shāngdiàn* (department store)
旅馆	*lǚguǎn* (hotel)
饭店	*fàndiàn* (restaurant)

入口	*rùkǒu* (entrance)
出口	*chūkǒu* (exit)
银行	*yínháng* (bank)
邮局	*yóujú* (post office)
大学	*dàxué* (college)

Here are some additional characters that you will see on signs for museums.

博物馆	*bówùguǎn* (museum)
故宫	*GùGōng* (Forbidden City)
革命	*gémìng* (revolution)
历史	*lìshǐ* (history)
生活	*shēnghuó* (life)
有名	*yǒumíng* (famous)

D. SHĒNGCÍ

bànfǎ	method
bāngmáng	to help
bāngzhù	to help
bówùguǎn	museum
cāntīng	cafeteria
chuántǒng	tradition
dàrén	adult
děng děng	etc.
diāokè	sculptures
dōngxi	thing
guǎn	building, mansion
gǔdài	ancient
GùGōng	the Forbidden City
huàr	painting
jiànzhù	architecture
liǎojiě	to understand
máfan	annoying
shēnghuó	life
wàibīn	foreign guest
yǒumíng	famous
zuòjiā	writer

SUPPLEMENTARY VOCABULARY 7:
AROUND TOWN

biànli shāngdiàn	convenience store
gāosù gōnglù	highway
hōnglǜdēng	traffic light
lùdēngzhù	lamppost
rénxíng héngdàoxiàn	crosswalk
shízì lùkǒu	intersection
shūdiàn	bookstore
tíngchēchǎng	parking lot
túshūguǎn	library
xìyuàn	theater

LIÀNXÍ

A. Replace *bāngzhù* in the following sentences with *bāngmáng*.

    1. *Qǐng bāngzhù wǒ.*
    2. *Tā xǐhuan bāngzhù tā de péngyou.*
    3. *Nǐ bú yào bāngzhù huàirén.*
    4. *Rúguǒ nǐ bāngzhù wǒ de huà, wǒ jiù gěi nǐ qián.*

B. Combine the following pairs of sentences using *rúguǒ . . . de huà, jiù . . .* and then translate into English.

    1. *Wǒ qù chīfàn. Wǒ qǐng nǐ.*
    2. *Zhāng jīnglǐ qù. Wǒ bú qù.*
    3. *Nǐ de háizi xuéxí. Wǒ de háizi xuéxí.*

C. Fill in the blanks according to the English equivalents.

    1. *Nǐ _____ Běijīng ma?*
       Do you know Beijing well?
    2. *Tā bù _____ nǐ de míngzi.*
       He doesn't know your name.
    3. *Wǒ xǐhuan shuìjiào, xiūxi, _____.*
       I like to sleep, to rest, etc.
    4. *Nǐ kě bu kěyi _____.*
       Can you help?

D. Write the following in Chinese characters.

1. The Forbidden City is very famous.
2. I like museums.
3. Chinese tradition is quite interesting.

WÉNHUÀ ZHÙJIĚ

Lu Xun (1881–1936) was a writer who was one of the first in China to advocate stronger ties with the West as well as equality for all citizens of China. His voice spoke for many as the dynastic system came to an end in 1911 and education was popularized. He advocated using colloquial Chinese instead of classical Chinese in schools in order to give everyone access to education. His famous works include *The Diary of a Madman* and *The Story of Ah Q*. His themes were centered on criticizing the decadence of imperial China and promoting ways to modernize China through the introduction of Western concepts and science. His was a strong voice during a tumultuous transitional period in China and his works still resonate today.

DÁÀN

A. 1. *Qǐng bāng wǒ de máng.* 2. *Tā xǐhuan bāng tā de péngyou máng.* 3. *Nǐ bú yào bāng huàirén de máng.* 4. *Rúguǒ nǐ bāng wǒ máng de huà, wǒ jiù gěi nǐ qián.*

B. 1. *Rúguǒ wǒ qù chīfàn de huà, wǒ jiù qǐng nǐ.* If I go out to dinner, I'll invite you. 2. *Rúguǒ Zhāng jīnglǐ qù de huà, wǒ jiù bú qù.* If Manager Zhang goes, then I won't go. 3. *Rúguǒ nǐ de háizi xuéxí de huà, wǒ de háizi jiù xuéxí.* If your kid studies, then mine does.

C. 1. *liǎojiě* 2. *zhīdào* 3. *děng děng* 4. *bāngmáng*

D. 1.北京故宫很有名。 2.我喜欢博物馆 3.中国传统很有意思。

DÌ ÉRSHÍQĪ KÈ
Lesson 27
ZÀI FĒIJĪCHĂNG. At the Airport.

A. DUÌHUÀ

Tā LÁI LE!

Sally's sister Joan arrives at the Beijing airport and goes through customs.

JOAN: **Zhè shì wǒ de hùzhào hé qiānzhèng.**

GUĀNYUÁN: **Nǐ shuō de hěn dìdào.**

JOAN: **Bù gǎndāng. Wǒ Zhōngwén shuō bù liǎo.**

GUĀNYUÁN: **Nǐ yǒu méiyǒu Zhōngwén míngzi?**

JOAN: **Yǒu. Wǒ lái zhèr yǐqián yǒu Zhōngwén lǎoshī jiào wǒ Zhōu Níng.**

GUĀNYUÁN: **Zhōu xiǎojie, nǐ cóng nǎr lái?**

JOAN: **Měiguó.**

GUĀNYUÁN: **Nǐ láiguò Zhōngguó jǐ cì?**

JOAN: **Zhè shì wǒ dì yī cì lái. Wǒ tīngshuō Zhōngguó de fēngjǐng hěn měi, rén yě hěn yǒuhǎo.**

GUĀNYUÁN: **Duì. Nín yīnggāi qù kànkan Zhōngguó de Chángchéng, lí Běijīng hěn jìn. Zhōngguó de huǒchē yě hěn hǎo. Wǒmen de huǒchē hěn duō, hěn fāngbiàn, hé biéde guójiā de huǒchē bù yíyàng.**

JOAN: **Wǒ dāngrán yào kàn Chángchéng. Xièxie nǐ.**

SHE'S HERE!

JOAN: Here is my passport and my visa.

OFFICIAL: You speak so correctly!

237

JOAN: Thanks, but I really can't speak Chinese.

OFFICIAL: Do you have a Chinese name?

JOAN: Yes. Before I came here, my Chinese teacher called me Zhou Ning.

OFFICIAL: Miss Zhou, where are you coming from?

JOAN: America.

OFFICIAL: How many times have you been to China?

JOAN: This is my first time. I've heard that there are beautiful things to see in China and that the people are quite friendly.

OFFICIAL: True. You have to go see the Great Wall, it's very close to Beijing. The trains in China are great, too. We have a lot of trains—they are quite convenient. Not like other country's trains.

JOAN: I'll certainly go to the Great Wall. Thanks!

B. YǓFǍ HÉ YÒNGFǍ

1. A *HÉ* B *YÍYÀNG*

When you want to say that something is the same as something else, use the expression A *hé* (and) B *yíyàng* (to be the same). You can say that something is not the same as something else by using the negation particle *bù*: A *hé* B *bù yíyàng*. In this construction, *yíyàng* can function as the main verb as follows.

Měiguó hé Zhōngguó bù yíyàng.
    America and China are not the same.

Wǒ hé wǒ de nánpéngyou bù yíyàng.
    My boyfriend and I are not alike.

Yíyàng can also modify an adjectival verb, but only in the positive. In English, we might say this as "A and B are equally [adjective]" or "A is as [adjective] as B."

Měiguó hé Zhōngguó yíyàng yǒu yìsi.
    America and China are equally interesting.

Wǒ hé tā yíyàng gāo.
    I am just as tall as he is.

Niŭyuē de fēijīchăng hé Běijīng de fēijīchăng yíyàng luàn.
   The airport in New York and the airport in Beijing are equally disorganized.

2. DESCRIBING AN ACTION WITH *DE LIĂO* AND *BÙ LIĂO*

In lesson 10, you learned how to describe an action using a verb plus *de* or *bù* plus an adjective. If you replace the adjective in that construction with the particle *le* (which in this case is pronounced *liăo*), you have a verb ending which implies that the verb can be done or is being done (with *de liăo*) or that the verb cannot be done or isn't being done (with *bù liăo*). This expression can only be used with action verbs, not adjectival verbs. Don't forget that with verb-object verbs or with a verb and its object, you must repeat the verb again after the object before you can attach such an expression.

Tā chīfàn chī bù liăo.
   He is unable to finish (his) meal.

Wŏ shuō Zhōngguóhuà shuō bù liăo.
   I can't speak Chinese.

Wŏ zuò gōnggòng qìchē zuò de liăo.
   I can take the bus.

You can also place the object of a sentence before the subject in this type of sentence.

Zhège cài wŏ chī bù liăo.
   I can't eat this dish. [Literally, this dish I cannot eat.]

Zhōngguóhuà wŏ shuō bù liăo.
   I can't speak Chinese. [Chinese I can't speak.]

Gōnggòng qìchē wŏ zuò de liăo.
   I can take the bus. [The bus I can take.]

3. THE EXPRESSION *TĪNGSHUŌ*

Remember that *tīng* means "to listen" and *shuō* means "to speak." So it is not surprising that the verb *tīngshuō* means "to hear it said."

Wŏ tīngshuō Zhōngguó de fēngjǐng hěn hǎo.
   I've heard that Chinese scenery is nice.

Wŏ tīngshuō nǐ hěn cōngmíng.
   I hear you are very clever.

C. HÀNZÌ

Practice writing these new characters and sentences.

飞机 （飛機）	*fēijī* (airplane)
场	*chǎng* (field)
火车 （火車）	*huǒchē* (trains)
站	*zhàn* (station)
哪儿	*nǎr* (where?)

我坐飞机到美国去。
Wǒ zuò fēijī dào Měiguó qù.
   I'm flying to the U.S.

北京的火车站很好。
Běijīng de huǒchēzhàn hěn hǎo.
   The train station in Beijing is quite good.

飞机场在哪儿？
Fēijīchǎng zài nǎr?
   Where's the airport?

D. SHĒNGCÍ

Chángchéng	the Great Wall
dìdào	authentic, standard
fēijī	plane
fēijīchǎng	airport
fēngjǐng	scenery
guānyuán	an official
hǎiguān	customs
huǒchē	train
huǒchēzhàn	train station
qiānzhèng	visa
ruǎnwò	soft sleeper
ruǎnzuò	soft seat
tèbié	particular
tíngliú	to stay
tīngshuō	to hear it said
yìngwò	hard sleeper
yìngzuò	hard seat
yíyàng	to be the same
yǒuhǎo	friendly

LIÀNXÍ

A. Complete the following dialogues according to the clues in parentheses.

1. A: *Nǐ de Yīngwén shuō de hěn* _____. (standard)
   B: _____. (you flatter me)
2. A: *Wǒ míngtiān qù Zhōngguó.*
   B: *Nǐ yǐqián qù* _____ *Zhōngguó ma?* (Have you gone before?)
   A: *Méiyǒu. Zhè shè wǒ* _____ *yí* _____. (first time)
   B: *Nǐ dǎsuàn qù Zhōngguó* _____? (How long?)
   A: _____ (two weeks)

B. Put the words in the correct order.

EXAMPLE: *shēngrì/ wǒ/ jīntiān/ bàba/ shì/ de*
          Jīntiān shì wǒ bàba de shēngrì.

1. *shuō/ dìdào/ tā/ de/ hěn*
2. *lái/ tā/ Běijīng/ cóng*
3. *sì/ cì/ wǒ/ guò/ qù/ Zhōngguó*
4. *Běijīng/ wǒ/ qù/ yǐqián/ guò*
5. *chénggōng/ xīwàng/ nǐ/ shēngyì/ de*

C. Match the sentence in group A with its translation in group B.

Group A	Group B
1. *Nǐ lái lǚyóu háishì bànshì.*	a. I have studied Chinese before.
2. *Zhōngguórén hěn yǒuhǎo.*	b. Do you come for travel or for business?
3. *Nǐ dǎsuàn tíngliú duōjiǔ?*	c. This is the fifth time.
4. *Wǒ yǐqián xuéguò Zhōngwén.*	d. How long do you plan to stay?
5. *Zhè shì dì wǔ cì.*	e. Chinese people are very friendly.

D. Write the Chinese characters for these places.

1. train station
2. post office
3. airport
4. bank
5. department store
6. restroom

E. Write these in *pīnyīn*.

1. 他要不要坐火车到北京去？
2. 我不想坐飞机。
3. 我们的火车站没有热水。

WÉNHUÀ ZHÙJIĚ

The rail system in China is extensive and makes travel between cities quite convenient. This is *the* mode of travel for the Chinese and for foreigners—traveling across the countryside in a train is a great way to see the country. Trains are scheduled on a daily basis between most major cities and the departure and arrival times are surprisingly precise considering the number of trains and the number of routes. Buying a train ticket in China is much easier now that they have implemented a computerized ticketing system. You can buy a train ticket at major hotels in China or at CITS, the government-sponsored travel agent. Many train stations also have special ticketing offices for foreigners where purchasing a ticket is fast and easy. Chinese trains have four types of seats. The hard seat (*yìngzuò*) compartment is by far the least expensive, but also the least comfortable. You can reserve a seat in this compartment, but they tend to cram as many people in as possible—smoking and throwing trash on the floor also seem to be allowed so a hard seat trip for longer than two hours is not recommended. Some trains, usually the shorter-distance trains, have soft seat (*ruǎnzuò*) compartments which are comfortable and more civilized. For longer trips you might choose the hard sleeper (*yìngwò*) compartment, where you can sleep staked up with five other people who may or may not want to play cards and drink throughout the night. But it is an experience and the bunks are comfotable with pillow and blanket provided. The soft sleeper (*ruǎnwò*) compartment is the most luxurious and the most expensive. Here you will be housed in small rooms with three other travelers with four very comfortable bunks. A nice way to travel.

DÁÀN

A. 1. *dìdào, Bù gǎndāng* 2. *guò, dì, cì, duōjiǔ, Liǎng ge xīngqī.*

B. 1. *Tā shuō de hěn dìdào.* 2. *Tā cóng Běijīng lái.* 3. *Wǒ qùguò Zhōngguó sì cì.* 4. *Wǒ yǐqián qùguò Běijīng.* 5. *Xīwàng nǐ de shēngyì chénggōng.*

C. 1.b 2.e 3.d 4.a 5.c

D. 1.火车站 2.邮局 3.飞机场 4.银行 5.商店 6.厕所

E. 1. *Tā yào bú yào zuò huǒchē dào Běijīng qù?* 2. *Wǒ bù xiǎng zuò fēijī.*
   3. *Wǒmen de huǒchēzhàn méiyǒu rè shuǐ.*

DÌ ÈRSHÍBĀ KÈ
Lesson 28
SÒNG LǏWÙ. Giving Gifts.

A. DUÌHUÀ

ZÀI SÙSHÈ.

Sally discusses gift giving in China with her roommate, Xiaoying.

SHĀLÌ: Jīntiān wǒ de péngyou Lǐ Wén qǐng wǒ qù tā jiā chīfàn. Wǒ hěn gāoxìng, suǒyǐ mǎile yí ge zhōng sòng gěi tā māma. Kěshì tā māma bú yào, shuō wǒ sòng cuò le.

XIǍOYĪNG: Nǐ bù yīnggāi sòng zhège lǐwù.

SHĀLÌ: Wèishénme?

XIǍOYĪNG: Yīnwèi sòng zhōng gēn Zhōngguó zì "sòngzhōng" tóngyīn. Duì tā lái shuō, nǐ sòng tā zhōng jiù hǎoxiàng yào tā zǎo yìdiǎn sǐ yíyàng.

SHĀLÌ: Wǒ de tiān! Wǒ gēnběn méi xiǎng dào zhè yìdiǎn.

XIǍOYĪNG: Suǒyǐ nǐ sòng lǐwù gěi Zhōngguó péngyou de shíhòu yídìng yào hěn xiǎoxīn.

SHĀLÌ: Hái yǒu shénme biéde jìnjì wǒ xūyào zhùyì ma?

XIǍOYĪNG: Bǐfāng shuō, "sì" gēn "sǐ" de fāyīn hěn xiàng. Suǒyǐ, xǐshì bāo hóngbāo de shíhòu, wǒmen bú sòng gēn "sì" yǒu guān de shùmù.

SHĀLÌ: Hái yǒu ne?

XIǍOYĪNG: Péngyou jiànmiàn zhǐ wòshǒu, bù yōngbào, yě bù qīn miànjiá.

SHĀLÌ: Nánguài jīntiān wǒ wèile gǎnxiè Lǐ māma qǐng wǒ, qīn le qīn tā de liǎn. Tā hǎoxiàng bù hǎoyìsi hěn nánwéiqíng. Wǒ yǐwéi tā bù xǐhuan wǒ.

XIǍOYĪNG: **Bù! Zhè shì zhōng xī wénhuà de chāyì.**

SHĀLÌ: **Wǒ yīnggāi duō liǎojiě yìxiē, yǐmiǎn yǐhòu zài nào xiàohuà.**

IN THE DORM.

SALLY: My friend Li Wen invited me to her house today to eat. I was very happy so I bought a clock for her mother as a gift. But her mother didn't want it and said I was wrong to give it to her.

XIAOYING: You shouldn't have given her that gift.

SALLY: Why?

XIAOYING: Because the pronunciation of "giving a clock" is the same as "making arrangements for the burial of one's parent" in Chinese. For her, getting a clock means the same as hoping she will pass away soon.

SALLY: Oh my god! I had no idea!

XIAOYING: You really need to be careful when giving a gift to a Chinese friend.

SALLY: Are there any other taboos I need to be aware of?

XIAOYING: For example, the pronunciation of "four" is similar to "death." When giving money for a wedding, we don't give currency in any amount with "four."

SALLY: What else?

XIAOYING: We only shake hands when we see our friends. No hugging or kissing on the cheek.

SALLY: No wonder Mrs. Li was so embarrassed when I kissed her face to thank her for inviting me to her house. I thought she didn't like me.

XIAOYING: Oh no, these are just the differences between Chinese and Western cultures.

SALLY: I should learn more about it to avoid making such a fool of myself in the future.

B. YǓFǍ HÉ YÒNGFǍ

1. THE ADVERB GĒNBĚN

The word *běn* literally means "the root of the tree." As in English, it can metaphorically mean "basic" or "fundamental." *Gēnběn* (basically, fundamentally) comes directly after the subject of a sentence and is most often found with a negative. In sentences like *tā gēnběn bú è*, the most accurate translation of *gēnběn* is "just" or "simply": "he just isn't hungry."

Wǒ gēnběn méi xiǎngdào zhè yìdiǎn.
   I just didn't think about this at all.

Wǒ gēnběn bù dǒng nǐ shuō de huà.
   I just did not understand what you said.

Tā gēnběn bù tóngyì nǐ de yìjiàn.
   He simply does not agree with your idea.

Tāmen gēnběn bú yuànyì zhù lǚguǎn.
   They are simply not willing to stay at a hotel.

2. THE ADJECTIVE MǍN

The adjective *mǎn* (full) can be placed before a noun to indicate "all of" that noun. The adverb *dōu* often follows nouns modified by *mǎn*.

Jiàrì de shíhòu, mǎn jiē (dōu) shì rén.
   During the holidays, all the streets are full of people.

Tā gōngzuò tài duō, mǎn shǒu dōu zāng le.
   He works so much that his hands are all dirty.

Tā mǎn liǎn bù gāoxìng.
   His unhappiness is all over his face.

3. VERB REDUPLICATION AND THE PARTICLE LE

In complex sentences where the second clause or phrase is dependent upon the first, *le* is often added between the reduplicated verb to stress this relationship. Remember that verbs are reduplicated to make the action more prominent in the sentence.

Wǒ qīn le qīn tā de liǎn, tā hěn bù gāoxìng.
   I gave her a kiss on the cheek and she was quite unhappy.

Tā bǎ bàozhǐ kàn le kàn, jiù zǒu le.
  He took a look at the newspaper and left.

Tā zhǐ shì wò le wò wǒ de shǒu, méiyǒu shuō shénme huà.
  He just shook my hand and didn't say anything.

4. THE CONJUNCTION *YǏMIǍN*

Yǐmiǎn (in order to avoid) is placed at the beginning of the second phrase of a sentence when the second phrase explains why the first phrase must be so.

Wǒ yào zǎo yìdiǎnr qǐlái, yǐmiǎn chídào.
  I want to get up a little earlier so I won't be late.

Wǒmen yīnggāi xiànzài jiù qù, yǐmiǎn tā xiān dào le.
  We should go now so that she won't get there first.

5. CHINESE EXCLAMATIONS

Exclamations in any language are usually based on shared cultural knowledge. In China, *tiān* (sky) has symbolism similar to the Western cultures' god or heaven. So, Chinese has similar exclamations to "oh my god!" or "heavens" in English.

Wǒ de tiān!
  Oh my god!

Tiān!
  Heavens!

Eggs also have a certain amount of symbolism in China—many derogatory terms contain the word *dàn* (egg). You might hear the following terms shouted out by children on the playground—they are not polite, but they are also not the worst words in Chinese.

Huàidàn!
  Rotten egg! [Jerk!]

Bèndàn!
  Stupid egg! [Idiot!]

C. HÀNZÌ

Here are some new characters.

宿舍　　　　　　　　　*sùshè* (dormitory)

应该（應該）   *yīnggāi* (should)

送   *sòng* (to give)

礼物（禮物）   *lǐwù* (gift)

文化   *wénhuà* (culture)

Sentence practice:

我送给你礼物。
Wǒ sòng gěi nǐ lǐwù.
   I'm giving you a gift.

中国文化很有意思。
Zhōngguó wénhuà hěn yǒu yìsi.
   China's culture is very interesting.

你应该住在宿舍。
Nǐ yīnggāi zhù zài sùshè.
   You should live in the dormitory.

D. SHĒNGCÍ

bāo	to wrap
bǐfāng shuō	for example
chāyì	difference
chídào	to arrive late
fāyīn	pronunciation, to pronounce
hóngbāo	red gift envelope full of money
jiànmiàn	meet
jīhuì	opportunity
jìnjì	taboo
liǎn	face
lǐwù	gift
mǎn	the whole
miànjiá	cheek
nánguài	no wonder
nánwéiqíng	embarrassment, shyness
nào xiàohuà	make a fool of oneself
qīn	to kiss
shùmù	number
sòngzhōng	to attend a dying family member
tóngyīn	same pronunciation
wèile	for the sake of

248

Wǒ de tiān!	Oh my goodness!
wòshǒu	to shake hands
xǐshì	happy event
yǐmiǎn	in order to prevent
yǐwéi	to think (usually mistakenly)
yōngbào	to hug
yǒu guān	to have something to do with
zhōng	clock
zhùyì	pay attention to

LIÀNXÍ

A. Which of the following sentences are true based on the dialogue?

1. *Lǐ wén de māma fēicháng xǐhuan Shālì sòng de zhōng.*
2. *Zhōngguórén bāo hóngbāo de shíhòu, bù sòng gēn sì yǒu guān de shùmù.*
3. *Zài Zhōngguó, hǎo péngyou jiànmiàn yídìng yào yōngbào.*
4. *Lǐ wén de māma bù xǐhuan Shālì, suǒyǐ tā bú yào Shālì qīn tā miànjiá.*

B. Choose from the words below and fill in the blanks.

suǒyǐ hǎoxiàng zhǐ chāyì yǐmiǎn

1. *Jīntiān wǒ _____ hē shuǐ, bù hē kāfēi, yě bù hē jiǔ.*
2. *Sòng lǐwù yǐqián yào duō zhùyì,_____ nào xiàohuà.*
3. *Tā jīntiān mǎn liǎn bù gāoxìng, _____ shì tā bàba mà tā le.*
4. *Yīnwèi nǐ shàng cì qǐng wǒ chīfàn, _____ zhè cì wǒ qǐng nǐ chī.*
5. *Péngyou jiànmiàn bù yōngbào, yě bù qīn miànjiá shì zhōngxī de _____.*

C. Translate the following into *pīnyīn* using the phrases provided.

1. You need to take care of your body so that you won't get sick. (*yǐmiǎn*)
2. I didn't understand what you said at all. (*gēnběn*)
3. I should understand more about it to avoid making a fool of myself. (*nào xiàohuà*)

D. Translate into English.

1. 你应该送给他礼物。
2. 我在宿舍学习。
3. 他的脸红的。
4. 你不要送钟。

WÉNHUÀ ZHÙJIĚ

The characteristics of the Chinese language make for some very interesting cultural attitudes and superstitions. Because one word can mean so many things depending on its tone as well as the context in which it is used, homonyms take on extra significance. The number four is especially inauspicious as the word for "four" *(sì)* sounds the same as the word for death *(sǐ),* although they have different tones. Thus, it is considered impolite to give gifts in any multiple of four. The word for "pear" *(lí)* has the same sound as one word meaning "to leave" *(lí)*—don't bring pears to anyone in the hospital who may not want to think about "leaving" this world. Instead, bring apples *(píngguǒ). Píngguǒ* contains the same sound as *píngān* (peace and prosperity). If you are invited to a Chinese person's house for dinner, it is always nice to bring some kind of round fruit—apples, lychees, kiwis, etc. Round food brings good luck—you will see a variety of round moon cakes and dumplings during important festivals like Chinese new year and weddings.

DÁÀN

A. Statement 2 is true.

B. 1. *zhǐ* 2. *yǐmiǎn* 3. *hǎoxiàng* 4. *suǒyǐ* 5. *chāyì*

C. 1. *Nǐ yào zhùyì shēntǐ yǐmiǎn shēngbìng.* 2. *Wǒ gēnběn (tīng) bù dǒng nǐ shuō de huà.* 3. *Wǒ yīnggāi duō liǎojiě (yìxiē), yǐmiǎn yǐhòu nào xiàohuà.*

D. 1. You should give him a present. 2. I'm studying in my dormitory. 3. His face is red. 4. You don't want to "give a clock."

DÌ ÈRSHÍJIǓ KÈ
Lesson 29
MIÀNZI. The Concept of Face.

A. DUÌHUÀ

ZÀI BÀNGŌNG SHÌ.

David Stone is curious about the Asian concept of "face" so he asks his friend Wang Bing about it during their lunch break.

SHÍ: **Wáng Bīng, wǒ de yí ge péngyou jīntiān shuō wǒ yīnggāi zhùyì miànzi. Nà shì shénme yìsi?**

WÁNG BĪNG: **Nǐ bú yào ràng bié rén diū miànzi.**

SHÍ: **Wǒ hái shì bù dǒng nà shì shénme yìsi.**

WÁNG BĪNG: **Yìsi jiù shì měi yí ge rén yǒu tāmen zìjǐ de yìjiàn, zìjǐ de shìqing yào zuò. Rúguǒ nǐ shuō tāmen de yìjiàn huòzhě shìqing shì cuò de, tāmen jiù diū miànzi.**

SHÍ: **Suǒyǐ wǒ bù yīnggāi pīpíng bié rén ma?**

WÁNG BĪNG: **Bù. Wǒ gěi nǐ yí ge lìzi. Yǒu yí cì wǒmen de gōngsī de yí ge wàibīn yào bāngzhù wǒmen bǎ bàogào fānyì chéng yīngwen. Kěshì, yí ge Zhōngguórén yǐjīng fānyìhǎo le. Nèige Zhōngguórén diū miànzi yīnwèi dàjiā dōu zhīdào wàibīn fānyì de bǐjiào hǎo.**

SHÍ: **O. Míngbái yìdiǎnr le! Xièxie.**

AT THE OFFICE.

STONE: Wang Bing, today a friend told me I should pay attention to "face." What does that mean?

WANG BING: You shouldn't cause other people to lose face.

STONE: I still don't know what that means.

WANG BING: That basically means that everyone has their own ideas and things that they want to do. You shouldn't do anything that implies that what they do or what they think is wrong. Then they lose face.

STONE: So I shouldn't criticize people?

WANG BING: That's not it. I'll give you an example. Once an American worker at our company wanted to help us translate a report into English. But a Chinese person had already translated it, so he lost face because everyone knew that the American's translation was better.

STONE: Oh. I understand a bit better now! Thanks.

B. YǓFǍ HÉ YÒNGFǍ

1. CAUSATIVE SENTENCES WITH *RÀNG*

Ràng (to make) is used in causative constructions in much the same way as "to make" is used in English, as in "She made me tell!" It is placed after the subject and before the agent that is acting on the subject.

Nǐ bú yào ràng bié rén diū miànzi.
    You shouldn't make other people lose face.

Tā ràng tā jiějie zuò cuòshì.
    He made his older sister make a mistake.

Qǐng nǐ ràng wǒ gāoxìng.
    Please make me happy.

2. VERB + *CHÉNG*

When *chéng* (to become) is attached to certain verbs such as *xiě* (to write), *fānyì* (to translate) or *biàn* (to change), it functions like a resultative verb ending (see lesson 25). It must be followed by a noun that shows what the subject or object has turned into or become. This construction is often found with the preposition *bǎ* (to take), which you learned about in lesson 10.

Tā bǎ bàogào fānyì chéng yīngwén.
    She translated the report into English.

Tā bǎ tā shuō de huà xiě chéng yí ge huàjù.
    He turned what she said into a play.

3. NEGATIVE SUGGESTIONS: *BÚ YÀO* VS. *BIÉ*

In lesson 9, you learned that *bié* is used in negative suggestions or commands, as in the following examples.

Nǐ bié shuōhuà!
   Don't talk!

Bié zǒu!
   Don't go!

Using *bú yào* (to not want) after the subject of a sentence also implies a negative suggestion, but softens the tone as you might want to if you help someone out by telling them not to do something.

Nǐ bú yào ràng bié rén diū miànzi.
   You shouldn't make other people lose face.

Qǐng nǐmen bú yào shuōhuà.
   Please stop talking [the lecture is about to begin].

4. "TO UNDERSTAND": *DǑNG* VS. *MÍNGBÁI*

You already know that *dǒng* means "to understand." *Míngbái* also means "to understand" and is usually interchangeable with *dǒng*, but also has the connotation that something has "come to light." Interestingly, the first syllable, *míng*, means "bright" and the second syllable, *bái*, means "white." The following two sentences are similar in meaning.

Wǒ míngbái nǐ shuō de huà.
Wǒ dǒng nǐ shuō de huà.
   I understand what you are saying.

But if someone has been listening to a detailed explanation of something, as in this lesson's dialogue, the response would be *míngbái*.

Wǒ míngbái le!
   It's clear to me now!

Remember that the particle *le* suggests that this is a change of state, that someone has just understood someone's meaning.

C. HÀNZÌ

New characters.

面子	*miànzi* (face)
让（讓）	*ràng* (to make)
别	*bié* (negative suggestion particle)
翻译	*fānyì* (to translate)
比较	*bǐjiào* (relatively)
丢	*diū* (to lose)

Sentence practice.

你不要让别人丢面子。
Nǐ bú yào ràng bié rén diū miànzi.
    Try not to make other people lose face.

别说话！
Bié shuōhuà!
    Don't talk.

做翻译没有意思。
Zuò fānyì méiyǒu yìsi.
    Translating is not interesting.

D. SHĒNGCÍ

biérén	other people; another person
chéng	into
diū	to lose
diūliǎn, diū miànzi	to lose face
dǒng	understand
fānyì	to translate
fùzá	complicated
huàjù	a theatrical play
lìzi	example
pīpíng	to criticize
ràng	to make, to cause
shìqing	things, events
wàibīn	foreign guest, visitor
xiǎoshuō	novel

yìjiàn	ideas
yìsi	meaning
zìjǐ	one's own

LIÀNXÍ

A. Translate the following into *pīnyīn*, incorporating the word in parentheses.

    1. I simply don't understand your meaning. (*gēnběn, míngbái*)
    2. Her happiness is all over her face. (*mǎn*)
    3. We should eat now so that we won't be hungry later. (*yǐmiǎn*)

B. Which reasons for losing face are presented in the dialogue?

    1. *Nǐ bú yào pīpíng bié rén.*
    2. *Nǐ bú yào bǎ píngguǒ sòng gěi nǐ de péngyou.*
    3. *Nǐ bú yào zài zuò bié rén fānyì de bàogào.*
    4. *Nǐ bú yào gàosu bié rén tāmen zuò cuò le.*
    5. *Nǐ bú yào qǐng nǐ de péngyou qù chīfàn.*

C. Place the following sets of words into the correct order to make correct sentences.

    1. *ràng/ rén/ bié/ nǐ/ diū/ miànzi/ bié*
    2. *xiǎoshuō/ tā/ yīngwén/ bǎ/ fānyì/ chéng*
    3. *bù/ shuō/ míngbái/ huà/ wǒ/ de/ nǐ*
    4. *bù/ nǐ/ yào/ qǐng/ huà/ shuō*

D. Translate the following into English.

    1. 你的宿舍很好看。
    2. 别丢面子！
    3. 我喜欢作翻译。

WÉNHUÀ ZHÙJIĚ

Losing face is a concept more prevalent in Asian countries than it is in the West—it is important to take care not to make people lose face when you are in China. This mainly involves making an effort not to highlight someone else's mistakes. For example, if you redo work that a Chinese colleague has already done, your colleague loses face because it is assumed that the work he or she did was incorrect. Criticizing someone directly to his or her face is a blatant way to cause someone to lose face. Little or implied critiques are also best avoided—even if a Chinese person gives directions to a place that are not the most efficient, it is best to leave it alone or the direction giver will lose face. If you decline an invitation to someone's home for dinner and you are later seen dining in a restaurant, that person loses face as well. It is best to err on the side of overpoliteness—remember, if you cause someone to lose face, you lose face as well and this can cause problems even in close friendships.

DÁÀN

A. 1. *Wǒ gēnběn bù míngbái nǐ de yìsi.* 2. *Tā mǎn liǎn gāoxìng.* 3. *Wǒmen yīnggāi xiànzài chīfàn yǐmiǎn yǐhòu è.*

B. 3, 4 are presented in the dialogue.

C. 1. *Nǐ bié ràng bié rén diū miànzi.* 2. *Tā bǎ xiǎoshuō fānyì chéng yīngwén.* 3. *Wǒ bù míngbái nǐ shuō de huà.* 4. *Qǐng nǐ bú yào shuōhuà.*

D. 1.Your dormitory is pretty. 2. Don't lose face! 3. I like to translate.

DÌ SĀNSHÍ KÈ
Lesson 30

KÀNBÌNG. Visiting a Doctor.

A. DUÌHUÀ

ZÀI YĪYUÀN.

Mr. Stone isn't feeling well, so he goes to visit the doctor.

SHÍ: **Wáng Dàifu, wǒ shēntǐ hěn bù shūfu, hǎoxiàng bìng le.**

DÀIFU: **Shì a! Nǐ de liǎnsè bú tài hǎo. Gàosù wǒ, nǐ bèi chóng yǎo le ma?**

SHÍ: **Méiyou. Wǒ tóutòng, quán shēn fālěng, pēntì dǎ bù tíng. Zuówǎn shuìjiào de shíhòu yìzhí késòu.**

DÀIFU: **Nǐ zhāngkāi zuǐ, ràng wǒ kànkan . . . Nǐ de hóulóng hónghong de, shì fāyán le. Lái, ràng wǒ liángliang tǐwēn.**

YĪ FĒN ZHŌNG YǏHÒU, DÀIFU BǍ WĒNDÙJÌ NÁ CHŪLÁI.

SHÍ: **Zěnmeyàng? Wǒ shì bú shì gǎnmào le?**

DÀIFU: **Duì, érqiě hái yǒu diǎnr fāshāo ne.**

SHÍ: **Yào bú yào dǎzhēn? Kě bù kěyǐ zhǐ chīyào?**

DÀIFU: **Dǎzhēn hǎo de bǐjiào kuài.**

SHÍ: **Méi guānxi. Wǒ pà dǎzhēn, níngyuàn chīyào.**

DÀIFU: **Hǎo ba! Wǒ kāi zhāng yàofāng, nǐ qù ná yào ba.**

SHÍ: **Xièxie.**

AT THE HOSPITAL.

STONE: Dr. Wang, I don't feel well, I think I'm sick.

DOCTOR: Yes, your complexion is not very good. Tell me, were you bit by an insect?

STONE: No. I have headaches. My whole body feels cold and I can't stop sneezing. Last night I kept coughing when I was sleeping.

DOCTOR: Open your mouth and let me see. . . . Your throat is red and inflamed. Let me take your temperature.

A MINUTE LATER, THE DOCTOR CHECKS THE THERMOMETER.

STONE: Well, do I have a cold?

DOCTOR: Yes, and you have a fever.

STONE: Do I need to get a shot? Can I just take pills?

DOCTOR: You'll get better faster if you have a shot.

STONE: That's all right. I'm afraid of shots. I would rather take pills.

DOCTOR: Okay. I'll write a prescription and you can pick up your medication.

STONE: Thanks.

B. YǓFǍ HÉ YÒNGFǍ

1. THE ADJECTIVE *QUÁN*

The adjective *quán* (whole) is similar to the adjective *mǎn* (full). The minor difference is that when *quán* is added to a noun, it means the whole of or all of the parts of the noun while *mǎn* implies the noun as a whole.

Tāmen quán jiā dōu chūguó le.
  The whole family went abroad.

Xīnnián de shíhòu, quán gōngsī dōu fàngjià.
  The whole company has a vacation during New Year's.

Wǒ shēngbìng le. Quán shēn bù shūfu.
  I'm sick. Every part of my body hurts.

2. THE *SHÌ . . . LE* CONSTRUCTION

You've already learned about the *shì . . . de* construction. The particle *le* replaces *de* in this construction in order to show that the statement is confirming a previous assumption.

Tā hǎoxiàng shì bìng le.
He does indeed seem sick.

Nǐ de hóulóng shì fāyán le.
Your throat is in fact inflamed.

3. PASSIVE SENTENCES WITH *BÈI*

Most passive sentences in Chinese are formed using *bèi* (by) after the subject. *Bèi* can be on its own or followed by the person or thing acting on the subject. The basic structure of these sentences is subject + *bèi* + agent + verb.

Wǒ bèi chóng yǎo le.
I was bitten by insects.

Wǒ bèi yǎo le.
I was bitten.

Nǐ yǒu méiyǒu bèi qiú dǎdào?
Were you hit by the ball?

Nǐ yǒu méiyǒu bèi dǎdào?
Were you hit?

4. THE EXPRESSION *LÁI . . .*

Lái (come on) is a colloquial expression used at the beginning of a sentence meant to cajole someone into doing something.

Lái, nǐ duō chī shūcài ba.
Come on, you need to eat more vegetables.

Lái, wǒmen zǒu.
Come on, we're going.

C. HÀNZÌ

New characters.

医院	*yīyuàn* (hospital)
大夫	*dàifu* (doctor)
感冒	*gǎnmào* (to have a cold)
打针	*dǎzhēn* (to get a shot)
药	*yào* (medicine)

Sentence practice.

我去看病。

Wǒ qù kànbìng.

    I'm going to see the doctor.

我不喜欢打针。

Wǒ bù xǐhuan dǎzhēn.

    I don't like to get shots.

请你给我药吃。

Qǐng nǐ gěi wǒ yào chī.

    Please give me some medicine.

D. SHĒNGCÍ

bìng	illness
bù shūfu	to feel ill
chīyào	to take medicine
chūguó	to go abroad
dǎzhēn	to get a shot
fālěng	to shiver, to tremble
fāshāo	to have a fever
fāyán	to become inflamed
gǎnmào	a cold, to catch a cold
hóulóng	throat
jiǎnchá	to examine
jiǎo	foot
kāi yàofang	write a prescription
kànbìng	to see a doctor
késòu	to cough
liǎnsè	complexion
liáng	to measure
níngyuàn	would rather
pà	to fear
pēntì	to sneeze
quán	entire, whole
shēntǐ	body, health
shūfu	comfortable
téng	ache, pain
tíng	to stop
tǐwēn	body temperature

tóu	head
tóutòng	headache
wēndùjì	thermometer
yīshēng	doctor
zhāngkāi	to open
zuǐ	mouth

LIÀNXÍ

A. Answer the following questions based on the dialogue.

1. *Dàifu shuō Shí zěnme le?*
2. *Shuōshuo Shí nǎr bù shūfu?*
3. *Jiéguǒ Shí shì dǎzhēn háishì chīyào. Wèishénme?*
4. *Ná yào yǐqián yào qǐng yīshēng kāi shénme?*

B. Rewrite the following sentences using the *shì . . . le* construction to express emphasis.

1. *Wǒ xiǎng wǒ gǎnmào le.*
2. *Wáng xiānsheng hǎoxiàng chū qù le.*
3. *Wǒ xiǎng wǒ de jiǎo bèi chóng yǎo le.*
4. *Tā qù kàn dàifu le.*
5. *Nǐ fāshāo le.*

C. Translate the following into English.

1. *tóutòng*
2. *hóulóng fāyán*
3. *gǎnmào*
4. *fāshāo*
5. *dǎ pēntì*
6. *bìng*
7. *bù shūfu*

WÉNHUÀ ZHÙJIĚ

Although Western medicine is gaining some ground in China, *qìgōng* doctors can be found in any village. *Qìgōng* is a type of Chinese medicine that is preventive in nature. It is based on maintaining a balance of *qì* (life force) in the body. Basically, every body contains levels of good *qì* and bad *qì*, and when these are out of balance disorders or sicknesses can occur. A *qìgōng* doctor will look at the aura of his or her patient (the aura being levels of *qì* emanating off the body) to see the movement and color of *qì*. If something seems out of balance, a special diet or special exercises, similar to *tàijí quán* exercises, will be prescribed. Sometimes the *qìgōng* doctor uses his hands to manipulate *qì* by stroking the air about an inch above an effected body part, thus restoring it to normal. To a mind conditioned by the Western concept of medicine, this may seem odd. But it does seem to work.

DÁÀN

A. 1. *Dàifu shuō Shí gǎnmào le, érqiě hái yǒu diǎnr fāshāo.* 2. *Shí tóutòng, quánshēn fālěng, pēntì dǎ bù tíng. Wǎnshàng hái késòu.* 3. *Shí zhǐ chīyào. Yīnwèi tā pà dǎzhēn.* 4. *Yào qǐng yīshēng kāi yàofāng.*

B. 1. *Wǒ xiǎng wǒ shì gǎnmào le.* 2. *Wáng xiānsheng hǎoxiàng shì chū qù le.* 3. *Wǒ xiǎng wǒ de jiǎo shì bèi chóng yǎo le.* 4. *Tā shì qù kàn dàifu le.* 5. *Nǐ shì fāshāo le.*

C. 1. headache 2. an inflammation in the throat 3. to have a cold 4. to have a fever 5. to sneeze 6. sick 7. to not feel well

FÙXÍ 6

A. Change these sentences into the passive using *bèi*.

    1. *Chóng yǎo le wǒ.*
    2. *Háizi máfan dàrén.*
    3. *Dàifu gěi wǒ jiějie jiǎnchá.*

B. Translate into *pīnyīn*.

    1. My little sister is sick so I want to help her.
    2. If he goes, then I'm not going.
    3. His whole face is unhappy.
    4. I don't like to get shots.
    5. How can he be that tall?

C. Match the *pīnyīn* to the English.

    1. *gǎnmào*   a. inflammation
    2. *fāshāo*   b. take medicine
    3. *chīyào*   c. headache
    4. *dǎzhēn*   d. a cold
    5. *tóutòng*   e. a fever
    6. *fāyán*   f. shots

D. Add the radicals to these characters according to the English equivalents.

    1. ___ (to speak)
    2. ___ (to wash)
    3. ___ (money)

E. Write the equivalent in Chinese characters.

    1. *yīyuàn*
    2. *gémìng lìshǐ bówùguǎn*
    3. *dàifu*
    4. *gùgōng*

F. Translate into English.

1. 我的宿舍很不舒服。
2. 我感冒了。
3. 我不要去医院。

DÁÀN

A. 1. *Wǒ bèi chóng yǎo le.* 2. *Dàrén bèi háizi máfán.* 3. *Wǒ jiějie bèi dàifu jiǎnchá.*

B. 1. *Wǒ mèimei shēngbìng le suǒyǐ wǒ yào bāngzhù tā.* 2. *Rúguǒ tā qù de huà, wǒ jiù bú qù.* 3. *Tā mǎn liǎn bu gāoxìng.* 4. *Wǒ bù xǐhuan dǎzhēn.* 5. *Tā zěnme nàme gāo?*

C. 1.D 2.E 3.B 4.F 5.C 6.A

D. 1. 言 2. 氵 3. 釒

E. 1.医院 2.革命历史博物馆 3.大夫 4.故宫

F. 1. My dormitory is very uncomfortable. 2. I have a cold. 3. I don't want to go to the hospital.

Early Chinese poems were written in classical Chinese, a form of the language that was used exclusively by scholars much as Latin was used in early European history. Classical Chinese is more abbreviated than modern Chinese, with one classical character carrying the meaning of several modern characters. Although the grammar of classical Chinese is much different from the Chinese you are learning, you should be able to guess at the meaning of classical poetry if you know the characters. Read aloud the following poem from the 8th century A.D. to experience the musicality of classical Chinese poetry.

空	山	不	见	人
kōng	*shān*	*bú*	*jiàn*	*rén*
empty	mountain	not	see	people
但	闻	人	语	响
dàn	*wén*	*rén*	*yǔ*	*xiǎng*
only	hear	people	language	sound
返	景	入	深	林
fǎn	*jǐng*	*rù*	*shēn*	*lín*
return	image	enters	deep	forest
复	照	青	苔	上
fù	*zhào*	*qīng*	*tái*	*shàng*
again	shines	green	moss	on

DÌ SĀNSHÍYĪ KÈ
Lesson 31

YÀO. Medicine.

A. DUÌHUÀ

ZÀI YÀODIÀN.

While shopping in the streets one afternoon, Ming's sister suddenly feels sick. Ming goes to a pharmacy to buy some medicine for her sister.

MÍNG: **Xiānsheng, wǒ mèimei tūrán hěn bù shūfu, zěnme bàn?**

DIÀNYUÁN: **Zěnme le?**

MÍNG: **Tā juéde quánshēn wúlì, ěxīn xiǎng tù, zǒu qǐ lù lái, tóuhūn yǎnhuā.**

DIÀNYUÁN: **Dùzi téng bù téng? Huì bú huì chī huài le?**

MÍNG: **Bú huì ba! Wǒmen zhōngwǔ chī de dōngxi shì yíyàng de.**

DIÀNYUÁN: **Nǐmen zài tàiyáng xià zǒu le duōjiǔ?**

MÍNG: **Dàgài yǒu liǎng, sān ge zhōngtóu.**

DIÀNYUÁN: **Kàn yàngzi nǐ mèimei kěnéng shì zhòngshǔ le. Jīntiān wàitóu zhème rè, nǐmen liǎng dōu méi dài màozi, hěn róngyì zhòngshǔ.**

MÍNG: **Tā kěyǐ chī shénme yào?**

DIÀNYUÁN: **Nǐ ràng nǐ mèimei xiān zuò zài yīnliáng de dìfāng xiūxi xiūxi, zài chī diǎnr réndān, mǒ diǎnr qīngliáng yóu. Tā hěn kuài jiù huì shūfu qǐlái.**

MÍNG: **Hǎo. Wǒ zhǐhǎo mǎi yì bāo réndān hé yì píng qīngliáng yóu.**

DIÀNYUÁN: **Bié wàngle mǎi jǐ píng kuàngquán shuǐ. Xiàtiān yào duō hē shuǐ a!**

———————

MING: Sir, my sister is sick all of a sudden. What should I do?

CLERK: What happened?

MING: She feels weak and like she is going to throw up. When she starts to walk, she feels dizzy and her head spins.

CLERK: Does she have stomach pains? Did she eat something bad?

MING: It can't be that! We ate the same things this afternoon.

CLERK: How long have you been walking under the sun?

MING: Probably two or three hours.

CLERK: It appears as if your sister is suffering a heatstroke. It's really hot outside and neither of you is wearing a hat. It's easy to get a heatstroke that way.

MING: Can she take any medicine?

CLERK: Have your sister rest under some shade, and then give her some medicated breath fresheners and put some pain-relieving oinment on her forehead. She will feel much better soon.

MING: Fine. I'll buy one pack of fresheners and one bottle of oinment.

CLERK: Don't forget to get a few bottles of mineral water. You need to drink a lot of water during the summer.

B. YǓFǍ HÉ YÒNGFǍ

1. THE EXPRESSION *KÀN YÀNGZI*

Kàn yàngzi (judging from appearances or circumstances) can be used with people or situations. It is placed either before or after the subject of a sentence.

Kàn yàngzi, tā shì bú huì lái le.
  It appears that he is not coming.

Tā kàn yàngzi hěn lèi.
  He seems very tired.

Wǒmen kàn yàngzi bù néng qù le.
It seems that we can't go now.

2. PERSON/THING + *ZĚNME LE?*

Questions with *zěnme le* are asked to express concern for a person or thing based on the situation at hand. For example, if a child is being jostled in a crowd, one might ask, *Zhège xiǎohái zěnme le?* (Is that child all right?)

Nǐ de chēzi zěnme le? Nǐ jīntiān zěnme méi kāi?
What's up with your car? Why didn't you drive it today?

Tā de māo zěnme le? Bìng le ma?
Is his cat okay? Is it sick?

3. *NǍ YǑU ZHÈME/NÀME . . . ?*

Nǎ, a shortened form of *nǎr* (where), and *yǒu* (to have) together with *zhème* or *nàme* have an idiomatic sense meaning "How can a person or thing be so . . . ?" These questions rhetorically express a point and aren't meant to be answered as such.

Tā nǎ yǒu nàme gāo?
How can he be that tall?

Zhè chǎng yīnyuèhuì nǎ yǒu zhème rèmén?
How can this concert be so popular?

Tāmen nǎ yǒu nàme wǎn.
I can't believe they were that late.

C. HÀNZÌ

New characters.

舒服	*shūfu* (comfortable)
怎么办？	*zěnme bàn* (What should we do?)
矿泉水	*kuàngquán shuǐ* (mineral water)
太阳	*tàiyáng* (sun)
知道	*zhīdào* (to know)

Sentence practice.

你的家很舒服。
Nǐ de jiā hěn shūfu.
    Your home is comfortable.

你知道不知道？
Nǐ zhīdào bù zhīdào?
    Do you know?

我喜欢矿泉水。
Wǒ xǐhuan kuàngquán shuǐ.
    I like mineral water.

太阳很热。
Tàiyáng hěn rè.
    The sun is very hot.

D. SHĒNGCÍ

dài	to wear, to bring
dōngxī	thing
dùzi	stomach, tummy
ěxīn	to be nauseated, nauseating
huài	bad
kěnéng	possible
kuàngquán shuǐ	mineral water
māo	cat
mǒ	to apply (like a cream)
níngyuàn	would rather
píng	bottle
qīngliáng	cool and refreshing
réndān	lozenges
tàiyáng	the sun
tóuhūn yǎnhuā	dizzy and spinning
tù	to vomit
tūrán	suddenly
wàitou	outside
wúlì	to be feeble, lacking energy
yàodiàn	pharmacy
yíyàng	the same
yīnliáng	shady and cool

yóu	oil
zhòngshǔ	heatstroke
zǒulù	to walk

LIÀNXÍ

A. Which of the following sentences are true based on the dialogue?

1. *Míng zhōngwǔ chī huài le, suǒyǐ quánshēn bù shūfu.*
2. *Yàodiàn diànyuán yào Míng de mèimei xiān chī wǔfàn.*
3. *Míng bāng mèimei mǎile réndān hé qīngliáng yóu.*
4. *Míng de mèimei xǐhuan hē kuàngquán shuǐ.*

B. Connect the following clauses using the *yī . . . jiù* construction.

1. *Māma xiào qǐlái. Dìdi gāoxìng.*
2. *Mèimei zhàn qǐlái. Mèimei juéde tóuhūn yǎnhuā.*
3. *Yīshēng zǒu jìn lái. Wǒ juéde bù shūfu.*
4. *Wǒ chīfàn. Dùzi téng.*
5. *Xiǎo Lín shuō qǐ huà lái, shuō bù wán.*

C. Translate the following sentences into *pīnyīn*.

1. I feel sick all of a sudden.
2. What's happened?
3. I feel dizzy and my head is spinning.
4. I think you are suffering a heatstroke.
5. You need to drink a lot of water during the summer.

D. Write the characters for the underlined *pīnyīn* words.

1. *Míng de mèimei xǐhuan hē kuàngquán shuǐ.*
2. *Wǒ bù zhīdào nǐ de míngzi.*
3. *Nǐmen zài tàiyáng xià zǒu le dūojiǔ?*

WÉNHUÀ ZHÙJIĔ

In China, medicines are distributed freely for almost every kind of minor discomfort. Herbal remedies are quite common for everything from a headache to a hangnail. Be careful about telling people your various aches and pains because they will undoubtedly have a long, involved explanation of what kind of herb to chew on or what pill to take based on the wisdom of their own ancestors. Antibiotics are also freely distributed in China, even for the slightest of colds. Kids with the sniffles are often subjected to several intravenous antibiotic drips rather than rest and TV. Traditional Chinese medicine and herbal remedies have begun to gain wider acceptance in the West, but be sure to bring your own prescription drugs and other medicinal needs to China if it will make you more comfortable.

DÁÀN

A. Statement 3 is true.

B. 1. *Māma yí xiào qǐlái, dìdi jiù gāoxìng.* 2. *Mèimei yí zhàn qǐlái, jiù juéde tóuhūn yǎnhuā.* 3. *Yīshēng yì zǒu jìn lái, wǒ jiù juéde bù shūfu.* 4. *Wǒ yì chīfàn, dùzi jiù téng.* 5. *Xiǎo Lín yì shuō qǐ huà lái, jiù shuō bù wán.*

C. 1. *Wǒ tūrán hěn bù shūfu.* 2. *Zěnme le?* 3. *Wǒ juéde tóuhūn yǎnhuā.* 4. *Wǒ xiǎng nǐ zhòngshǔ le.* 5. *Xiàtiān nǐ yīnggāi duō hē shuǐ.*

D. 1. 喜欢, 矿泉水　2. 知道　3. 太阳

DÌ SĀNSHÍÈR KÈ
Lesson 32

JIÉQÌNG. Holidays.

A. DUÌHUÀ

ZÀI JÙNFĒNG DE JIĀ.

Mr. Stone discusses Chinese holidays with a friend.

SHÍ: Jùnfēng, míngtiān shì shénme rìzi? Wèishénme yínháng hé yóujú dōu bù kāi mén? Wǒ běnlái yào qù yínháng qǔqián. Xiànzài děi děng dào hòutiān le.

JÙNFĒNG: Míngtiān shì nónglì bāyuè shíwǔ hào "Zhōngqiū jié". Zhè shì wǒmen Zhōngguó chuántǒng de sì dà zhòngyào jiérì zhīyī, suǒyǒu de gōngsī dōu fàngjià yì tiān.

SHÍ: Zhōngqiū jié? Wǒ zhīdào le. Nǐmen zài zhège jiérì chī yuèbǐng, duì bú duì?

JÙNFĒNG: Duì! Rénmén zài zhè tiān dōu xǐhuan chīle wǎnfàn yǐhòu, zuò zài yuànzi lǐ xīnshǎng yuèliang, chī yuèbǐng.

SHÍ: Yàoshì nà tiān xiàyǔ zěnme bàn?

JÙNFĒNG: Jiù zài fángzi lǐ chī a! Zhè shì yìzhǒng fēngsú, zuì zhòngyào de shì ràng quán jiārén tuánjù zài yìqǐ.

SHÍ: Zhōngguó rén hái yǒu nǎxiē zhòngyào de chuántǒng jiéqìng? Yǒu shénme tèbié de huódòng?

JÙNFĒNG: Chūntiān zuì zhòngyào de shì sìyuè wǔhào de "Qīngmíng jié." Zhè tiān quán jiā yào yìqǐ qù jìbài sǐqù de qīnrén hé zǔxiān.

SHÍ: Xiàtiān de jiérì ne?

JÙNFĒNG: Shì nónglì wǔyuè wǔrì de "Duānwǔ jié." Hěn duō rén zài zhè tiān huá lóngzhōu, chī zòngzi.

SHÍ: Ràng wǒ cāicai. "Zhōngqiū jié" shì qiūtiān de jiérì. Dōngtiān nǐmen jiù qìngzhù nónglì xīnnián, duì bú duì?

272

JÙNFĒNG: **Duì. Cóngqián de xīnnián zhìshǎo yào guò shíwǔ tiān, dào Yuánxiāo jié chīle yuánxiāo cái jiéshù. Zài xīnnián qījiān, dàjiā chuān xīnyī, dài xīnmào, hái yǒu gèzhǒng xīnnián huódòng. Xiǎo háizi gāoxìng jí le. Tāmen kěyǐ ná hóngbāo.**

SHÍ: **Zhè gēn wǒmen de Shèngdàn jié yíyàng, fēicháng rènào. Wǒ zhēn xīwàng zài Zhōngguó de xīnnián zài lái Zhōngguó yícì!**

JÙNFĒNG: **Hǎo a! Dào shíhòu wǒ yídìng dài nǐ hǎohao guàngguang!**

AT JUNFENG'S HOUSE.

STONE: Junfeng, what day is it tomorrow? Why won't the bank and post office be open? I wanted to withdraw money tomorrow, but now I'll have to wait until the day after.

JUNFENG: Tomorrow is the eighth month and fifteenth day in the Chinese lunar calendar, Mid-Autumn festival. It's one of the four major holidays, and every company will be closed for the day.

STONE: Oh, I've heard of the Mid-Autumn festival. You eat moon cakes on this holiday, right?

JUNFENG: Right. People like to sit in the yard after dinner, eat mooncakes and enjoy the moonlight.

STONE: What if it rains on that day?

JUNFENG: Well, they eat in the house of course. It is only a custom. The most important thing is to have the whole family together.

STONE: What are China's other traditional festivals? What kinds of special activities do you do?

JUNFENG: The most important holiday in the spring is the Tomb Sweeping festival on the fourth month and fifth day in the lunar calendar. The whole family gets together to pay their respects to their late relatives and ancestors.

STONE: What about in the summer?

JUNFENG: We have the Dragon festival on the fifth month and fifth day of the lunar calendar. People row dragon boats and eat rice tamales on that day.

STONE: Let me guess. The Mid-Autumn festival is the holiday in the fall and Chinese New Year is celebrated in winter, right?

JUNFENG: Yes. Since the past, New Year's has lasted for at least fifteen days, until the fifteenth day of the first lunar month, when people eat special rice cakes. During New Year's period, everyone wears new clothes and new hats and participates in all kinds of events. Little kids are especially happy because they get "red envelopes."

STONE: It's the same as Christmas—full of activity. I hope to come back to China during the New Year celebration!

JUNFENG: Great! I'll definitely take you around.

B. YǓFǍ HÉ YÒNGFǍ

1. MORE ABOUT *RÀNG*

Ràng (to make, to let) can also be used in commands or suggestions as follows. Here, the implied subject is *nǐ* (you).

Ràng wǒ cāicai.
   Let me guess.

Ràng nǐ de háizi zuòzuo gōngkè.
   Make your child do his homework.

2. THE ADVERB *BĚNLÁI*

You already know that *běn* means "root." The adverb *běnlái* (originally) comes after the subject of a sentence to indicate the original state or intention of the subject. The implication when *běnlái* is used is that this original state or intention has since changed. The following examples will help illustrate the meaning of this construction.

Wǒ běnlái yào qù yínháng qǔqián.
   I originally wanted to go to the bank to take out money [but now the bank is closed].

Tā běnlái yào xiě xiǎoshuō.
   At first, she wanted to write short stories [but now she is a banker].

3. THE CONSTRUCTION *SUŎYŎU DE . . . DŌU*

The construction *suǒyǒu de . . . dōu* is used when talking about "all" of a particular thing. As with most words that imply "all," *suǒyǒu* occurs in conjunction with *dōu*.

Suǒyǒu de péngyou, wǒ dōu bàifǎng guò le.
   I have visited all of my friends.

Tā duì suǒyǒu de shì dōu hěn yǒu xìngqù.
   He is interested in everything.

Wǒmen bǎ suǒyǒu de dōngxī dōu tuì huíqu ba.
   Let us return everything.

Suǒyǒu de kèrén dōu dào le ma?
   Have all the guests arrived?

4 THE CONJUNCTION *DÀO . . . CÁI*

Dào (to arrive) when used with *cái* (then) forms a conjunction pair used to say something will not or did not happen until a specific event occurs or occurred. The order of these events in a sentence is the reverse of what it is in English.

Chūnjié guò dào Yuánxiāo jié cái jiéshù.
   The New Year celebration does not end until after the Yuanxiao festival.

Tā dào shàng dàxué, cái dào Zhōngguó lái.
   He did not come to China until he was in college.

Wǒ yào dào xiàtiān cái huíqu.
   I will not return until the summer.

C. HÀNZÌ

New characters.

春	*chūn* (spring)
秋	*qiū* (autumn)
冬	*dōng* (winter)
夏	*xià* (summer)
天	*tiān* (day)
日子	*rìzi* (day)

Sentence practice.

夏天有什么节日？

Xiàtiān yǒu shénme jiérì?

　　What holidays are there in summer?

我妈妈不喜欢冬天。

Wǒ māma bù xǐhuan dōngtiān.

　　My mother doesn't like the winter.

D. SHĒNGCÍ

bài	to worship
chuántǒng	tradition
chūntiān	spring
cóngqián	previously, formerly
dōngtiān	winter
Duānwu jié	Dragon festival
fàngjià	to take a holiday
fēngsú	custom
gèzhǒng	each kind
huá	to row
jìbài	to worship
jiéqìng	festival
jiérì	festival day
nónglì	the Chinese lunar calendar
qíjiān	time period
qìngzhù	to celebrate
qiūtiān	autumn
qǔqián	to withdraw money
rènào	lively and exciting
Shèngdàn jié	Christmas
tuánjù	to gather together
xiàtiān	summer
yàoshì	if, suppose
yuèbǐng	moon cakes
yuànzi	backyard
zhìshǎo	the least
Zhōngqiū jié	Mid-Autumn festival
zòngzi	Chinese tamale
zǔxiān	ancestor

A. Fill in the blanks based on the dialogue.

1. *Xiǎoháize dōu xǐhuan _____ yīnwèi tāmen kěyǐ ná hóngbāo.*
2. *Chūntiān zuì zhòngyào de jiérì shì _____.*
3. *Zhōngguórén zài _____ chī yuèbǐng, zài Yuánxiāo jié chī _____.*
4. *Zài Qīngmíng jié quán jiā yào yìqǐ qù jìbài sǐqù de qīnrén hé _____.*

B. Use the *suǒyǒu de . . . dōu* construction to write the following sentences in *pīnyīn*.

1. She is interested in all of the basketball teams.
2. We have visited all of the French companies.
3. Is all of the medicine in your house?
4. All of the Chinese holidays are interesting.

C. Write the English eqivalents.

1. 春
2. 夏
3. 秋
4. 冬
5. 夏天的时候应该多喝矿泉水。
6. 冬天太冷啊！

WÉNHUÀ ZHÙJIĚ

Holidays are not celebrated with as much gusto in China as they are in the United States. Spring festival occurs during the winter break, when schools are already closed. However, there is a special holiday school closing on National Day (October 1st), which is the anniversary of the founding of Communist China. Other holidays are celebrated rather perfunctorily, but always with some kind of symbolic food—moon cakes, *yuè bǐng*, for the moon festival (round food is always considered lucky), and noodles, *miàntiáo*, on birthdays and anniversaries to symbolize longevity. One of the more interesting holidays is Ancestor Day where people go out on the street to burn paper money to send it to the beyond so their dead ancestors have money to buy food with. At every street corner on this day, you will see little fires attended by dutiful decendants all through the night.

DÁÀN

A. 1. *Xīnnián* 2. *Qīngmíng jié* 3. *Zhōngqiū jié, Yuánxiāo* 4. *Zǔxiān*

B. 1. *Tā duì suǒyǒu de lánqiúduì dōu hěn yǒu xìngqù.* 2. *Suǒyǒu de Fǎguó gōngsī, wǒmen dōu bàifǎngguò le.* 3. *Suǒyǒu de yào dōu zài nǐ de fángzi ma?* 4. *Suǒyǒu de Zhōngguó jiérì dōu hěn yǒu yìsi.*

C. 1. spring 2. summer 3. autumn 4. winter 5. During the summer, we should drink more mineral water. 6. Winter is too cold!

DÌ SĀNSHÍSĀN KÈ
Lesson 33

SHĒNTǏ. The Body.

A. DUÌHUÀ

ZÀI BÀNGŌNGSHÌ.

Mr. Ma causes some concern in the office because of a burn on his hand.

LIÚ: **Xiǎo Mǎ, nǐ de zuǒshǒu zěnme le?**

MǍ: **Zhēn dǎoméi. Zuótiān dào rèshuǐ de shíhòu, yí bù xiǎoxīn jiù bèi shuǐ tàngshāng le.**

LIÚ: **Kàn qǐ lái hěn yánzhòng. Nǐ qù kàn yīshēng le méiyǒu?**

MǍ: **Zhè shì xiǎo shì, hébì qù kàn yīshēng. Wǒ zìjǐ yǐjīng cā le tàngshāng yào le.**

LIÚ: **Bù xíng! Bù xíng! Nǐ kàn wǒ jiǎo shàng de zhègebā.**

MǍ: **Āiyā! Nǐ zěnme yǒu zhème dà de bā?**

LIÚ: **Wǒ de jiǎo bèi chóng yǎo le, běnlái yǐwéi méi shì, zìjǐ suíbiàn cā yào. Hòulái jiǎo zhǒng de yuè lái yuè dà, hái fāyán.**

MǍ: **Jiéguǒ ne?**

LIÚ: **Wǒ zhǐhǎo qù kàn yīshēng, huāle hěn duō qián. Érqiě hái bèi yīshēng màle yí dùn. Tā shuō yàoshì wǒ zǎo qù kàn, shāngkǒu jiù bú huì zhème zāo le.**

MǍ: **Kàn yàngzi, wǒ hái shì yīnggāi qù yīyuàn guàhào kàn yīshēng.**

LIÚ: **Duì a! Wǒ kàn nǐ xiànzài jiù qù ba.**

AT THE OFFICE.

LIU: Little Ma, what happened to your left hand?

MA: My bad luck! When I was pouring hot water yesterday, my hand accidentally got burned.

279

LIU: It looks serious. Did you go see a doctor?

MA: It's not a big deal. There's no need to see a doctor. I already put some burn ointment on it myself.

LIU: That's no good! Look at the scar on my foot.

MA: Wow! How did you get such a big scar?

LIU: An insect bit me and I thought it was nothing and I just put some stuff on it myself. Later, my foot got more swollen and inflamed.

MA: How did it turn out?

LIU: I had to see a doctor and ended up spending a lot of money. Moreover, the doctor also scolded me. The doctor said that if I had seen him earlier, the wound wouldn't have been so bad.

MA: Hmm . . . maybe I should go take a number in the hospital and wait to see a doctor.

LIU: I think so. I think you should go now.

B. YǓFǍ HÉ YÒNGFǍ

1. PASSIVE VERBS WITH *SHÒU*

Shòu, which expresses the idea of "receiving," "accepting" or "suffering," is added to certain verbs to make them passive.

shòu huānyíng	to be welcomed
shòu jiàoyù	to be educated
shòu pīpíng	to be criticized
shòushāng	to be wounded
shòu yǐngxiǎng	to be influenced

When used in a sentence, particles and adverbs such as *le* appear after *shòu* and before the main verb.

Wǒ chànggē de shíhou shòudào hěn duō pīpíng.
When I sing, I get a lot of criticism.

Wǒ fùqin shàngge xīngqī shòule shāng.
My father was injured last week.

2. MULTIPLE NEGATIVES

In Chinese, it is possible to repeat the negative particle *bù* in one sentence to negate each appropriate element. Examine the following examples.

Nǐ bú chàng bù xíng.
  It's not acceptable for you not to sing.

Dàifu shuō "bù chīyào bù hǎo."
  The doctor said that "it is not good not to take your pills."

3. THE CONSTRUCTION *YUÈ LÁI YUÈ* ADJECTIVE

The most common way in Chinese to say that a person or thing or state becomes more and more of an adjective is to use *yuè lái yuè* and the adjective. *Yuè* on its own means "to exceed," and *yuè lái yuè* is an idiom that can be translated "more and more."

Tā chàng de yuè lái yuè piàoliang.
  Her singing is becoming more and more beautiful.

Xiǎoyīng xuéxí de yuè lái yuè lèi.
  Xiaoying is getting more and more tired as she studies.

Wǒmen dōu yuè lái yuè è.
  We are getting hungrier and hungrier.

4. THE CONSTRUCTION *YUÈ* ADJECTIVE *YUÈ* ADJECTIVE

Lái can be replaced in the above construction with another adjective. The result is an expression which means the more that something becomes the first adjective, the more it becomes the second adjective.

Tā yuè dà yuè piàoliàng.
  The older she gets the prettier she gets.

Yuè kuài yuè hǎo.
  The faster the better.

Compare the following two sentences.

Wǒ yuè lái yuè pàng.
  I'm getting fatter and fatter.

Wǒ yuè chī yuè pàng.
  The more I eat the fatter I get.

5. THE EXPRESSION *YÍ BÈIZI*

Yí bèizi (all along, all one's life) is used to say that a person has done something or has wanted to do something for their whole life. It is placed directly after the subject of the sentence.

Wǒ mèimei yí bèizi yào jiāoshū.
My little sister has always wanted to be a teacher.

Tā yí bèizi bù xǐhuan zài kǎ-lā-ok chànggē.
He has never liked to sing karaoke.

C. HÀNZÌ

New characters.

受	*shòu* (to receive)
批评	*pīpíng* (criticize, criticism)
唱歌	*chànggē* (to sing)
越来越	*yuè lái yuè* (more and more)

Sentence practice.

别批评我。
Bié pīpíng wǒ.
Don't criticize me.

他受到很多批评。
Tā shòudào hěn duō pīpíng.
He gets a lot of criticism.

他唱歌唱得很好。
Tā chànggē chàng de hěn hǎo.
She sings very well.

我们越来越不舒服。
Wǒmen yuè lái yuè bù shūfu.
We are getting more and more uncomfortable.

D. SHĒNGCÍ

bā	scar
běnlái	originally
búbì	need not, there is no need

cā	to apply to the skin
chóng	insect
dào	to pour
fāyán	to be infected
guàhào	to register, take a number
hébì	there is no need
huā (qián)	to spend money
jiǎo	foot
jiéguǒ	result, outcome
mà	to scold, to curse
màiguāng	to sell out
shòushāng	to get injured
suíbiàn	as one pleases
tàngshāng	to burn
yánzhòng	serious
yǎo	to bite
yīshēng	doctor
yīyuàn	hospital
yòu	right (direction)
yòushǒu	right hand
yuè lái yuè	more and more
zāo	to be a mess
zhǐhǎo	to have to
zhǒng	to be swollen
zuǒ	left
zuǒshǒu	left hand

SUPPLEMENTARY VOCABULARY 8: PARTS OF THE BODY

tóu	head
é	forehead
yǎnjīng	eyes
yǎnmáo	eyelashes
méimao	eyebrow
miànjiá	cheek
bízi	nose
chún	lip
zuǐba	mouth
yáchǐ	teeth

shétou	tongue
xiàba	chin
húxū	beard
xiǎohúzi	moustache
érduo	ear
bíkǒng	nostril
bózi	neck
xiōngqiāng	chest
rǔfáng	breast
bèi	back
jiānbǎng	shoulder
wèi	belly, abdomen
yāo	waist
pìgu	buttocks
tuǐ	leg
xīgài	knee
jìng	shin
jiǎo	foot
jiǎohòugēn	heel
jiǎozhǐ	toe
shǒubei	arm
zhǒu	elbow
shǒuzhǐ	finger
wàn	wrist
zhǐjia	fingernail
dàmǔzhǐ	thumb
pífū	skin
jǐngqián	throat
xīn	heart
fèi	lungs
wèi	stomach
cháng	intestines
yīnjíng	penis
yīndào	vagina
gāngmén	anus
xuě	blood
jīròu	muscle
gǔtou	bone
tóugàigǔ	skull
gǔgé	skeleton

LIÀNXÍ

A. Answer the following questions based on the dialogue.

1. *Xiǎo Mǎ de zuǒshǒu zěnme le?*
2. *Xiǎo Mǎ shòushāng yǐhòu qù kàn yīshēng le méiyǒu? Wèishénme?*
3. *Lǎo Liú de jiǎo zěnme le?*
4. *Yīnwèi méi qù kàn yīshēng, lǎo Liú de jiǎo zěnme le?*
5. *Zhège duìhuà gàosù wǒmen yàoshì shòushāng le yídìng yào zěnme bàn?*

B. Fill in the blanks, using the words below.

yuè lái yuè hébì běnlái yǐwéi zhǐhǎo yàoshì

1. *Wǒ* _____ *yào qù kàn diànyǐng de, kěshì péngyou lái kàn wǒ, jiù méi qù le.*
2. _____ *nǐ bú qù kàn diànyǐng, wǒ yě bú qù kàn.*
3. *Nǐ de Zhōngguóhuà shuō de* _____ *hǎo. Nǐ yídìng cháng shuō, duì bú duì?*
4. *Nǐ jiā lí wǒ zhèr hěn jìn,* _____ *yào zuò chūzūchē ne? Nǐ zǒu lái ba.*
5. *Wǒ* _____ *nǐ yào lái wǒ jiā, suǒyǐ cái huíjiā děng nǐ.*
6. *Yīnyuèhuì de piào dōu màiguāng le. Wǒmen* _____ *qù kàn diànyǐng.*

C. Change into passive sentences using *bèi*.

1. *Jīntiān gēge méi qù shàngkè, māma mà tā le.*
2. *Rè shuǐ tàngshāngle wǒ de zuǒ jiǎo.*
3. *Chóng yǎole dìdi de liǎn.*
4. *Wǒ qǔdéle zhè jiā ruǎnjiàn gōngsī de dàilǐ quán.*

D. Fill in the missing characters based on the English translations.

1. 我不 ___ 。
   I am uncomfortable.
2. 他的母亲 ___ 了伤。
   His mother got injured.
3. 你应该到 ___ 去。
   You should go to the hospital.

WÉNHUÀ ZHÙJIĚ

People in China are generally very private. They don't discuss their problems even with their closest friends—marital problems, money problems, confusion about life, all are kept within the home. Everyday health problems, on the other hand, are a big topic of conversation. Any wound or sniffle is subjected to all kinds of suggestions for cures. What to eat, what to put on it—there are endless possibilities that people aren't afraid of sharing.

DÁÀN

A. 1. *Tā de zuǒshǒu bèi rè shuǐ tàngshāng le.* 2. *Tā méi qù kàn. Tā shuō zhè shì xiǎo shì, hébì qù kàn yīshēng.* 3. *Tā de jiǎo bèi chóng yǎo le.* 4. *Hòulái jiǎo zhǒng de yuè lái yuè dà, hái fāyán.* 5. *Yàoshì shòushāng le, yídìng yào qù yīyuàn guàhào kàn yīshēng.*

B. 1. *běnlái* 2. *yàoshì* 3. *yuè lái yuè* 4. *hébì* 5. *yǐwéi* 6. *zhǐhǎo*

C. 1. *Jīntiān gēge méi qù shàng kè, bèi māma mà le.* 2. *Wǒ de zuǒ jiǎo bèi rè shuǐ tàngshāng le.* 3. *Dìdi de liǎn bèi chóng yǎo le.* 4. *Zhè jiā ruǎnjiàn gōngsī de dàilǐquán bèi wǒ qǔdé le.*

D. 1. 舒服 2. 受 3. 医院

DÌ SĀNSHÍSÌ KÈ
Lesson 34
QÌHÒU. Climate.

A. DUÌHUÀ

<small>ZÀI BĚIJĪNG SHĪFÀN DÀXUÉ.</small>

Sally and Xiaoying, both students at Beijing Normal University, talk about weather.

XIĂOYĪNG: **Shālì, nǐ jiāxiāng de huánjìng zěnmeyàng?**

SHĀLÌ: **Wǒ zhù zài Měiguó de Nán Jiāzhōu. Nàr de qìhòu hěn hǎo. Yì nián sìjì cóng bú xiàxuě.**

XIĂOYĪNG: **Nà gēn Zhōngguó nánfāng hěn xiàng, yǒu Nán Jiāzhōu nàme nuǎnhuo.**

SHĀLÌ: **Zhōngguó nánfāng gēn běifāng de qìhòu yǒu shénme chābié?**

XIĂOYĪNG: **Zhōngguó nánfāng de qìwēn gāo, yǒu běifāng de liǎng bèi gāo. Huánjìng yě bǐjiào cháoshī. Běifāng chūn xià qiū dōng sìjì fēnmíng. Dōngtiān bǐjiào cháng, huì guāfēng, yě huì xiàxuě.**

SHĀLÌ: **Běijīng de dōngtiān tài lěng le. Wǒ dì yí cì lái de shíhòu, Běijīng xiàle dà xuě. Wǒ de yīfu dài de bú gòu, lěng de zhí fādǒu, hòulái hái gǎnmào le.**

XIĂOYĪNG: **Nǐ yīnggāi qiūtiān lái. Běijīng de qiūtiān zuì měi. Tiānqì bù lěng yě bú rè, fēicháng shūfu.**

SHĀLÌ: **Wǒ shàng cì jiù shì qiūtiān lái de. Wǒ jìde shù shàng de yèzi dōu hóng le, zhēnde fēicháng piàoliang.**

XIĂOYĪNG: **Nǐ xiànzài duì Běijīng de tiānqì xíguàn bù xíguàn? Xíguàn xīn de qìhòu qǐmǎ yě yào bàn nián. Nǐ xíguàn bù xíguàn?**

SHĀLÌ: **Xiànzài xíguàn le.**

XIAOYING: Sally, what is the area around your hometown like?

SALLY: I live in southern California. The temperature there is quite nice—it doesn't snow all year long.

XIAOYING: That sounds a lot like the south of China. The weather there is as warm as southern California.

SALLY: What are the differences between the north and south of China?

XIAOYING: The temperature in China's south is high, twice as hot as in the north, and the environment is quite humid. In the north, all the seasons are different. The winters are long and very windy and snowy.

SALLY: The winters in Beijing are too cold! When I first came here, there was a lot of snow and I didn't have the right kind of clothes so I was shivering and caught a bad cold.

XIAOYING: You should come in the autumn, that's the prettiest time in Beijing. It's not too cold and not too hot, quite comfortable.

SALLY: The last time I came was in autumn and the leaves turned bright red. It was very pretty.

XIAOYING: Are you used to the weather in Beijing now? Getting used to a new climate takes at least half a year. Are you used to it?

SALLY: Oh yes, it's much better.

B. YǓFǍ HÉ YÒNGFǍ

1. YǑU . . . NÀME . . .

This construction is used to express that two things or two people have the same quality or property. This concept is expressed in English with "as . . . as . . . ," as full as, as much as, etc. The structure in a sentence is noun + *yǒu* + noun + *nàme* + verb. As with other sentences with *yǒu* (to have) as the main verb, the negative is formed by adding *méi* before *yǒu*. Questions can be formed by adding *ma* at the end of a sentence or with *yǒu méiyǒu*.

Zhōngguó nánfāng yǒu Jiāzhōu nàme nuǎnhuo.
   The south of China is as temperate as California.

Zhāng xiānsheng yǒu Lǐ xiānsheng nàme gāo.
Mr. Zhang is as tall as Mr. Li.

Wǒ méiyǒu tā nàme yǒu shíjiān.
I don't have as much time as he does.

Nǐ yǒu méiyǒu tā nàme máng?
Are you as busy as she is?

2. *YǑU . . . BÈI . . .*

This construction is used to express that a noun is a certain number of times (*bèi*) more of something than another noun. These types of sentences are formed in this way: noun + *yǒu* + noun + number + *bèi* + (*nàme*) + adjective. *Nàme* (as) is optional in these types of sentences.

Běijīng yǒu Měiguó Luódé Dǎo de liǎng bèi dà.
Beijing is twice as big as Rhode Island.

Wǒ jiā dào gōngsī yǒu nǐ jiā dào gōngsī de sān bèi yuǎn.
It is three times as far from my house to work than it is from your house.

Nǐ de xuéxiào yǒu tā de xuéxiào liǎng bèi dà ma?
Is your school twice as big as his?

3. THE ADVERB *QǏMǍ*

Qǐmǎ (at least) comes after the subject of the sentence and is usually followed by *yě* (also).

Xuéhǎo hànyǔ qǐmǎ yě yào sān nián.
It takes at least three years to learn Chinese well.

Nǐ qǐmǎ yě děi qù kànkan tā.
You at least have to go see him.

Zhè zhǒng píngguǒ yí ge qǐmǎ yě yào yí kuài qián.
Each of this type of apple costs at least one yuan.

4. EXPRESSING NORTH, SOUTH, EAST, WEST

The terms for points of the compass are *běi* (north); *nán* (south); *dōng* (east), and *xī* (west). In directional phrases in English, north and south come before east and west; i.e., northeast and southwest. In Chinese, the opposite is the case: *dōng* and *xī* come before *běi* and *nán*.

Zhōngguó dōngběi hěn lěng.
The northeast of China is cold.

Xīnán yǔ xià de hěn duō.
It rains a lot in the southwest.

C. HÀNZÌ

New characters.

北	*běi* (north)
南	*nán* (south)
东	*dōng* (east)
西	*xī* (west)
方	*fāng* (place)
最	*zuì* (most)

Sentence practice:

中国西方最有意思。
Zhōngguó xīfāng zuì yǒu yìsi.
The west of China is the most interesting.

我要去美国西南。
Wǒ yào qù Měiguó xīnán.
I want to go to the southwest of the U.S.

美国东北秋天很美。
Měiguó dōngběi qiūtiān hěn měi.
Autumn in the northeast of the U.S. is pretty.

D. SHĒNGCÍ

běifāng	north
cháoshī	humid
chūn	spring
cóngbù	never
dìlǐ	geography
dōng	winter
fādǒu	to shiver, tremble
fēnmíng	distinct
guāfēng	windy

huánjìng	environment
Jiāzhōu	California
liángkuài	cool
nánfāng	south
nuǎnhuo	warm
qìhòu	climate
qìwēn	air temperature
shù	tree
sìjì	four seasons
wēndù	temperature
xiàxuě	to snow
xuě	snow
yèzi	leaves
zhēnde	really, truly
zhí	continuously

LIÀNXÍ

A. Fill in the blanks according to the dialogue.

1. *Nán Jiāzhōu de qìhòu hěn hǎo, cóng bú xià _____.*
2. *Zhōngguó _____ de tiānqì bǐjiào nuǎnhuo.*
3. *Zhōngguó běifāng _____ sìjì fēnmíng.*
4. *Běijīng de qiūtiān zuì _____. Tiānqì bù _____ yě bù _____.*
5. *Dōngtiān yīfu chuān bú gòu, huì lěng de zhí _____.*

B. Choose from the words below to fill in the blanks.

fēnmíng nuǎnhuo běifāng xiàxuě cóngbù zhēnde

Mr. Lǐ lives in Suzhou in southern China. Mr. Wang lives in Xi'an in northern China.

Wáng: *Lǐ xiānsheng, Sūzhōu nàr de qìhòu zěnmeyàng?*
Lǐ: *Nàr de tiānqì bǐjiào _____, yìnián sìjì _____ xiàxuě. Xi'ān ne?*
Wáng: *Xi'ān zài Zhōngguó de _____, sìjì _____. Dōngtiān cháng _____.*
Lǐ: *Nǐ yīnggāi lái Sūzhōu wánr. Wǒmen nàr _____ fēicháng piàoliàng.*
Wáng: *Wǒ yídìng huì qù.*

C. Answer the following questions with the words provided in parentheses.

1. *Nǐ xíguàn xiàxuě de tiānqì ma (duì . . . xíguàn)*
2. *Nán Jiāzhōu chūntiān de tiānqì lěng háishì rè? (bù . . . yě bù)*
3. *Měiguó běifāng de dōngtiān guā bù guāfēng? xià bú xià xuě? (yòu . . . yòu)*
4. *Zhōngguó de nánfāng xià bú xiàxuě? (cóngbù)*

D. Write the following in Chinese characters.

1. The north is the coldest.
2. The southeast is the most interesting.
3. My hospital is the most comfortable.

WÉNHUÀ ZHÙJIĚ

The weather is a source of many conversations in China, much like anywhere else. One phrase that you will hear quite often in the north in winter is *duō chuān yīfú!* (Wear more clothes!) No one wants to catch a cold and in China the way to prevent this is to wear six pairs of wool long underwear and big overcoats. The weather in China is much like the weather in the United States. Beijing has very hot summers and very cold winters, like New York, and the south is hot and humid all year, like Florida. You can buy any kind of weather gear, raincoats, etc., in China—except shoes! If you need warm boots, bring your own. Shoe sizes are much smaller in China than in the United States.

DÁÀN

A. 1. *xuě* 2. *nánfāng* 3. *chūn, xià, qiū, dōng* 4. *měi, lěng, rè* 5. *fādǒu*

B. *nuǎnhuo, cóngbù, běifāng, fēnmíng, xiàxuě, zhēnde*

C. 1. *Wǒ duì xiàxuě de tiānqì xíguàn.* 2. *Nán Jiāzhōu de tiānqì bù lěng yě bù rè.* 3. *Měiguó běifāng de dōngtiān yòu guāfēng yòu xiàxuě.* 4. *Zhōngguó de nánfāng cóngbù xiàxuě.*

D. 1.北方最冷。 2.东南最有意思。 3.我的医院最舒服。

DÌ SĀNSHÍWǓ KÈ
Lesson 35
YĪFÚ. Clothes.

A. DUÌHUÀ

XIÀYǓ LE!

The weather has changed dramatically lately in Beijing. Wang Ling and her friend Chen Qing talk about the rapid changes.

WÁNG LÍNG: **Zuìjìn de tiānqì zhēn guài. Yīhuǐr chū tàiyáng, rè de bù dé liǎo; yīhuǐr yòu lěng de yào chuān wàitào.**

CHÉN QĪNG: **Gāngcái qìxiàng yùbào hái shūo míngtiān yào kāishǐ xiàyǔ ne.**

WÁNG LÍNG: **Nánguài zhè jǐ tiān zhème mēn. Búgùo xià diǎn yǔ yě hǎo, tiānqì bǐjiào liángkuài.**

CHÉN QĪNG: **Kěshì chūmén de shíhòu hěn máfan. Bù zhīdào dàodǐ yīnggāi chuān hòu yìdiǎnr de yīfu, háishì báo yìdiǎnr de yīfu; yě bù zhīdào yīnggāi bù yīnggāi dài yǔsǎn.**

WÁNG LÍNG: **Qíshí xià diǎn yǔ yě tǐng yǒu yìsi de.**

CHÉN QĪNG: **Wǒ kě bù juéde. Shàngge xīngqī wǒ chuān le yíjiàn xīn yīfu chūmén. Hūrán qīngpén dàyǔ. Wǒ wàngle dài sǎn, yíxiàzi jiù chéng le "luò tāng jī," xīn yīfu yě bàofèi le.**

WÁNG LÍNG: **Zhèyàng nǐ cái kěyǐ zài mǎi yíjiàn ya!**

IT'S RAINING!

WANG LING: The weather's been very strange lately. One minute the sun is out and it's extremely hot. The next minute it is so cold that we need to wear coats.

CHEN QING: The weather forecast just reported that it's going to rain tomorrow.

293

WANG LING: No wonder it's been so humid. Well, it would be better to get some rain—it'll get cooler.

CHEN QING: But it's inconvenient when going out. I never know when to wear heavy clothes or light clothes and also whether or not to bring an umbrella.

WANG LING: Actually, I think it's kind of fun to get wet.

CHEN QING: I don't feel the same way. Last week I wore new clothes to go out and suddenly it was raining cats and dogs. I forgot to bring an umbrella and was drenched in no time. My clothes were ruined.

WANG LING: Now you have an excuse to buy new clothes!

B. YŮFǍ HÉ YÒNGFǍ

1. THE EXPRESSION *YĪHUĬR . . . YĪHUĬR*

Yīhuĭr . . . yīhuĭr (one moment . . . the next moment) can express that two things are happening at the same time or that one thing follows another surprisingly quickly.

Xiǎo háizi yīhuĭr chànggē, yīhuĭr tiàowǔ, wánde hěn gāoxìng.
   The children sang and danced; they had a good time.

Jīntiān tiānqì yīhuĭr rè, yīhuĭr lěng, bù zhīdào yào chuān shénme yīfu.
   One minute it's hot, one minute it's cold. I just don't know what to wear.

Tā yīhuĭr shuō yào qù, yīhuĭr shuō búqù, tā dàodǐ qù búqù?
   One minute he says he's going, the next minute that he's not going — is he or not?

2. RESULTATIVE VERBS WITH LONGER DESCRIPTIVE PHRASES

You have already learned about several types of resultative verbs. Remember that these verbs follow the construction verb + *de* + adjective, like in the sentence *wǒ chī de wán* (I am able to finish eating). A more complex type of this sentence includes an entire phrase after the particle *de* that explains in detail the result of the action of the verb.

Jīntiān lěng de yào chuān wàitào.
   It is so cold today that I want to wear an overcoat.

294

Tā máng de méiyǒu shíjiān shuìjiào.
He is so busy that he doesn't have time to sleep.

Tā gāoxìng de bù néng shuìjiào.
He was too happy to fall asleep.

3. *DE BÙ DÉ LIǍO*

De bù dé liǎo (extremely) is a common colloquial expression used in place of a descriptive phrase in complex resultative expressions.

Zhè bù diànyǐng, tā xǐhuan de bù dé liǎo.
He really likes this movies.

Jīntiān de tiānqì rè de bù dé liǎo.
The weather today is extremely hot.

Zhè zhǒng shì, máfan de bù dé liǎo, wǒ bù xiǎng zuò.
This thing is extremely annoying, I don't want to do it.

4. *KĚ*

Kě is an important little word that doesn't have a meaning in and of itself, but serves in many different situations to add emphasis. It can be placed in front of any verb or adjective to imply "very." In this case, *kě* is a much stronger choice than *hěn* (very) as it also expresses surprise.

Jīntiān tiānqì kě lěng a!
I can't believe it's so cold today!

Nǐ de chéngjī kě zhēn hǎo!
I can't believe your grades are so good!

When *kě* is used as an adverb in a complex sentence, it also expresses surprise and contradiction.

Tā bù xǐhuan, wǒ kě xǐhuan.
He doesn't like it, but I sure do!

Tā wàngle dài yǔsǎn, wǒ kě méi wàng!
He forgot his umbrella, but I didn't.

Tā dǒng, wǒ kě bù dǒng.
He understands, but I don't!

Wǒ kě méiyǒu shuōguò zhè zhǒng huà.
Of course, I could never say this kind of thing!

C. HÀNZÌ

New characters.

天气	*tiānqì* (weather)
热	*rè* (hot)
冷	*lěng* (cold)
暖和	*nuǎnhuo* (temperate)
下雨	*xiàyǔ* (to rain)
凉快	*liángkuài* (cool)

Sentence practice.

今天(的)天气很冷。

Jīntiān (de) tiānqì hěn lěng.

It's very cold today.

下雨了！

Xiàyǔ le!

It's raining!

今年秋天的天气很凉快。

Jīnnián qiūtiān de tiānqì hěn liángkuài.

The autumn was quite cool this year.

D. SHĒNGCÍ

báo	light, thin
bàofèi	dregs, scraps
bù dé liǎo	extremely
dàodǐ	finally, in the final analysis
guài	strange
hòu	thick
hūrán	suddenly
juéde	to feel, to think
liángkuài	cool (temperature)
luò tāng jī	like a drowned rat, drenched
mēn	humid and stuffy
nánguài	no wonder
qíshí	in fact, actually
qìxiàng yùbào	weather forecast
qīngpén dàyǔ	a heavy rain

296

qǔxiào	to ridicule
xiàxuě	to snow
xiàyǔ	to rain
yīhuǐr	a little while, in a moment
yíxiàzi	all of a sudden
yǔ	rain
yǔsǎn	umbrella

SUPPLEMENTARY VOCABULARY 9: CLOTHES

chángkù	pants
duǎnkù	shorts
fēngyī	raincoat
hànshān	T-shirt
jiákè	jacket
kùzi	pants
máoyī	sweater
màozi	hat
nèiyī	underwear
niúzǎikù	jeans
pídài	belt
qiúxié	tennis shoes, sneakers
qúnzi	skirt
shǒutào	gloves
tuōxié	slippers
wàitào	coat
wàzi	socks
xiézi	shoes
yīfu	dress
yùndòngshān	sweatshirt

LIÀNXÍ

A. Fill in the blanks based on the dialogue.

1. *Zuìjìn de tiānqì zhēn _____. _____ rè, yīhuǐr _____.*
2. *_____ yùbào shuō míngtiān huì _____, suǒyǐ chūmén bié wàngle dài sǎn.*
3. *Chén qīng _____ le dài sǎn, suǒyǐ chéng le _____.*
4. *Wáng Líng xǐhuan xiàyǔ. Tā shuō _____ yě tǐng yǒu yìsi de.*

B. Translate the following sentences into English.

1. *Zhè jǐ tiān de tiānqì mēn de bù dé liǎo.*
2. *Wǒ yǐwéi jīntiān huì hěn rè, qíshí hěn lěng.*
3. *Míngtiān wǒ dàodǐ yīnggāi chuān hòu yìdiǎn de yīfu, háishì báo yìdiǎn de yīfu?*

C. Write the English equivalents.

1. 热
2. 天气
3. 得不得了
4. 闷
5. 凉快
6. 冷
7. 有意思
8. 舒服

WÉNHUÀ ZHÙJIĚ

Clothing styles have changed in China over the years, as they have everywhere else. During the Cultural Revolution of the 1960s and 1970s, everyone wore the same plain "Mao" suit, the clothes of the masses. You might still spot one of these outfits in certain parts of China, but in the bigger cities clothes are much more modern. Jeans are highly desirable, especially among young people. Generally, though, people dress more formally in China than they do in the U.S. Women wear long skirts and high-heeled shoes even when they go out for a walk in the park. Men favor polyester slacks and button-down shirts. It is not recommended to show too much skin in China—short skirts and shorts are becoming more common, but attitudes are still on the traditional side. Just look around at what other people are wearing to get a sense of what is appropriate.

DÁÀN

A. 1. *guài, yīhuǐr, lěng* 2. *Qìxiàng, xiàyǔ* 3. *wàng, luòtāng jī* 4. *línyǔ*

B. 1. These past few days have been extremely humid and stuffy. 2. I thought it was going to be hot today but it turned out to be very cold. 3. Should I wear heavy or light clothes tomorrow?

C. 1. hot 2. weather 3. extremely 4. humid 5. cool 6. cold 7. interesting 8. comfortable

FÙXÍ 7

A. Write the following in *pīnyīn*.

1. The weather is becoming colder and colder.
2. The taller she gets, the more beautiful she gets.
3. Clothes are getting more and more expensive.
4. Your hair just gets longer and longer!

B. Select *ràng, bèi* or *shòu* to fill the spaces. When there is more than one alternative, give them all.

1. _____ *jiàoyù de rén piānjiàn yīnggāi shǎo yìxiē.*
2. *Wǒ gàosù tā bié zhèyàng zuò, suǒyǐ* _____ *tā mà le yíxià.*
3. *Háizi dōu hěn róngyì* _____ *piàn.*

C. Combine the two sentences using *de* + a descriptive verb phrase.

1. *Jīntiān de tiānqì hěn lěng. Wǒ yào chuān hěn duō yīfu.*
2. *Zhè ge kǎoshì hěn nán. Wǒ bú huì kǎo de hǎo.*
3. *Dàifu hěn cōngmíng. Wǒ yào tīng tā de huà.*

D. Translate the following into English.

1. *Zhāng xiānsheng yǒu Lǐ xiānsheng nàme gāo.*
2. *Nǐ de xuéxiào yǒu tā de xuéxiào de liǎng bèi dà ma?*
3. *Zhōngguó nánfāng yǒu Jiāzhōu nàme nuǎnhuo.*

E. Choose from the words below to fill in the blanks.

běnlái yíbèizi hébì gēnběn

1. *Tā* _____ *shì hǎo rén.*
2. *Wǒ* _____ *yào qù yínháng lǐng qián.*
3. *Tā* _____ *bú huì hē niúnǎi.*
4. *Nǐ* _____ *yě děi qù kànkan tā.*

F. Translate the signs below into Chinese characters.

> NO SMOKING
>
> EXIT
>
> CLOSED
>
> SHANGHAI PARK

G. Write the English equivalents.

1. 春天
2. 秋天
3. 冬天
4. 夏天
5. 上海
6. 公园
7. 东北
8. 西南

DÁÀN

A. 1. *Tiānqì yuè lái yuè lěng.* 2. *Tā yuè gāo yuè piàoliang.* 3. *Yīfu yuè lái yuè guì.* 4. *Nǐ tóufa yuè lái yuè cháng a!*

B. 1. *shòu* 2. *bèi* 3. *bèi*

C. 1. *Jīntiān de tiānqì lěng de yào chuān hěn duō yīfu.* 2. *Zhège kǎoshì nán de bú huì kǎo de hǎo.* 3. *Dàifu cōngmíng de yào tīng tā de huà.*

D. 1. Mr. Zhang is as tall as Mr. Li. 2. Is your school twice as big as hers? 3. The south of China is as warm as California.

E. 1. *gēnběn* 2. *hébì* 3. *yí bēizi* 4. *běnlái*

F. 1. 勿吸烟 2. 出口 3. 不开放 4. 上海公园

G. 1. spring 2. autumn 3. winter 4. summer 5. Shanghai 6. park 7. northeast 8. southwest

DÌ SĀNSHÍLIÙ KÈ
Lesson 36

QÙ GŌNGYUÁN. A Trip to the Park.

A. DUÌHUÀ

ZÀI SHÀNGHǍI DE WÀITĀN.

Amy and David Stone take a trip to Shanghai with their friends the Wangs.

WÁNG TÀITAI: Wǒ tīngshuō Wàitān de hěnduō jiànzhù gēn xīfāng de hěn xiàng. Shì zhēnde ma?

AÌMÉI: Shì zhēnde. Shànghǎi zhēn shì "dōngfāng de Bālí."

WÁNG TÀITAI: Zhège chéngshì shì Zhōngguó zuì kāifàng de. Hái yǒu Màidāngláo, hái kěyǐ mǎi dào suǒyǒu xīfāng de yīfu, qìchē, chǎnpǐn, děng děng. Xīfāng de yǐngxiǎng yǒu hǎochù, yě yǒu huàichù.

AÌMÉI: Wǒ tóngyì. Wǒmen zài Zhōngguó de shíhòu liǎojie dào dōngfāng de sīxiǎng yǒu hěn duō gēn xīfāng bù yíyàng. Háizi zài zhèr hěn zhòngyào, "xiǎo huángdì" méi yǒu bǎomǔ. Měiguó rén xǐhuan bǎ àiwù yǎng zài jiā lǐ. Hǎoxiàng Zhōngguórén méiyǒu àiwù.

WÁNG TÀITAI: Duì le. Wǒmen juéde yǎng àiwù yǒu yìdiǎnr qíguài. Ránér, xiànzài ne yǒu de rén xǐhuan yǎng xiǎogǒu. Érqiě, yú biǎoshì xìngyùn.

AÌMÉI: Wǒ tǐng xǐhuan àiwù. Wǒmen zài Měiguó yǒu yì zhī māo.

WÁNG TÀITAI: Hǎo. Wǒmen qù kànkan gōngyuán de yú chítáng ba.

———————————

ON THE BUND.

MRS. WANG: I've heard that the buildings along the Bund are a lot like those in the West. Is that true?

AMY: Yes. Shanghai really is the "Paris of the East."

302

MRS. WANG: This is the most open city in China. There's also McDonald's here and you can buy all kinds of Western clothes, cars and other products. Western influence has good points but it also has bad points.

AMY: I agree. While we've been in China, I've learned that Eastern thought is very different from Western. Children are important here: no baby-sitters for the "little emperors"! Americans also like to keep pets at home. It seems like Chinese people don't have any.

MRS. WANG: True. We think that raising pets is a little strange. However, some people are keeping puppies now. Also, fish symbolize good fortune.

AMY: I love pets. We have a cat in the U.S.

MRS. WANG: Great. Let's go look at the park's fishpond.

B. YǓFǍ HÉ YÒNGFǍ

1. *HǍOCHÙ* AND *HUÀICHÙ*

Hǎo (good) and *huài* (bad) can both be paired with *chù* (strong point) to mean, respectively, "good point" or "bad point." Each of these terms takes the verb *yǒu* (to have) and they often appear together.

Jiéhūn yǒu hǎochù yě yǒu huàichù.
Getting married has it good points and its bad points.

Hē jiǔ yǒu shénme hǎochù?
What are the good points of drinking?

Nǐ wèishénme juéde zhège dìfang yǒu huàichù?
Why do you think this place has such bad points?

2. THE CONJUNCTION *RÁNÉR*

The conjunction *ránér* (however) usually appears at the beginning of a sentence to contradict the previous sentence.

Wǒmen juéde yǎng àiwù yǒu yìdiǎnr qíguài. Ránér, xiànzài yǒu de rén xǐhuan yǎng xiǎogǒu.
We think that raising pets is a little strange. However, now there are people who like to raise puppies.

Tā bù xǐhuan chī niúròu. Ránér, tā yǒu de shíhòu qù Màidāngláo.
He doesn't like to eat beef. However, sometimes he goes to McDonald's.

3. MORE ABOUT CHINESE EXPRESSIONS

Expressions in every language are based on the culture. In this lesson's dialogue, you learned the expression *"xiǎo huángdì,"* which means "little emperor." In the past, emperors were the highest rulers in China. Today, little emperors are spoiled children who command all the attention of their parents.

Other Chinese expressions and words come from the concept of *yīn* and *yáng*, which are the two opposing elements of the universe. *Yīn* represents, to express it in very simplistic terms, the feminine forces of the universe, while *yáng* represents the masculine forces. *Yīn* is written with a moon radical (see *hànzì* section) and *yáng* is written with a sun radical. Much of Chinese philosophy is based on maintaining a balance between *yīn* and *yáng*. The following terms and expressions will illustrate how these concepts are evidenced in the language.

yīnyáng guàiqì
    deliberately enigmatic [literally, "yin and yang strangely matched"]

yīnliáng
    shady and cool

yīnsēn
    gloomy

yángsǎn
    parasol

tàiyáng
    sun

C. HÀNZÌ

Radicals are the parts of Chinese characters that most directly relate to the meaning. If you learn what some of the most common radicals mean, you might be able to determine the general meaning of a character. The radical of a character is usually the left-hand series of strokes.

Radicals are also important to know when you learn to use a Chinese dictionary. When you look up a character in a dictionary, you first need to count the number of strokes in the radical, then find the radical in a table to find where it is located on another table. Then you count the strokes in the rest of the character and find it in another table which will tell you the page number where you can locate the meaning of the word. It is a complicated process! To give you a head start, look at the following radicals to see what kind of meaning they lend to a character.

氵 Characters with this radical have something to do with water or liquid.

海	*hǎi* (ocean)
河	*hé* (river)
酒	*jiǔ* (liquor)
上海	*Shànghǎi* [literally, "on the ocean"]

犭 This radical relates to animals.

狗	*gǒu* (dog)
猫	*māo* (cat)

钅 This one has to do with metal.

钱	*qián* (money)
铁	*tiě* (iron)

月 This is the moon radical which indicates a *yīn* element.

阴	*yīn*

日 Here is the sun radical for *yáng*.

阳	*yáng*

讠 This radical indicates that the character involves language.

说	*shuō* (to speak)
话	*huà* (speech)
语言	*yǔyán* (language)

D. SHĒNGCÍ

àiwù	pets
Bālí	Paris
bǎomǔ	baby-sitter
biǎoshì	symbolize
chǎnpǐn	products
chítáng	pond
dàgài	probably

dōngfāng	the East, Asia
érqiě	in addition
gōngyuán	park
gǒu	dog
hǎochù	good characteristics
huàichù	bad characteristics
huángdì	emperor
kāifàng	open, open-minded
Màidāngláo	McDonald's
māo	cat
Ōuzhōu	Europe
ránér	however
tóngyì	to agree
Wàitān	the bund in Shanghai
xìngyùn	good fortune
yǎng	to raise
yǐngxiǎng	influence
zhī	[measure word for animals]

SUPPLEMENTARY VOCABULARY 10: ANIMALS

hǔ	tiger
láng	wolf
lǘ	donkey
mǎ	horse
niǎo	bird
niú	cow
qīngwā	frog
shé	snake
shī	lion
shǔ	mouse
tù	rabbit
xiàng	elephant
xiǎogǒu	puppy
yīng	eagle

LIÀNXÍ

A. Translate into English.

1. *Wǒ ài nǐ. Ránér wǒ bú yào gēn nǐ jiéhūn.*
2. *Tā cóng Shànghǎi huílái le. Ránér tā hái méiyǒu gěi wǒ dǎ diànhuà.*
3. *Tā de háizi hěn hǎo. Ránér yǒu de shíhòu tā shì xiǎo huángdì.*

B. Match the *pīnyīn* to the English.

1. *mǎ*   a. rabbit
2. *tù*   b. elephant
3. *shǔ*   c. wolf
4. *xiàng*   d. horse
5. *láng*   e. cow
6. *niú*   f. mouse

C. Answer these questions using characters.

1. 你喜欢不喜欢狗？
2. 你去过上海没有？
3. 你知道阴阳是什么意思吗？

D. Write the radical that corresponds to these categories.

1. metal
2. water
3. sun
4. animals
5. language
6. moon

WÉNHUÀ ZHÙJIĚ

The concept of owning a pet is quite new in China. A fish tank in the home or family-run business is thought to bring good luck; there are also practical advantages to having fresh fish around for meals. The resistance to pets in general is probably practical as well—why buy more food for the household than you need to? Recently, having a small dog as a pet has become something of a status symbol. These dogs are expensive and show that there is an excess of food in the house. Crickets, which symbolize longevity, are sometimes kept by children. In the southern parts of China, you will see men selling crickets in little baskets: they string hundreds of them together on poles and walk around the streets making a lot of noise.

You have probably heard that people in China enjoy dining on good dog every once in a while. While you can get stir fried dog or a nice dog stew if you want it, many Chinese people don't go in for it. Most expensive restaurants have "exotic" items like dog or cat, but they are not culinary staples in China.

DÁÀN

A. 1. I love you. However, I don't want to marry you. 2. She came back from Shanghai. However, she still hasn't called me. 3. His kid is great. However, sometimes he's a "little emperor."

B. 1.d 2.a 3.f 4.b 5.c 6.e

C. 1.我（不）喜欢狗。2.我（沒有）去过上海。3.我（不）知道阴阳的意思。

D. 1. 钅 2. 氵 3. 日 4. 犭 5. 讠 6. 月

DÌ SĀNSHÍQĪ KÈ
Lesson 37

MIÁOSHÙ. Giving Descriptions.

A. DUÌHUÀ

ZÀI SHŪDIÀN DE FÚWÙ TÁI QIÁN.

Mrs. Zhang lost sight of her son at the bookstore so she went to the information desk to ask for help.

ZHĀNG TÀITAI: **Xiānsheng, wǒ de érzi bú jiàn le. Zěnme bàn? Qǐng bāng wǒ zhǎozhao.**

JǏNGWÈI: **Tàitai, bié zhāojí. Nǐ xiān gàosù wǒ, nǐ de érzi jiào shénme míngzi? Zhǎng de shénme yàngzi? Jīnnián jǐsuì le?**

ZHĀNG TÀITAI: **Tā jiào Zhāng Xiǎomíng. Jīnnián jiǔ suì. Tā zhǎng de bú tài gāo, dàgài yì mǐ sān bā. Rén shòushou de.**

JǏNGWÈI: **Tā chuān shénme yīfu?**

ZHĀNG TÀITAI: **Tā chuān yí jiàn bái shàngyī, yì tiáo lán duǎnkù, hé yí jiàn huáng wàitào. Wǒmen gāngcái zài nàr kànkan shū. Yì zhuǎnyǎn, tā jiù bú jiàn le.**

JǏNGWÈI: **Zhāng tàitai, bié zhāojí. Wǒ mǎshàng tōngzhī dàjiā yìqǐ zhǎo.**

XIǍOMÍNG: **Māma! Wǒ yào mǎi zhè běn shū!**

ZHĀNG TÀITAI: **Xiǎomíng, nǐ pǎo dào nǎr qù le? Māma jí huài le.**

XIǍOMÍNG: **Wǒ qù kànkan nèibiān piàoliang de shū. Wǒ yě kàndào jǐ zhāng zhǐ. Wǒmen kě bù kěyǐ mǎi?**

ZHĀNG TÀITAI: **Wǒmen yì zhāng zhǐ dōu bù mǎi. Xiǎomíng, nǐ yǐhòu juéduì bù kěyǐ dàochù luàn pǎo. Zhīdào ma?**

XIǍOMÍNG: **Duìbùqǐ, māma.**

AT THE BOOKSTORE'S INFORMATION DESK.

MRS. ZHANG: Sir, my son has disappeared. What should I do? Please help me look.

SECURITY GUARD: Don't worry, ma'am. First tell me, what's your son's name? What does he look like? How old is he?

MRS. ZHANG: His name is Zhang Xiaoming. He's nine years old and isn't very tall, about 1.3 meters. He's also quite thin.

SECURITY GUARD: What is he wearing?

MRS. ZHANG: He's wearing a white shirt, blue shorts and a yellow jacket. We were just over there looking at books. All of a sudden, he disappeared.

SECURITY GUARD: Stay calm, Mrs. Zhang. I'll immediately notify everybody to look together.

XIAOMING: Mom! I want to buy this book!

MRS. ZHANG: Xiaoming, where did you run to? Mom was worried sick.

XIAOMING: I was looking at those pretty books. I also saw some paper. Can we buy some?

MRS. ZHANG: We are not going to buy a single sheet. Xiaoming, don't ever wander around by yourself again. Understand?

XIAOMING: Sorry, Mom.

B. YǓFǍ HÉ YÒNGFǍ

1. REDUPLICATION OF MEASURE WORDS

Repeating *yī* plus a measure word after the noun gives the meaning "one after another."

Gōngrén yí ge yí ge dōu qù gōngzuò.
   The workers go to work one after the other.

Tā yì běn yì běn de xiě xiǎoshuō.
   He writes novels one after the other.

2. XIÀNG VS. HǍOXIÀNG

The verbs *xiàng* and *hǎoxiàng* seem similar, but there are subtle differences in meaning. *Xiàng* means "to resemble" and *hǎoxiàng* means "to seem."

Tā xiàng tā bàba.
  He looks like his father.

Nàge lǎoshī bú xiàng zhège lǎoshī.
  That teacher is not like this teacher.

Hǎoxiàng yào xiàyǔ.
  It looks like it's going to rain.

Nǐ hǎoxiàng bìng le.
  You seem sick.

3. REVIEW OF THE USES OF *LE*

Remember that the most significant use of *le* is to indicate that an event has already taken place or has changed in some way. This roughly corresponds to the past tense in English. Usually when *le* is placed at the end of a sentence, it indicates a specific past event.

Xiǎomíng, nǐ pǎo dào nǎr qù le?
  Xiaoming, where did you go?

Māma jí huài le.
  Mom was worried.

Wǒ wǎnfàn chīhǎo le.
  I finished eating dinner.

Le can also follow a verb immediately to show that something happened at a nonspecific point in the past.

Wǒ chīle hěn duō.
  I ate a lot.

When a change is about to occur, *le* is also used to indicate a change of state and is placed at the end of a sentence.

Huǒchē kuài zǒu le.
  The train is about to leave.

311

The construction *tài . . . le* is not related to the above concept of change of state or past tense but rather is used to emphasize a point.

Wǒ tài lèi le!
  I'm so tired!

Nèi běn shū tài hǎo le!
  That book is great!

C. HÀNZÌ

Read these new characters.

书店	*shūdiàn* (bookstore)
纸	*zhǐ* (paper)
张	*zhāng* (measure word for paper)
象	*xiàng* (to resemble)
笔	*bǐ* (pen)

Sentence practice.

我要买一张纸。
Wǒ yào mǎi yì zhāng zhǐ.
  I want to buy a piece of paper.

你好象我的弟弟。
Nǐ hǎoxiàng wǒ de dìdi.
  You resemble my little brother.

D. SHĒNGCÍ

bái	white
bàn	to handle, to manage
běn	measure word for books, volume
dài	to bring
dàjiā	everybody
dàochù	at all places, everywhere
duǎnkù	shorts
érzi	son
fúwù tái	information booth
guòlái	to come over
huáng	yellow

jí	to worry, worried
jǐngwèi	security guard
juéduì	absolutely
lán	blue
mǐ	meter [unit of measurement]
pǎo	to run
shàngyī	top (shirt)
shòu	thin
shūdiàn	bookstore
tōngzhī	to inform
yàngzi	appearance
yíqiè	everything
zhāng	[measure word for paper]
zhǎng	to grow
zhāojí	to be worried
zhǐ	paper
Zhuǎnyǎn	in the twinkle of an eye

LIÀNXÍ

A. Answer the following questions with the descriptive phrases provided in parentheses.

1. *Nǐ chànggē chàng de zěnmeyàng? (pàoliang)*
2. *Jīntiān de lánqiú dǎ de zěnmeyàng? (jīngcǎi)*
3. *Zhāng tàitai de yú zuò de zěnmeyàng? (hǎochī)*
4. *Nǐ dìdi chē kāi de zěnmeyàng? (kuài)*

B. Introduce the following items with the words provided in parentheses.

1. *Nǐ gēge* _____. (a bit thin)
2. *Tā de chē* _____. (sort of small)
3. *Wǒ jīntiān* _____. (kind of tired)
4. *Zhè jiàn shàngyī* _____. (yellowish)

C. Fill in the blanks using the given quantity and proper classifiers.

1. _____ *shàngyī* (2)
2. _____ *kùzi* (1)
3. _____ *dàyī* (3)

4. _____ *màozi* (5)
5. _____ *lǐngdài* (4)
6. _____ *wàzi* (10)

D. Translate the following sentences into *pīnyīn*.

1. What does your father look like?
2. Never run around by yourself.
3. Don't worry. Everything is fine.
4. In the twinkle of an eye, Mr. Wang disappeared.

E. Write the English equivalents.

1. 书店
2. 一本书
3. 三张纸
4. 好象

WÉNHUÀ ZHÙJIĚ

At many department stores and small stores in China, you will find different desks for different purposes. These might be an information desk where you can ask for help finding various items (even children!). The system for purchasing items is also different in China—there is a two-step process: First, you take your items to a desk in whatever department or area in which they are found. The sales clerk will hold on to your items and give you a receipt to take to the cashier, a desk that is usually enclosed with glass. There you will pay for your items and be given another receipt that you have to take back to the area where you found the items in order to have them returned to you. At large stores, people collect receipts from every area before they pay and then go back and get everything they bought. It can be a long process!

DÁ ÀN

A. 1. *Wǒ chànggē chàng de hěn piàoliang.* 2. *Jīntiān de lánqiú dǎ de hěn jīngcǎi.*
   3. *Zhāng tàitai de yú zuò de hěn hǎochī.* 4. *Wǒ dìdi chē kāi de hěn kuài.*

B. 1. *Nǐ gēge shòushou de.* 2. *Tā de chē xiǎoxiao de.* 3. *Wǒ jīntiān lèilei de.*
   4. *Zhè jiàn shàngyī huánghuang de.*

C. 1. *liǎng jiàn* 2. *yì tiáo* 3. *sān jiàn* 4. *wǔ dǐng* 5. *sì tiáo* 6. *shí shuāng*

D. 1. *Nǐ de bàba zhǎng de shénme yàngzi.* 2. *Juéduì bù kěyǐ zìjǐ dàochù luàn pǎo.*
   3. *Bié zhāojí. Yíqiè dōu méi shì le.* 4. *Yì zhuǎnyǎn, Wáng xiānsheng jiù bújiàn le.*

E. 1. bookstore 2. one book 3. three pieces of paper 4. to seem

DÌ SĀNSHÍBĀ KÈ
Lesson 38
JIÀOYÙ. Education.

A. DUÌHUÀ

ZÀI SHÍ JIĀ.

The Stones are going back to the United States soon. Junmin goes over to their house to apologize for not being able to see them off at the airport because his son is preparing to take the all-important college entrance exams.

JŪNMÍN: **Míngtiān wǒ děi péi háizi qù gāokǎo, suǒyǐ bù néng dào jīchǎng sòng nǐ. Zhēn bàoqiàn, xiān zhù nǐ yílù píngān.**

SHÍ: **Méi guānxi. Nǐ gāngcái shuō nǐ háizi yào kǎo shénme?**

JŪNMÍN: **Tā jīnnián gāozhōng bìyè, yào cānjiā gāoxiào liánhé zhāoshēng. Zài Zhōngguó, xiǎng shàng dàxué děi kǎo gāokǎo.**

SHÍ: **Kǎole gāokǎo yǐhòu, zěnmeyàng?**

JŪNMÍN: **Děng kǎoshì chéngjī shōudào yǐhòu, xuéshēng jiù ànzhào fēnshù de gāodī, xuǎnzé zìjǐ xiǎng shàng de dàxué.**

SHÍ: **Kǎo bú shàng dàxué, zěnme bàn?**

JŪNMÍN: **Dì èr nián kěyǐ chóng kǎo, huòzhě shàng zhíyè jìshù xuéxiào.**

SHÍ: **Shàng xiǎoxué huòzhě zhōngxué yě yào kǎo ma?**

JŪNMÍN: **Yào kǎo gāozhōng. Zhǐyǒu xiǎoxué hé chūzhōng shì yìwù jiàoyù, bú yòng kǎo.**

SHÍ: **Wǒ juéde Zhōngguórén hěn zhòngshì jiàoyù, yě fēicháng zūnjìng lǎoshī.**

JŪNMÍN: **Shì a! Wǒmen cháng shuō "yí rì wéi shī, zhōngshēng wéi fù."**

AT THE STONES'.

JUNMIN: I need to go with my son to take the college entrance exam tomorrow so I can't see you off at the airport. I'm really sorry; I'll wish you bon voyage in advance.

STONE: Don't worry about it. Which exam did you say your son is going to take?

JUNMIN: He graduates from high school this year and needs to take the college entrance exam. In China, you have to take the college entrance exam in order to go to college.

STONE: What happens after he takes the exam?

JUNMIN: After getting their scores, students will choose the colleges they would like to go to depending on how well they did.

STONE: What if a student doesn't pass?

JUNMIN: He can try again the following year or go to a vocational school.

STONE: Do you need to take exams to get into primary or middle schools?

JUNMIN: We need to take an exam in order to get into high school, but primary and junior middle schools are both compulsory.

STONE: I think the Chinese pay special attention to education and also really respect their teachers.

JUNMIN: That's right. We often say "being a teacher for one day is like being a father for life."

B. YǓFǍ HÉ YÒNGFǍ

1. THE VERB *ZHÙ*

Zhù (to wish) is used mainly in sentences expressing good wishes for another person.

Zhù nǐ shēngrì kuàilè.
  Happy birthday to you!

Zhù nǐ yílù píngān.
  Bon voyage! (Literally, "Wishing you a road of peace.")

2. THE VERB *ÀNZHÀO*

The verb *ànzhào* means "to do according to," as in the following examples.

Nǐ yīnggāi ànzhào Zhāng jīnglǐ shuō de huà zuò.
    You should act according to what Manager Zhang says.

Nǐ ànzhào tā de fāngfǎ zuò shì, jiù bú huì cuò.
    If you work according to his methods, you can't go wrong.

Ànzhào tā de kànfǎ, nǐ bù yīnggāi huíqù.
    According to what he says, you shouldn't go back.

3. THE ADVERB *ZHǏHǍO*

The adverb *zhǐhǎo* is made up of *zhǐ* (only) and *hǎo* (good) and is used to indicate that that there is no other choice or possibility in a situation. It is found in a sentence directly after the subject of the first or second clause. Remember that the subject of the second clause can be deleted.

Tā bú qù, zhǐhǎo wǒmen qù.
    He won't go, so we had better go.

Wǒ yǐjīng méiyǒu gānjìng de yīfu le, zhǐhǎo xiànzài xǐ yīfu.
    I don't have any clean clothes, so I have no choice but to do laundry now.

Wǒ méiyǒu qián le, zhǐhǎo xiàng tā jiè qián.
    I don't have any more money, so the only thing I can do is borrow from him.

4. THE ADVERB *CHÓNG*

Chóng (again) is placed directly before the main verb of a sentence.

Nǐ zhège zuòcuò le, yīnggāi chóng zuò.
    You did this wrong, you should do this again.

Wǒ xiǎng chóng kàn zhè běn shū.
    I want to read this book again.

5. THE CONJUNCTION *ZHǏYÀO . . . JIÙ*

The conjunction *zhǐyào . . . jiù* can be translated as part of an "as long as . . . then" or "because . . . therefore" construction.

Zhǐyào tā lái, wǒ jiù gāoxìng le.
    As long as he comes, I will be happy.

Zhǐyào rènzhēn, jiù méiyǒu shénme zuò bù hǎo de.
As long as you work hard, there is nothing you can't do.

C. HÀNZÌ

New characters.

祝你一路平安。	*zhù nǐ yílù píngān* (bon voyage)
考试	*kǎoshì* (test)
机场	*jīchǎng* (airport)
飞机	*fēijī* (airplane)
不用	*bú yòng* (not necessary)

D. SHĒNGCÍ

ànzhào	according to
chéngjī	score, grade
chóng	over again
chūzhōng	junior high school
fēnshù	score
fù	father (classical)
gāodī	difference in degree
gāokǎo	college entrance exam
gāozhōng	high school
shōudào	to receive
suàn	to count
wéi	to become
xiǎoxué	primary school
yí bèizi	all your life
yílù píngān	bon voyage
yìwù jiàoyù	compulsory education
zhīshì	knowledge
zhíyè	occupation
zhōngshēng	the entire life
zhòngshì	to pay attention to, to attach importance to
zūnjìng	to pay respect to

SUPPLEMENTARY VOCABULARY 11:
SCHOOL SUBJECTS

dìlǐxué	geography
fǎxué	law
huàxué	chemistry
jǐhéxué	geometry
jīngjìxué	economics
kēxué	science
lìshǐ	history
shēngwùxué	biology
shùxué	math
wénxué	literature
wùlǐxué	physics
yǔyánxué	linguistics
zhéxué	philosophy
zhèngzhì xué	political science

LIÀNXÍ

A. Which of the statements are true based on the dialogue?

1. *Zhōngguórén hěn zhòngshì jiàoyù yě zūnjìng lǎoshī.*
2. *Zài Zhōngguó, xiǎoxué, chūzhōng hé gāozhōng dōu shì yìwù jiàoyù.*
3. *Zhōngguó xuéshēng xiǎng shàng dàxué, yídìng yào kǎo gāokǎo.*
4. *Zhōngguó xuéshēng kǎole gāokǎo yǐhòu, shénme dàxué dōu kěyǐ shàng.*

B. Which word or phase does not seem to fit in the group?

EXAMPLE: měi/ piàoliang/ hǎokàn/ gāoxìng

1. *xiǎoxué/ zhōngxué/ dàxué/ zhíyè*
2. *zhòngshì/ zhùyì/ suíbiàn*
3. *kāi wánxiào/ qǔxiào/ nào xiàohuà*
4. *bù gǎndāng/ bàoqiàn/ duìbùqǐ/ bù hǎo yìsi*

C. Respond to the following using the words provided in parentheses.

1. *Liú xiānshēng míngtiān qù Měiguó, nǐ yīnggāi shuō shénme? (Zhù...)*
2. *Wǒ gāokǎo kǎo de hái búcuò. Xiànzài yào zěnme bàn? (Ànzhào)*

3. *Xiǎo Wáng méi kǎoshàng dàxué. Xiànzài yīnggāi zěnme bàn? (zhǐhǎo)*
4. *Xiǎo Liú jīnnián gāozhōng bìyè. Tā xiǎng shàng dàxué, yīnggāi zěnme bàn? (děi)*

WÉNHUÀ ZHÙJIĚ

The competition among high school seniors to get into the best Chinese colleges is intense. Less than 10 percent of all of China's students are able to secure a place in a university, let alone in one of the best like Beijing University or Fudan University. The only criterion for getting into college is a grueling exam. Students put in long hours studying for this exam, and the pressure to succeed can be overwhelming. Suicide rates among students who do not pass is a problem. The students who do pass are then allowed to make a list of colleges that they want to attend, depending on their scores, and then they are eventually assigned schools. Education reform is increasingly becoming a priority in China—75 percent or so of the entire population lives in the countryside and has little opportunity for education beyond grammar school.

DÁÀN

A. 1.T 2.F 3.T 4.F

B. 1 *zhíyè* 2. *suíbiàn* 3. *nào xiàohuà* 4. *bù gǎndāng*

C. 1. *zhù nǐ yílù píngān* 2. *Nǐ kěyǐ ànzhào chéngjī xuǎnzé zìjǐ xiǎng shàng de dàxué.* 3. *Tā zhǐhǎo chóngkǎo huòzhě qù shàng zhíyè jìshù xuéxiào.* 4. *Tā děi kǎo gāokǎo.*

DÌ SĀNSHÍJIǓ KÈ
Lesson 39
TÁN JIĀNGLÁI. Talking About the Future.

A. DUÌHUÀ

ZÀI CHÁ GUǍN.

Xiaoying is going to graduate from college soon. Her American friend Sally is curious about the job-searching process in China.

SHĀLÌ: Xiǎoyīng, nǐ zài guò yí ge yuè yào bìyè le. Yǐhòu dǎsuàn zuò shénme?

XIǍOYĪNG: Hái méi juédìng. Wǒ xiǎng xiān xiěxie lǚlìbiǎo. Yàobùrán, qǐng bàba wèn tā péngyou de dānwèi yǒu méiyǒu kòngquē.

SHĀLÌ: Wǒ yǐwéi nǐmen bú yòng zhǎo gōngzuò. Xuéxiào huì bāng nǐmen ānpái gōngzuò dānwèi.

XIǍOYĪNG: Yǐqián shì zhèyàng de. Kěshì, xiànzài yǒu kòngquē de dānwèi yuè lái yuè shǎo, zhǐhǎo zìjǐ zhǎo.

SHĀLÌ: Zhōngguó de gōngsī jiěgù bù jiěgù zhíyuán?

XIǍOYĪNG: Jīběnshàng, zhèngfǔ jīguān shì bù jiěgù de. Kěshì, xiànzài hěn duō sīrén de gōngsī huì jiěgù rén.

SHĀLÌ: Nǐ zìjǐ zhǎo gōngzuò nán bù nán?

XIǍOYĪNG: Zhǐyào kěn gànhuó, yīnggāi bú tài nán.

SHĀLÌ: Nǐ dǎsuàn zài shénme gōngsī gōngzuò?

XIǍOYĪNG: Wǒ xiǎng zài zhōngwài hézī qǐyè gōngzuò. Yì fāngmiàn kěyǐ xuéxí rúhé gēn wàiguó rén zuò mǎimài, yì fāngmiàn kěyǐ shíjì liǎojiě wàimào yèwù wǎnglái de qíngkuàng.

SHĀLÌ: Nǐ de Zhōngwén hé Yīngwén dōu hěn hǎo, érqiě màoyì yòu shì nǐ de zhuānyè, wǒ xiāngxìn nǐ yídìng kěyǐ zhǎodào yí ge lǐxiǎng de gōngzuò.

XIǍOYĪNG: Xīwàng rúcǐ.

322

AT A TEAHOUSE.

SALLY: Xiaoying, you're going to graduate in a month. What do you plan to do?

XIAOYING: I haven't decided yet. I want to write a résumé first. Otherwise I'll ask my father if there are any vacancies at his friends' works units.

SALLY: I thought in China you didn't need to find jobs on your own—that your school would arrange a work unit for you.

XIAOYING: That's the way it was before. But now there are fewer work units with open positions. Most people have to look for jobs on their own.

SALLY: Do employees get fired in Chinese companies?

XIAOYING: Basically, there are no layoffs in government organizations. However, private companies will fire employees these days.

SALLY: Is it hard to find a job by yourself?

XIAOYING: As long as a person is willing to work hard, he shouldn't have a problem finding a job.

SALLY: What kind of company do you plan to work for?

XIAOYING: I would like to work for a joint-venture company. On one hand, I can learn how to do business with foreigners and, on the other hand, I can begin to understand the business activities related to international trade.

SALLY: Both your English and Chinese are good. Besides, trading is your specialty. I'm sure you'll find the ideal job.

XIAOYING: I hope so.

B. YǓFǍ HÉ YÒNGFǍ

1. ADDING *SHÀNG* TO A NOUN OR ADJECTIVE TO MAKE AN ADVERB

You can add *shàng* (above, on) to many nouns or adjectives to make an adverb. There is no rule for which nouns or adjectives can be changed in this way—just think about the nouns and adjectives that we tend to add "ly" to in English; there are similarities.

jīběnshàng
basically

lìshǐshàng
historically

jīngjìshàng
economically

zhèngzhìshàng
politically

These adverbs can be placed in a sentence either before or after the subject.

Lìshǐshàng, Zhōngguó hěn yǒu yìsi.
Historically, China is very interesting.

Wǒ jīběnshàng bù xǐhuan tā.
I basically don't like him.

2. YÌ FĀNGMIÀN . . . YÌ FĀNGMIÀN

The expression *yì fāngmiàn . . . yì fāngmiàn* is similar to "on one hand . . . on the other hand" in English. It is used to connect two phrases that have the same subject.

Wǒ yì fāngmiàn kěyǐ xuéxí rúhé gēn wàiguórén zuò mǎimài, yì fāngmiàn kěyǐ shíjì liǎojiě wàimào yèwù wǎnglái de qíngkuàng.
On one hand, I can learn how to do business with foreigners and, on the other hand, I can begin to understand the business activities related to international trade.

3. YǏWÉI VS. XIǍNG

You already know that *xiǎng* means "to think." You can use *yǐwéi* (to have an opinion) when you want to tell someone what you think in a more humble manner. *Yǐwéi* implies that you are aware of the possibility that you might be incorrect.

Wǒ xiǎng nǐ chī tài duō le!
I think you eat too much!

Wǒ yǐwéi nǐ chī tài duō le.
I think perhaps you eat too much.

C. HÀNZÌ

New characters.

单位	*dānwèi* (work unit)
难	*nán* (difficult)
容易	*róngyì* (easy)
安排	*ānpái* (to arrange)
将来	*jiānglái* (future)

Sentence practice:

说中国话不容易。

Shuō Zhōngguóhuà bù róngyì.

It is not easy to speak Chinese.

说中国话很难。

Shuō Zhōngguóhuà hěn nán.

It is quite difficult to speak Chinese.

他要找工作单位。

Tā yào zhǎo gōngzuò dānwèi.

He wants to find a work unit.

D. SHĒNGCÍ

ānpái	to arrange
dānwèi	work unit
díquè	indeed, really
gànhuó	to work
guójì	international
hézī	joint venture
jīběnshàng	basically
jīguān	organization
jiěgù	to lay off, to fire
kěn	willing to
kòngquē	vacancy; a job opening
lǐxiǎng	ideal
lǚlìbiǎo	résumé
mǎimài	trade, business
màoyì	trade
qǐyè	enterprise, business

qíngkuàng	situation
rúcǐ	such, in this way
rúhé	how, what
shíjì	realistic
shíjìshàng	realistically
wàimào	foreign trade
wǎnglái	dealings, comings and goings
yàobùrán	otherwise
yèwù	vocation, business
zhèngfǔ	government
zhíyuán	office worker

SUPPLEMENTARY VOCABULARY 12: PROFESSIONS

diàngōng	electrician
fúwùyuán	waiter, waitress
hǎiyuán	sailor
hùshì	nurse
jǐngchá	policeman
lǜshī	lawyer
miànbāo shīfu	baker
mùgōng	carpenter
nóngfū	farmer
shāngrén	business person
shèyǐngshī	photographer
shòuhuòyuán	salesman
yǎnyuán	actor
yínhángjiā	banker
yìshùjiā	artist

LIÀNXÍ

A. Mark the statements T (true), F (false) or X (no way to know) based on the dialogue.

1. *Xiànzài zhōngguó dàxuéshēng bìyè yǐhòu dōu bú yòng zhǎo gōngzuò. Xuéxiào huì bāngmáng ānpái gōngzuò dānwèi.*
2. *Xiǎoyīng xīwàng zài zhōngwài hézī qǐyè gōngzuò.*

3. *Zhōngguó de gōngsī dōu bù jiěgù zhíyuán.*
4. *Xiǎoyīng hé Shālì de zhuānyè dōu shì màoyì.*

B. Answer the following questions using the words provided in parentheses.

1. *Wèishénme Xiǎoyīng xīwàng zài zhōngwài hézī qǐyè gōngzuò? (yì fāngmiàn . . . yì fāngmiàn)*
2. *Zhōngguó zhèngfǔ jīguān dàodǐ jiěgù bù jiěgù zhíyuán? (jīběnshàng)*
3. *Tīngshuō Zhōngguó yǐqián huì bāng xuéshēng ānpái gōngzuò dānwèi (díquè)*
4. *Wèishénme xiànzài de dàxuéshēng kāishǐ zìjǐ zhǎo gōngzuò? (zhǐhǎo)*

C. Fill in the blanks using the words below.

yì fāngmiàn yàobùrán rúcǐ jīběnshàng zhǐhǎo

1. *Wǒ xīwàng _____ xuéxí Yīngwén, yì fāngmiàn zài màoyì gōngsī gōngzuò.*
2. *_____ měi ge xiǎng shàng dàxué de Zhōngguó xuéshēng dōu děi kǎo gāokǎo.*
3. *Jīntiān wǒ de chē huài le, _____ zuò gōnggòng qìchē qù xuéxiào.*
4. *Nǐ yīnggāi rènzhēn gànhuó, _____ nǐ de gōngsī huì jiěgù nǐ de.*
5. A: *Wǒ xiāngxìn nǐ yídìng kěyǐ shàng Běijīng dàxué.*
   B: *Xīwàng _____.*

WÉNHUÀ ZHÙJIĚ

It used to be that in Communist China all jobs were assigned to people by the government. The *dānwèi* (work unit) that a person was assigned to was that person's sole source of livelihood, health care and housing during his or her lifetime. Often a worker was assigned a job that had nothing to do with his or her training—choice was not an opinion. Of course, things change and today in China there are many more options. The government still assigns jobs to people out of college, but these jobs are usually in line with the expertise of the worker. The *dānwèi* still provides health care and housing and a worker must request to change to another work unit if he wants to; sometimes heavy fines are levied if someone wants to leave his or her work unit too soon. The option to look for one's own job is becoming more feasible—in this case, the process is much like it is in the United States—contacts, contacts, contacts.

DÁÀN

A. 1.F 2.T 3.F 4.X

B. 1. *Yīnwèi tā xīwàng yì fāngmiàn xuéxí gēn wàiguórén zuò mǎimài, yìfāngmiàn shíjì liǎojiě guójì yèwù wǎnglái de qíngkuàng. 2. Jīběnshàng, tāmen shì bù jiěgù zhíyuán de. 3. Yǐqián díquè rúcǐ. 4. Yīnwèi xiànzài yǒu kòngquē de dānwèi yuè lái yuè shǎo, dàxuéshēng zhǐhǎo zìjǐ zhǎo gōngzuò le.*

C. 1. *yì fāngmiàn* 2. *jīběnshàng* 3. *zhǐhǎo* 4. *yàobùrán* 5. *rúcǐ*

DÌ SÌSHÍ KÈ
Lesson 40
YÀNHUÌ. A Banquet.

A. DUÌHUÀ

ZÀI WÁNG JIĀ.

Amy and David Stone are leaving Beijing for good, so the Wangs invite them over for a farewell dinner.

WÁNG TÀITAI: **Lái chīfàn ba. Jiǎozi bāo hǎo le, zhèngzài zhǔ. Xiān hē jiǔ ba.**

WÁNG XIĀNSHENG: **Zhè píng jiǔ búcuò, shì báijiǔ, hézī qǐyè de chǎnpǐn. Zhōngguó jiǔ yìbān shì tián de, dànshi wǒmen zhīdào nǐmen bú tài xǐhuan hē tián de. Hǎo, gānbēi! Zhù nǐmen yílù píngān, zǎorì huílái!**

DÀWÈI: **Zhù nǐmen shēntǐ jiànkāng.**

AÌMÉI: **Nǐ de fàn měi yí cì dōu tèbié hǎochī. Wǒ xīwàng huí Měiguó yǐhòu huì chī de dào nàme hǎo de fàn.**

WÁNG TÀITAI: **Nǐ bú yào kèqi.**

WÁNG XIĀNSHENG: **Nǐmen zài Zhōngguó dāile yì nián le. Yìnxiàng zěnmeyàng?**

DÀWÈI: **Wǒ xiǎng huíqù yǐhòu wǒ huì xiǎng wǒ Zhōngguó péngyou hé tóngshì. Wǒmen zài zhèr hěn mǎnyì. Gānbēi!**

AÌMÉI: **Yǒu méi yǒu wǒmen zài Měiguó de dìzhǐ?**

WÁNG TÀITAI: **Méiyǒu.**

DÀWÈI: **Wǒ gěi nǐmen xiě xià lái.**

WÁNG XIĀNSHENG: **Hǎo. Gānbēi!**

MRS. WANG: Come eat. The dumplings are made, still being boiled. First have a drink.

MR. WANG: This bottle of liquor isn't bad, it's baijiu, the product of a joint venture. Chinese liquor is usually sweet, but we know you don't like sweet drinks very much. Good! Cheers! I wish you a safe journey and that you return soon!

DAVID: I wish you health.

AMY: Your food is always especially good. I hope I can eat this well once I return to America.

MRS. WANG: Don't be so polite.

MR. WANG: You stayed in China for a year. What was your impression?

DAVID: I think that I'll miss my Chinese friends and coworkers after I return. We've been very satisfied here. Cheers!

AMY: Do you have our address in America?

MRS. WANG: No.

DAVID: I'll write it for you.

MR. WANG: Good! Cheers!

B. YǓFǍ HÉ YÒNGFǍ

1. INDICATING FUTURE: *HUÌ* VS. *YÀO*

You already know that you can use *yào* (to want) to indicate that you will do something in the future. *Huì* (to be able to) also serves this function with a different implication. While *yào* implies that something will probably happen, *huì* implies that something possibly will happen. Thus, *huì* is generally used with feelings that someone might have in the future.

Wǒ huì xiǎng wǒ de Zhōngguó péngyou.
  I'll miss my Chinese friends.

Wǒ yào huí Měiguó qù.
  I'm going back to America.

2. *MĂNYÌ*

Mănyì (to be satisfied) is a commonly heard verb in China.

Wŏ zài Zhōngguó hĕn mănyì.
  I've been very happy here.

Wŏ mănyì wŏ de gōngzuò.
  I'm satisfied with my work.

3. MORE ABOUT *CHÉNGYŬ*

You will always impress your Chinese friends if you use idiomatic expressions, or *chéngyŭ*. Here are more *chéngyŭ* for you to learn.

yúmù hùnzhū
  To mislead someone [literally, "to try and pass a fish eye off as a pearl"].

zìqī qīrén
  To deceive oneself as well as others [literally, "cheat self, cheat others"].

C. HÀNZÌ

New characters.

宴会	*yànhuì* (banquet)
满意	*mănyì* (to be satisfied)
干杯	*gānbēi* (bottoms up!)

Sentence practice.

我们在中国很满意。
Wŏmen zài Zhōngguó hĕn mănyì.
We've been very satisfied in China.

你有没有我们在美国的地址？
Nĭ yŏu méiyŏu wŏmen zài Mĕiguó de dìzhĭ?
Do you have our address in the United States?

我会想我中国的朋友和同事。
Wŏ huì xiăng wŏ Zhōngguó de péngyou hé tóngshì.
I'll miss my Chinese friends and colleagues.

D. SHĒNGCÍ

báijiǔ	Chinese liquor
chǎnpǐn	product
dànshi	but, still, nevertheless
dìzhǐ	address
gānbēi	bottoms up! Cheers!
hézī	cooperative, joint
mǎnyì	satisfied
qǐyè	business venture
yànhuì	banquet
yìnxiàng	impression
zǎorì	early, soon
zhǔ	to boil

LIÀNXÍ

A. Match the *pīnyīn* to the English.

1. To deceive oneself as well as others. a. *yúmù hǔnzhū*
2. To mislead someone. b. *zìqī qīrén*

B. Translate the following into English.

1. *Wǒ zài Zhōngguó hěn mǎnyì.*
2. *Wǒ yì fāngmiàn yào huíjiā, yì fāngmiàn bú xiǎng zǒu.*
3. *Tā de Zhōngguó péngyou méiyǒu tā zài Měiguó de dìzhǐ.*
4. *Gānbēi!*

C. Write the character for the underlined words.

1. *Zhù nǐmen yílù píngān!*
2. *Wǒ huì xiǎng wǒ de <u>Zhōngguó</u> péngyou.*
3. *<u>Xièxie</u> Wáng xiānsheng.*
4. *Wǒmen zài Zhōngguó hěn <u>mǎnyì</u>.*

D. Write in characters.

1. Good-bye!
2. Your food is delicious.
3. We are going to America.

While you are in China, you will undoubtedly be treated to numerous banquets and dinners. The most important thing to remember at these events is to toast your hosts as often and as effusively as possible. Thank them for their hospitality and finish with a hearty *gānbēi* (bottoms up!). You should also wait to sit down when you first arrive at the banquet table until the host shows you your seat. Other rules of banquet etiquette are: never taste a dish until the host has sampled it first, and, when a toast is offered, it is polite to drink as much liquor as the toastee. Men are generally expected to drink but can decline. Women are not expected to drink. If you have spent a significant amount of time in China, it is a good idea to host your own banquet for the people who helped you most during your stay. You will be remembered fondly if you do.

DÁÀN

A. 1.b 2.a

B. 1. I've been very satisfied in China. 2. On the one hand, I want to go home, on the other hand, I don't want to leave. 3. Her Chinese friends don't have her address in the U.S. 4. Bottoms up!

C. 1.一路平安 2.中国 3.谢谢 4.满意

D. 1.再见！2.你的饭很好吃。3.我们要到美国去。

FÙXÍ 8

A. Place either *xiàng* or *hǎoxiàng* in the blanks as appropriate.

1. *Shí xiānsheng _____ lái Zhōngguó bànshì.*
2. *Wǒ jiějie hěn _____ wǒ bàba, wǒ bǐjiào _____ wǒ māma.*
3. *Nàge xuéshēng _____ bìng le.*
4. *Zhōngguórén _____ bù _____ Měiguórén.*

B. What do you say in the following cases? Choose from the expressions below.

1. Someone is about to embark on a long journey.
2. Someone is making fun of you.
3. It is somebody's birthday.
4. Someone is not looking well.
5. You are offering a toast.

a. *Nǐ zěnme le?*

b. *Zhù nǐ yílù píngān.*

c. *Zhù nǐ shēngrì kuàilè.*

d. *Bié gēn wǒ kāi wánxiào.*

e. *Gānbēi!*

C. Translate the following into *pīnyīn* using *bǎ* and *chéng* construction.

1. He exchanged his American currency for Chinese currency.
2. The teacher translated the news report into Chinese.

D. Fill in the blanks with characters according to the English translations.

1. 在中国找工作很 ____ 。
   It is difficult to find a job in China.
2. 在中国找工作很 ____ 。
   It is easy to find a job in China.
3. 你去不去 ____ ?
   Are you going to the bookstore?
4. 我会 ____ 你。
   I am going to miss you.

DÁÀN

A. 1. *hǎoxiàng* 2. *xiàng, xiàng* 3. *hǎoxiàng* 4. *hǎoxiàng, xiàng*

B. 1.B 2.D 3.C 4.A 5.E

C. 1. *Tā bǎ měijīn duìhuàn chéng rénmínbì.* 2. *Lǎoshī bǎ bàogào fānyì chéng Zhōngwén.*

D. 1. 难 2. 容易 3. 书店 4. 想

YUÈDÚ LIÀNXÍ (Reading Practice 4)

We leave you with China's national anthem.

Qǐlái, bù yuàn zuò núlì de rénmín!
Bǎ wǒmen de xuèròu zhùchéng wǒmen xīn de Chángchéng.
Měi ge rén dōu bèipò fāchū zuìhòu de hǒushēng.
Wǒmen wànzhòng yīxīn, màozhe dírén de pàohuǒ.
Qián jìn, qián jìn, qián jìn jìn . . .

núlì	slave
wànzhòng	"the masses"
pàohuǒ	gunfire

APPENDICES

A. COMMON MEASURE WORDS

PĪNYĪN	TYPE OF OBJECT	EXAMPLES
bǎ	objects with a handle, chairs	knife, umbrella, toothbrush, chair
bāo	pack	cigarettes
bēi	cup of something	tea, soda
běn	volume of reading	books, magazines
bù	a piece of something flat	film
fèn	newspaper	newspaper
fēng	flat, sealed	letters
gè	general	can be used with anything
jià	machines	television, radio, computer
jiān	room	living room, bedroom
jiàn	piece or article of something	clothing, luggage
jù	a phrase of language	remarks, sentences
juǎn	reel or spool	toilet paper, film
kē	trees	trees
kè	lessons or text	passage of text, lesson
kuài	piece	soap, land
liàng	wheeled vehicles	car, bicycle
píng	bottle of something	beer, soda
qún	crowd, group, flock	cows, bees
shǒu	passage of text	poem
tào	set	furniture, stamps
tiáo	long and winding objects, cartons of something	towel, noodle, street, cigarettes
wèi	person (polite)	teacher, stranger
zhāng	rectangular objects	table, sheet of paper, bed
zhī	long and thin objects	pencil, pen
zhī	animals, one of a pair of body parts	cat, dog, hand, leg
zuò	large, relatively permanent thing	mountain, skyscraper

B. TYPES OF QUESTIONS

1. QUESTION WORD QUESTIONS

shéi (who)
Nǐ qǐng shéi chīfàn?
  Whom did you invite to dinner?

shénme (what)
Nǐmen zuò shénme?
  What are you doing?

zěnme (how, why)
Nǐ zěnme dǎ tàijíquán?
  How do you do taichi?

zěnme-yàng (how)
Tā de háizi zěnmeyàng?
  How is his child?

wèishénme (why)
Nǐ wèishénme bú shàngbān?
  Why aren't you going to work?

duōshǎo (how much)
Nèi jiàn chènshān duōshǎo qián?
  How much does that shirt cost?

jǐ (how many)
Nǐ yǒu jǐ zhī bǐ?
  How many pens do you have?

nǎr (where)
Nǐ de lǎojiā zài nǎr?
  Where is your hometown?

něi (which)
Nǐ xǐhuan něi wèi lǎoshī?
  Which teacher do you like?

2. ALTERNATIVE QUESTIONS

Nǐ xǐhuan bù xǐhuan tā de chènshān?
  Do you like her shirt?

Nǐ māma yǒu méiyǒu zìxíngchē?
  Does your mother have a bicycle?

3. QUESTIONS WITH PARTICLES

Nǐ hǎo ma?
   How are you?

Wǒ hǎo, nǐ ne?
   I'm fine, and you?

4. TAG QUESTIONS

Wǒmen qù chīfàn, hǎo bù hǎo?
   Let's go eat, okay?

Tā zhèngzài dǎ diànhuà, shì bú shì?
   He's on the phone, right?

C. ADVERBS

běnlái	originally
cóng	from
cónglái	since
dōu	all
gāng (cái)	just
gēnběn	basically
hái	still
mǎshàng	at once, immediately
qǐmǎ	at least
yě	also
yìdiǎn	a little
yǐjīng	already
yòu	again
zài	again
zài	at
zhǐ	only
zhǐhǎo	had better

D. PARTICLES

1. QUESTION PARTICLES

ma
Nǐ è ma?
   Are you hungry?

ne

Wǒ hǎo. Nǐ ne?
    I'm fine. And you?

2. SUGGESTION PARTICLES

ba

Wǒmen huíjiā ba.
    Let's go home.

bié

Nǐ bié shuōhùa.
    Don't speak.

3. NEGATION PARTICLES

bù

Wǒ bù xǐhuan chī niúròu.
    I don't like to eat beef.

méi

Wǒ méiyǒu hěn duō qián.
    I don't have much money.

4. POSSESSION PARTICLE

de

Nà shì wǒ de shū.
    That's my book.

5. RESULTATIVE VERB PARTICLE

de

Nǐ shuō Zhōngwén shuō de hěn hǎo.
    You speak Chinese very well.

6. "TENSE" PARTICLES

le

Tài lèi le!
    Too exhausting!

Wǒ xuéle sānbǎi ge zì.
    I studied 300 characters.

Yínháng guānmén le.
   The bank just closed.

Huǒchē kuài zǒu le.
   The train is about to leave.

guò
Wǒ qùguò Zhōngguó.
   I have been to China.

zhe
Chuānghu kāizhe.
   The window is open.

GLOSSARY
CHINESE-ENGLISH

A

ài	love
àiwù	pets
āiyā	oh no! oh dear!
ānpái	to arrange
ànzhào	according to
āyí	auntie

B

ba	[suggestion particle]
bā	scar
bàba	dad
bái	white
bàifǎng	to pay a visit
bǎihuò shāngdiàn	department store
báijiǔ	Chinese liquor
Bālí	Paris
bàn	to do, to manage
bànfǎ	method
bāngmáng	to help
bàngqiú	baseball
bāngzhù	to help
bāo	to wrap
báo	light, thin
bàoàn	to report a crime
bàofèi	dregs, scraps
bāoguǒ	parcel, package
bǎomǔ	baby-sitter
bèi	back
běi	north
běifāng	north
běn	[measure word for books, volume]
běnlái	originally
bǐ	[comparison word]
biànhuà	a change
biǎo	meter
biǎoshì	symbolize
biǎoyǎn	to perform

biāozhǔn	standard
bié	don't
biéde	other
bǐfang shuō	for example
bǐjiào	relatively
bìng	illness
bīngqiú	ice hockey
bīng shuǐ	ice water
bǐsài	match, game, competition
bìyè	to graduate
bízi	nose
BōShìDùn	Boston
bù	not
bú cuò	not bad
bù dé liǎo	extremely
bù gǎndāng	you're welcome
bú jiàn le	to have disappeared
bówùguǎn	museum
bùtóng	different from, distinct from

C

cā	to apply to the skin
càidān	menu
cānguān	to visit, to look around
cāntīng	cafeteria
cǎo	grass
cèsuǒ	bathroom, toilet
chā	fork
chàbùduō	about
chǎng	spot, site, field
chángcháng	often
Chángchéng	the Great Wall
chángkù	pants
chǎnpǐn	products
cháo	dynasty
chǎo	to stir-fry
cháoshī	humid
chāozhòng	overweight
chāyì	difference
chē	car
chéng	into
chénggōng	succeed

chéngjī	score, grade
chènshān	shirt
chīfàn	to eat
chítáng	pond
chóng	over again
chóng	insect
chōutì	drawer
chuáng	bed
chuānghu	window
chuántǒng	tradition
chūchāi	to be on a business trip
chúfáng	kitchen
chūn	spring
chūnàyuán	bank teller
chūnjià	spring break
chùzhǎng	division head
chūzhōng	junior high school
chūzūchē	taxi
cóng	from
cóng bù	never
cónglái	never
cóngqián	previously, formerly
cuò	wrong
cuòguò	to miss an opportunity

D

dǎ	to play or do a sport
dǎzhēn	to get a shot
dàfang	with grace and ease
dàgài	probably
dài	to bring
dài	to wear
dàifu	doctor
dàjiā	everybody
dāng	to work as, serve as
dāngdì	local
dāngrán	of course
dānrén fáng	single room
dànshi	but, still, nevertheless
dānwèi	work unit
dānxīn	to worry
dāo	knife

dào	to pour
dàochù	everywhere
dàodǐ	finally, in the final analysis
dǎoméi	to be unfortunate
dǎsuàn	to plan
Dàtóng	a town in northern Shanxi province
dàxué	college
dāyìng	to promise, to agree
dàyuē	approximately
de	[possessive particle]
Déguó	Germany
Déguorén	German person
déi	to need to, to have to
dēng	lamp
děng děng	etc.
dēngpào	lightbulb
diǎn	[measure word for time, o'clock]
diǎn	point (as in decimal point)
diàn	electricity
diǎn (cài)	to order food (in a restaurant)
diàngōng	electrician
diànnǎo	computer
diànshì	television
diǎnyǎ	elegant and classic
diànyuán	retail sales person
diāo kè	sculptures
dìdao	perfect, standard (language)
dìdi	younger brother
dìlíxué	geography
dìng	to reserve (a room or a table)
dìnghūn	to get engaged
díquè	indeed, really
dìtǎn	rug
dìtiě	subway
diū	to lose
dìzhǐ	address
dìzhíxué	geology
dòng	cave
dǒng	to understand
dōng	east
dōng (tiān)	winter
dōngfāng	the East/Asia

dòngwù	animal
dòngwùyuán	zoo
dōngxi	thing
dōu	all
duǎnkù	shorts
duì	a team
duìhuàn	to exchange
duìbuqǐ	excuse me
duìhuàndān	currency exchange form
duìhuànlǜ	exchange rate
duìmiàn	opposite
duō	many
duōshǎo	how many
dú	to read
dùzi	stomach, tummy

E

è	to be hungry
Éguó	Russia
ěrduo	ears
érqiě	in addition
érzi	son
ěxīn	to be nauseous

F

fādǒu	to shiver, to tremble
Fǎguó	France
Fǎguórén	French person
fāngbiàn	to be convenient
fángjiān	room
fànguǎnr	restaurant
fàngsōng	relax
fángzi	house
fānyì	to translate
fāshāo	to have a fever
fáxué	law
fāyán	to be infected
fāyīn	pronunciation, to pronounce
fēicháng	very, extremely
fēijī	plane
fēijī chǎng	airport
Fēizhōu	Africa

fēn	cent
fēng	classifier for letters
fēngsú	custom
fēngyī	raincoat
fēngjǐng	scenery
fēnmíng	distinct
Fó	Buddha
Fójiào	Buddhism
fù	father (classical)
fùmǔ	parents
fùqīn	father
fúwù tái	information booth
fúwùyuán	server (in a restaurant)
fùzá	complicated

G

gài	to build
gǎi	to change
gǎibiàn	to change, a change
gānbēi	bottoms up! Cheers!
gāng	just
gānjìng	to be clean
gǎnkuài	quickly, at once
gǎnlǎn qiú	American football
gǎnmào	a cold, to catch a cold
gǎnxiè	to be grateful
gāo ěrfū qiú	golf
gāodī	difference in degree
gāokǎo	college entrance exam
gàosù	to tell
gāoxìng	glad, happy
gāozhōng	high school
ge	[general measure word]
gébì	neighboring
gēge	older brother
gēn	with
gēnběn	fundamental
gèzhǒng	each kind
gōngsī	company
gōngfu	kungfu
gōnggòng qìchē	public bus
gōngkè	homework

gōngyuán	park
gōngzuò	work, job
góu	dog
guāfēng	windy
guàhào	to register
guàhào xìn	registered letter
guài	strange
guǎn	mansion, building
guàng	to browse
guànjūn	champion
guānyuán	an official
gǔdài	ancient
gǔdiǎn	classical
Gùgong	the Forbidden City
guì	expensive
guì	honorable
gǔjī	historic site
guò	[particle implying "ever" or "never"]
guójí	nationality
guójì	international
guòlái	to come over
gùwèn	consultation, consultant

H

hǎi	ocean
hǎiguān	customs
hǎixiān	seafood
hǎiyuán	sailor
háizi	child/children
hángkōng	airmail
Hánguó	Korea
hànshān	T-shirt
Hànyǔ	Chinese language
Hànzì	Chinese characters
hǎo	good, fine
hǎochù	good characteristics
hǎojiǔ bújiàn	long time no see
hǎo kàn	good-looking
hǎoxiàng	to look like
hǎo yùn, xìng yùn	good fortune
hé	and
hé	river

hébì	there is no need
hēi	black
hējǔ	to drink alcohol
hěn	very
hézi	box
hézī	joint venture
hóng	red
hónglùdēng	traffic light
hóngbāo	red gift envelope full of money
hōnggān jī	clothes dryer
hóngshāo	cooked in soy sauce
hòu	back
hòu	thick
hóulóng	throat
hòunián	the year after next
hòutiān	day after tomorrow
hú	lake
hǔ	tiger
huà	speech
huà	painting
huá	to row
huā (qián)	to spend money
huábīng	skating
huài	bad
huàichù	bad characteristics
huàjù	a theatrical play
huàn	to change
huàn	to exchange
huáng	yellow
huángdì	emperor
huānyíng	to welcome
huàxué	chemistry
huì	to be able to
huì	to be likely to
huíjiā	to go home
hūnlǐ	wedding ceremony
huǒchē	train
huǒchēzhàn	train station
huòzhě	or
hūrán	suddenly
hùshi	nurse
hùxiāng	mutually, each other

J

jī	chicken
jīròu	chicken (meat)
jǐ	crowded
jǐ	how many
jì	to mail, to send
jiā	to add
jiákè	jacket
jiān	[measure word for rooms]
jiàn	[measure word for suitcases]
jiàn	to see
Jiānádà	Canada
jiǎngjià	to bargain
jiànmiàn	meet
jiànzhù	architecture
jiào	belief system
jiǎo	foot
jiǎo	ten cents
jiào	to be called, to be (first) named
jiāo	to teach
jiāoshū	to teach in a school
jiāotōng	traffic
jiǎozhǐ	toes
jiǎozi	dumplings
jiàqián	price
jiàrì	vacation, holiday
Jiāzhōu	California
jìbài	to worship
jīběnshàng	basically
jīdīng	chunks of chicken
jiēfēng	to treat a guests to a welcoming dinner
jiěgù	to lay off, to fire
jiéguǒ	result, outcome
jiéhūn	to get married
jiějie	older sister
jiérì	festival day
jiéshù	to end, to finish
jīguān	organization
jǐhéxué	geometry
jìhuà	a plan, to plan
jīhuì	opportunity
jìn	nearby

jìn lái	to come in
jīngcǎi	brilliant, wonderful
jǐngchá	policeman
jīngjìxué	economics
jìngjiǔ	to propose a toast
jīngjù	Chinese opera
jīnglǐ	manager
jìngzi	mirror
jìnjì	taboo
jīnnián	this year
jīntiān	today
jìshù	technical
jìsuànjī	computer
jiǔ	a long time
juéde	to feel, to think
juédìng	to decide
juéduì	absolutely
juésài	the final competition
jùtuán	theater company
jùxiào	drama school
jùyuàn	theater

K

kāishǐ	to start
kāihuì	to hold a meeting
kāishuǐ	boiled water
kāifàng	open, open-minded
kàn	to watch
kǎo	to roast, to barbeque
kénéng	possible
kèqì	to be polite
kěshì	but
késòu	to cough
kètīng	living room
kēxué	science
kěyǐ	to be able to
kōng	empty
kōngtiáo	air conditioner
kòngquē	vacant
kǒuyīn	accent
kǔ	to be bitter
kuài	dollar

kuài	fast
kuàizi	chopsticks
kuàngquán shuǐ	mineral water
kùzi	pants

L

là	to be spicy
lā	to play (certain instruments)
lā	to pull
lán	blue
láng	wolf
lánqiú	basketball
lǎojiā	hometown
láojià	excuse me, may I thank you
lǎoshí	honest, sincere
lǎoshī	teacher, professor
le	[particle]
lěng	cold
lí	between
lǐ	miles
liǎn	face
liàn	to practice
liàng	to be bright
liáng	to measure
liáng shuǐ	cool walter
liángkuài	cool (temperature)
liǎnsè	complexion
liǎojiě	to understand
lǐfú	evening gown
lǐngdài	necktie
lìngwài	in addition
línjū	neighbor
línyù	shower
lìshǐ	history
liúyì	to keep an eye on
lìzi	example
lóu	floor
lóushàng	upstairs
lóuxià	downstairs
lù	road
lǘ	donkey
luàn	to be messy

lǚkè	guest, traveler
lǚlìbiǎo	résumé
luòtāng jī	like a drowned rat
lùshī	lawyer
lǚxíng zhīpiào	traveler's checks
lùyùn	to send by land

M

ma	[question particle]
mǎ	horse
máfan	annoying
mǎi	to buy
mài	to sell
Màidāngláo	McDonald's
mǎimài	to do business
májiàng	mah-jongg
māma	mom
màn	slow
mǎn	the whole
máng	to be busy
mǎnyì	satisfied
máo	ten cents
māo	cat
máojīn	towel
màoyì	trade
máoyī	sweater
màozi	hat
méi	[particle for negation]
Měiguó	America
Měiguórén	American person
měijīn	U.S. currency
mèimei	younger sister
měitiān	every day
mén	door
mēn	humid and stuffy
mǐ	meter
miàn	face
miànbāo shīfù	baker
miànjiá	cheek
miàntiáo	noodles
mǐfàn	rice
míngnián	next year

míngtiān	tomorrow
mìshū	secretary
mǒ	to apply (like a cream)
mùgōng	carpenter
mùqián	presently
mǔqīn	mother

N

nǎ	which [interrogative form]
ná	to take
nà/nèi	that
nán	difficult
nán	south
Nán Měizhōu	South America
nánfāng	south
nánguài	no wonder
nánwéiqíng	embarrassment, shyness
nǎo	brain
nào xiàohuà	make a fool of oneself
ne	[question particle]
nèiyī	underwear
nǐ	you
niándài	era
niǎo	bird
nǐmen	you (plural)
nín	you (formal)
níngyuàn	would rather
niú	cattle
Niǔyuē	New York
niúzǎikù	jeans
nóngfū	farmer
nónglì	the Chinese lunar calendar
nuǎnhuó	warm

O

Ōuzhōu	Europe

P

pà	to fear
pàichūsuǒ	local police station
pán	plate [measure word]
pǎobù	to run

péngyou	friend
(dǎ) pēntì	to sneeze
piányi	inexpensive
piàoliang	pretty
pídài	belt
píng	bottle
píngguǒ	apple
píngxìn	ordinary mail
pīpíng	to criticize

Q

qī	knee
qí	to ride astride
qián	front
qián	money
qiáng	wall
qiánnián	the year before last
qiántiān	the day before yesterday
qiānzhèng	visa
qiàtán	to discuss, to talk
qìchē	bus
qǐchuáng	to get out of bed
qíguài	strange
qìhòu	climate
qījiān	time period
qīn	to kiss
qīng	green
qǐng	please, to invite
qīngcài	greens
qǐngjià	to ask for a day off, to ask for leave
qíngkuàng	condition, situation
qīnglǐ	to clean
qīngliáng	cool and refreshing
qīngpén dàyǔ	a heavy rain
qīngwā	frog
qǐngwèn	may I ask?
qìngzhù	to celebrate
qíshí	in fact, actually
qiū	autumn
qiúxié	tennis shoes
qìxiàng yùbào	weather forecast
qǐyè	business enterprise or venture

qíyú	the rest, the remainder
quán	entire, whole
quán	authority
qùnián	last year
qúnzi	skirt
qǔqián	to withdraw money
qǔxiào	to ridicule

R

ránér	however
ràng	to make, to cause
rè	to be hot
rè shuǐ	hot water
rén	person
rènào	lively and exciting
réndān	lozenges
rénmínbì	the currency of the PRC
rènshi	to recognize, to know (a person)
rì	sun, day
Rìběn	Japan
rìcháng shēnghuó	daily life, routine
rùjìng suísú	when in Rome, do as the Romans do
ruǎnjiàn	software
ruǎnwò	soft sleeper
ruǎnzuò	soft seat
rúcǐ	such, in this way

S

shāfā	sofa
shān	mountain
shàng	on
shàngge xīngqī	last week
shàngge yuè	last month
shàng xià	up and down
shàngbān	to start work
shàngchē	to get in the vehicle
shāngdiàn	store
shàngkè	to start class
shāngliang	to discuss
shāngrén	business person
shàngshàng ge xīngqī	the week before last
shàngshàng ge yuè	the month before last

shāngǔ	valley
shāngyè	business
shàngyī	top (shirt)
shǎo	few
shé	snake
shèyǐngshī	photographer
shēngbìng	to get sick
Shèngdàn jié	Christmas
shēnghuó	life
shēngrì	birthday
shēngwù xué	biology
shèngxia	to remain, to be left
shēngyi	business
shénme	what
shēntǐ	body, health
shétou	tongue
shì	city
shì	to be
shíchā	jet lag, time difference
shídài	times, era, epoch
shíjì	realistic
shíjìshàng	realistically
shíjiān	time
shìlì	municipally funded
shílì	strength
shīqiè	to have something stolen
shìqing	things, events
shítou	rock
shìyìng	to adapt, to fit
shǐyòng	to make use of
shīzi	lion
shǒu	hand
shòu	thin
shōují	to collect, to gather
shòushāng	to get injured
shōushi	to clean
shǒutào	gloves
shōuyīnjī	radio
shǒuzhǐ	fingers
shū	book
shǔ	mouse
shù	tree

shuāngrén fáng	double room
shūdiàn	bookstore
shūfu	comfortable
shùijiào	to go to sleep
shuǐyùn	to send by sea (shipping)
shùmù	number
shuō	to speak
shuōhuà	to speak
shúxī	to be familiar with someone or something
shùxué	math
shūzhuō	desk
sì	temple
sì jì	four seasons
sīshì	personal affairs
sīwà	stocking
sòngkè	to see guests to the door
sòngzhōng	to attend a dying family member
suān	to be sour
suàn	to calculate, to count
suàn le!	forget it!
suì	age
suíbiàn	as one pleases
suīrán	although
suìshu	age
suǒ	to lock
suǒyǐ	therefore
sùshè	dormitory

T

tā	he/she, him/her
tài	too
tàijí quán	taichi
tàitai	Mrs., wife
tàiyáng	the sun
tāmen	they, them (plural)
tāng	soup
tàng	to burn
tǎnzi	blanket
tào	[measure word for furniture]
tèbié	particular, special
téng	ache, pain
tiān	day

358

tián	to be sweet
tián	to fill out a form
tiān	sky
tiāntian	everyday
tiáo	[measure word for roads]
tiāo	to pick, to choose
tǐcāo	gymnastics
tiē	to paste, to stick
tǐng	extremely
tīng	to listen to
tíng	to stop
tīngshuō	to hear it said
tǐwēn	body temperature
tóngshì	colleague
tóngxué	classmate
tóngyì	to agree
tóngyīn	same pronunciation
tōngzhī	to inform
tóu	head
tōu	to steal
tóufa	hair
tóuhūn yǎnhuā	dizzy and spinning
tóutòng	headache
tǔ	old-fashioned, not stylish
tù	rabbit
tù	to vomit
tuánjù	to gather together
tuǐ	leg
tuìxiū	to retire
tuōxié	slippers

W

wàibì	foreign currency
wàibiān	outside
wàibīn	foreign guest
wàiguó	foreign country
wàiguó rén	foreign person
wàimào	foreign trade
wàitān	the Bund in Shanghai
wàitào	overcoat
wàitou	outside
wàng	to, toward

wǎngqiú	tennis
wǎnglái	dealings, comings and goings
wǎnshàng	evening
wàzi	socks
wèi	[polite measure word for people)
wéi	to become
wèihūn fū	fiance
wèihūn qī	fiancée
wèile	for the sake of
wèishēngjiān	bathroom
wèn	to ask
wēndù	temperature
wēndùjì	a thermometer
wèntí	problem
wénxué	literature
wǒ	I, me
Wǒ de tiān!	Oh my goodness!
wò shǒu	to shake hands
wǒmen	we, us
wòshì	bedroom
wúlì	to be feeble
wùlǐxué	physics
wūzi	a room

X

xī	west
xī yān	to smoke
xià	summer
xiàge yuè	next month
xiàyǔ	to rain
xiàbān	to get out of work
xiàchē	to get out of the vehicle
xiàge xīngqī	next week
xiàkè	to get out of class
xiǎng	to miss, to want to, to think
xiàng	elephant
xiànjīn	cash
xiānsheng	Mr., husband
xiànzài	now
xiǎo tíqín	violin
xiǎojie	Miss, young woman
xiàtiān	summer

xiàwǔ	afternoon
xiàxià ge xīngqī	the week after next
xiàxià ge yuè	the month after next
Xībānyá	Spain
xǐdícáo	sink
xièxie	thank you
xiézi	shoes
xīfāng	the west
xíguàn	habit, to be used to
xǐhuān	to like
xīn	heart
xìn	letter
xīn	new
xìnfēng	envelope
xìng	to be (last) named, last name
xīngqī	week
xīngqièr	Tuesday
xīngqīrì	Sunday
xīngqīsān	Wednesday
xīngqīsì	Thursday
xīngqītiān	Sunday
xīngqīwǔ	Friday
xīngqīyī	Monday
xīngqīliù	Saturday
xìngyùn	good luck, fortunate
xīnshǎng	to appreciate, to enjoy
xǐshì	happy events (usually a wedding)
xǐtiē	wedding invitation
xīwàng	(to) hope, wish
xǐyī diàn	dry cleaner
xǐyī jī	clothes washing machine
xǐyīfáng	laundry room
xuǎn	to choose
xué	to study
xuě	snow
xuéshēng	student
xuéxí	to study
xūyào	to need, to require

Y

yā	duck
yàjūn	second place finisher
yǎng	to raise (a child, an animal)

yàngzi	appearance
yànhuì	banquet
yǎnjīng	eye
yánsè	color
yǎnyuán	actor
yánzhòng	serious
yào	to want to, to plan to
yǎo	to bite
yàobùrán	otherwise
yàojǐn	important, pressing
yàoshi	key (door)
Yǎzhōu	Asia
yě	also
yèwù	vocation, business
yěxú	perhaps
yèzi	leaves
yí bèizi	all your life
yīhuǐr	a little while, in a moment
yīlù píngān	bon voyage
yī xiàzi	all of a sudden
Yìdàlì	Italy
yīfu	clothing
yígòng	all together
yīguì	closet
Yíhéyuán	the Summer Palace
yǐhòu	after
yìjiàn	ideas
yǐmiǎn	in order to prevent
yīng	eagle
yīnggāi	should
Yīngguó	England
yíngjiē	to meet
yìngwò	hard sleeper
yǐngxiǎng	influence
yíngyè yuán	clerk
yìngzuò	hard seat
yínháng	bank
yínháng jiā	banker
yīnliáng	shady and cool
yǐnliào	drink
yìnxiàng	impression
yīnyuè	music

yǐqián	before
yíqiè	everything
yīshēng	doctor
yìshùjiā	artist
yìsi	meaning
yǐwéi	to regard (something as)
yìwù jiàoyù	compulsory education
yīyàng	the same
yīyuàn	hospital
yīzhí	continuously
yǐzi	chair
yòng	to use
yōngbào	to hug
yòu	again
yòu	right
yǒu	to have
yóu	oil
yǒuguān	to have something to do with
yòu . . . yòu	both . . . and
yōudiǎn	strong point
yòuér yuán	kindergarten
yǒuhǎo	friendly
yǒumíng	famous
yóupiào	a stamp
yōuxiù	outstanding
yǒuyí	friendship
Yǒuyí Shāngdiàn	Friendship Store
yú	fish
yǔ	rain
yuán	dollar, yuan
yuǎn	far
yuán	park
yuán	round
yuànzi	courtyard, yard
yuè	month
yuē (huì)	appointment, to make arrangements for
yuè lái yuè	more and more
yuèbǐng	moon cakes
Yuènán	Vietnam
yǔfǎ	grammar
yùndòngshān	sweatshirt
yǔsǎn	umbrella
yǔyánxué	linguistics

Z

zài	again
zài	at
zàihu	to care
zàijiàn	good-bye
zāo	to be a mess
zāogāo	damn
zǎorì	an early day, soon
zǎoshàng	morning
zéi	thief
zěnme	how
zěnme huíshì?	what's up?
zhàn	station
zhāng	[measure word for paper]
zhǎng	to grow
zháojí	to be worried
zhège yuè	this month
zhège xīngqī	this week
zhēn	really
zhēnde	really, truly
zhèngfǔ	government
zhèngzài	occurs before a verb to indicate an action in progress
zhèngzhì xué	political science
zhí	straight
zhí	continuously
zhī	[measure word for certain animals]
zhǐ	paper
zhīdaò	to know
zhíde	to be worthwhile
zhǐhǎo	to have to
zhìshǎo	the least
zhīshì	knowledge
zhǐyào	so long as
zhíyè	occupation
zhōng	clock
zhōng	o'clock
zhǒng	to be swollen
zhǒng	kind, type, sort
Zhōngguó	China
Zhōngguóhuà	Chinese
Zhōngqiū jié	Mid-Autumn Festival

zhōngshēng	the entire life
zhòngshì	to pay attention to, to attach importance to
zhòngshǔ	heatstroke
Zhōngwén	Chinese
zhòngyào	to be important
zhǒu	elbow
zhōudào	thoughtful, considerate
zhǔ	to boil
zhù	to live
zhuǎn	turn
zhuàng	strong, healthy
zhuānjiā	expert
zhuānmén	specialized
zhǔnbèi	to prepare
zhuōzi	table
zhùyì	to pay attention to
zì	words, characters
zìjǐ	self, one's own
zīliào	data, information
zìxíngchē	bicycle
zìzhù	self-service
zǒng	always, invariably
zòngzi	Chinese tamale
zǒu	to go
zǒulù	to walk
zuì	guilt, sin
zuì	most
zuì xǐhuan	favorite
zuǐba	mouth
zuìhòu	the last, the final
zuìjìn	recently, lately
zūnjìng	to pay respect to
zuǒ	left
zuò	to do (for work)
zuò	to ride, to sit (for transportation)
zuòjiā	writer
zúqiú	soccer
zuǒshǒu	left hand
zuótiān	yesterday
zuǒyòu	about, more or less
zúxiān	ancestor

ENGLISH-CHINESE

A

about	chàbùduō
about, more or less	zuǒyòu
absolutely	juéduì
accent	kǒuyīn
according to	ànzhào
ache, pain	téng
actor	yǎnyuán
adapt, to fit	shìyìng
add	jiā
address	dìzhǐ
Africa	Fēizhōu
after	yǐhòu
afternoon	xiàwǔ
again	yòu
again	zài
age	suì
age	suìshu
agree	tóngyì
air conditioner	kōngtiáo, lěngqìjī
airmail	hángkōng
airport	fēijīchǎng
all	dōu
all of a sudden	yī xiàzi
all together	yígòng
all your life	yībèizi
also	yě
although	suīrán
America	Měiguó
American football	gǎnlǎnqiú
American person	Měiguórén
ancestor	zǔxiān
ancient	gǔdài
and	hé
animal	dòngwù
annoying	máfan
appearance	yàngzi
apple	píngguǒ
apply (like a cream)	mǒ

apply to the skin	cā
appointment	yuē (huì)
appreciate, to enjoy	xīnshǎng
approximately	dàyuē
architecture	jiànzhù
arrange	ānpái
artist	yìshùjiā
as one pleases	suíbiàn
Asia	Yàzhōu
ask	wèn
ask for a day off, to ask for leave	qǐngjià
at	zài
attend a dying family member	sòngzhōng
auntie	āyí
authority	quán
autumn	qiū

B

baby-sitter	bǎomú
back	bèi
back	hòu
backyard	hòu yuàn(zi)
bad	huài
bad characteristics	huàichù
baker	miànbāo shīfù
bank	yínháng
bank teller	chūnàyuán
banker	yínháng jiā
banquet	yànhuì
bargain	jiǎngjià
baseball	bàngqiú
basically	jīběnshàng
basketball	lánqiú
bathroom	wèishēngjiān
bathroom, toilet	cèsuǒ
be (occupation, role)	dāng
be	shì
be (last) named, last name	xìng
be a mess	zāo
be able to	huì
be able to	kéyǐ
be bitter	kǔ

be bright	liàng
be busy	máng
be called, to be (first) named	jiào
be clean	gānjìng
be convenient	fāngbiàn
be familiar	shúxī
be feeble	wúlì
be grateful	gǎnxiè
be hot	rè
be hungry	è
be important	zhòngyào
be infected	fāyán
be likely to	huì
be messy	luàn
be nauseous	éxīn
be on a business trip	chūchāi
be polite	kèqì
be sour	suān
be spicy	là
be sweet	tián
be swollen	zhǒng
be unfortunate	dǎoméi
be worried	zháojí
be worthwhile	zhíde
become	wéi
bed	chuáng
bedroom	wòshì
before	yǐqián
Beijing Opera	jīngjù
belief system	jiào
belt	pídài
between	lí
bicycle	zìxíngchē
biology	shēngwùxué
bird	niǎo
birthday	shēngrì
bite	yǎo
black	hēi
blanket	tǎnzi
blue	lán
body temperature	tǐwēn
body	shēntǐ

boil	zhǔ
boiling water	kāishuǐ
bon voyage	yīlù píngān
book	shū
bookstore	shūdiàn
Boston	Bō Shì Dùn
both . . . and	yòu . . . yòu
bottle	píng
bottoms up! Cheers!	gānbēi
box	hézi
brain	nǎo
brilliant	jīngcǎi
bring	dài
browse	guàng
Buddha	Fó
Buddhism	Fójiào
Buddhist	Fójiàotú
build	gài
burn	tàng
bus	qìchē
business	shāngyè
business	shēngyi
businessperson	shāngrén
but	kěshì
but, still, nevertheless	dànshi
buy	mǎi

C

cafeteria	cāntīng
calculate, to count	suàn
California	Jiāzhōu
calligraphy	shūfǎ
Canada	Jiānádà
car	chē
care	zàihu
carpenter	mùgōng
cash	xiànjīn
cat	māo
cattle	niú
cave	shāndòng
celebrate	qìngzhù
cent	fēn

chair	yǐzi
champion	guànjūn
change	biànhuà
change	gǎi
change	huàn
change, a change	gǎibiàn
cheek	miànjiá
chemistry	huàxué
chicken	jī
child/children	háizi
chin	xiàba
China	Zhōngguó
Chinese	Zhōngguóhuà
Chinese person	Zhōngwén
Chinese characters	hànzì
Chinese language	Hànyǔ
Chinese liquor	báijiǔ
Chinese lunar calendar	nónglì
Chinese opera	jīngjù
Chinese tamale	zòngzi
choose	xuǎn
chopsticks	kuàizi
Christmas	Shèngdàn jié
chunks of chicken	jīdīng
city	shì
classical	gǔdiǎn
classifier for letters	fēng
classmate	tóngxué
clean	qīnglǐ
clean	shōushi
clerk	yíngyè yuán
climate	qìhòu
clock	zhōng
closet	yīguì
clothes dryer	hōnggān jī
clothes washing machine	xǐyījī
cold	gǎnmào
cold	lěng
colleague	tóngshì
collect, to gather	shōují
college	dàxué
college entrance exam	gāokǎo

370

color	yánsè
come in	jìnlái
come over	guòlái
comfortable	shūfu
company	gōngsī
complexion	liǎnsè
complicated	fùzá
compulsory education	yìwù jiàoyù
computer	jìsuànjī, diànnǎo
condition	qíngkuàng
consultation, consultant	gùwèn
continuously	yīzhí
cooked in soy sauce	hóngshāo
cool (temperature)	liángkuài
cool and refreshing	qīngliáng
cool water	liángshuǐ
cough	késou
count	suàn
cow	niú
criticize	pīpíng
crowded	jǐ
currency exchange form	duìhuàndān
currency of the PRC	rénmínbì
custom	fēngsú
customs	hǎiguān

D

dad	bàba
daily life, routine	rìcháng shēnghuó
damn	zāogāo
data	zīliào
day	tiān
day after tomorrow	hòutiān
day before yesterday	qiántiān
dealings, comings and goings	wǎnglái
decide	juédìng
department store	bǎihuò shāngdiàn
desk	shūzhuō
difference	chāyì
difference in degree	gāodī
different	bùtóng

difficult	nán
discuss	shāngliang
discuss	qiàtán
distinct	fēnmíng
division head	chùzhǎng
dizzy and spinning	tóuhūn yǎnhuā
do business	mǎimài
do (for work)	zuò
do, to manage	bàn
doctor	dàifu
doctor	yīshēng
dog	gǒu
dollar	kuài
dollar, yuan	yuán
don't	bié
donkey	lǘ
door	mén
dormitory	sùshè
double room	shuāngrénfáng
downstairs	lóuxià
drama school	jùxiào
drawer	chōutì
dregs, scraps	bàofèi
dress	yīfu
drink	yǐnliào
drink alcohol	hēijǔ
dry cleaner	xǐyī diàn
duck	yā
dumplings	jiǎozi
dynasty	cháo

E

each kind	gèzhǒng
eagle	yīng
early day	zǎorì
ears	ěrduo
east	dōng
eat	chī
economics	jīngjìxué
elbow	zhǒu
electrician	diàngōng
electricity	diàn

elegant and classic	diǎnyǎ
elephant	xiàng
embarrassment	nánwéiqíng
emperor	huángdì
empty	kōng
end, to finish	jiéshù
England	Yīngguó
enterprise	qǐyè
entire life	zhōngshēng
entire, whole	quán
envelope	xìnfēng
environment	huánjìng
era	niándài
etc.	děng děng
Europe	Ōuzhōu
evening	wǎnshàng
evening gown	lǐfú
every day	měitiān
everybody	dàjiā
everyday	tiāntiān
everything	yíqiè
everywhere	dàochù
example	lìzi
exchange	duìhuàn
exchange	huàn
exchange rate	duìhuànlǜ
excuse me	duìbùqǐ
expensive	guì
expert	zhuānjiā
extremely	bù dé liǎo
extremely	tǐng
eye	yǎnjīng

F

face	liǎn
face	miàn
famous	yǒumíng
far	yuǎn
farmer	nóngfū
fast	kuài
father	fùqīn

father (classical)	fù
favorite	zuì xǐhuan
fear	pà
feel	juéde
festival	jiérì
few	shǎo
fiance	wèihūn fū
fiancée	wèihūn qī
fill out (a form)	tián (biǎo)
final competition	juésài
finally	dàodǐ
fingers	shǒuzhǐ
fish	yú
floor	lóu
foot	jiǎo
for example	bǐfáng shuō
for the sake of	wèile
Forbidden City	GùGōng
foreign country	wàiguó
foreign currency	wàibì
foreign guest	wàibīn
foreign person	wàiguó rén
foreign trade	wàimào
forget it!	suàn le!
fork	chā
four seasons	sì jì
France	Fǎguó
French person	Fǎguó rén
Friday	xīngqī wǔ
friend	péngyou
friendly	yǒuhǎo
friendship	yǒuyí
Friendship Store	Yǒuyí Shāngdiàn
frog	qīngwā
from	cóng
front	qián
fundamental	gēnběn

G

gather together	tuánjù
[general measure word]	ge
geography	dìlǐxué

geology	dìzhìxué
geometry	jǐhéxué
German person	Déguórén
Germany	Déguó
get a shot	dǎzhēn
get engaged	dìnghūn
get in the vehicle	shàngchē
get injured	shòushāng
get married	jiéhūn
get out of bed	qǐchuáng
get out of class	xiàkè
get out of the vehicle	xiàchē
get out of work	xiàbān
glad	gāoxìng
gloves	shǒutào
go	zǒu
go home	huíjiā
go to sleep	shuìjiào
golf	gāo érfūqiú
good characteristics	hǎochù
good fortune	hāoyùn, xìngyùn
good-looking	hǎo kàn
good, fine	hǎo
good-bye	zàijiàn
government	zhèngfǔ
government funded	shìlì
graduate	bìyè
grass	cǎo
Great Wall	Chángchéng
green	lǜ
grow	zhǎng
guest, traveler	lǚkè
gymnastics	tǐcāo

H

habit, to be used to	xíguàn
hair	tóufa
hand	shǒu
happy	gāoxìng
happy events (usually a wedding)	xǐshì
hard seat	yìngzuò
hard sleeper	yìngwò

hat	màozi
have	yǒu
have a fever	fāshǎo
have disappeared	bú jiàn le
have something to do with	yǒuguān
have something stolen	shīqiè
have to	zhǐhǎo
he/she, him/her	tā
head	tóu
headache	tóuténg
health	shēntǐ
hear it said	tīngshuō
heart	xīn
heatstroke	zhòngshǔ
heavy rain	qīngpén dàyǔ
help	bāngmáng
help	bāngzhù
high school	gāozhōng
historic site	gǔjì
history	lìshǐ
hold a meeting	kāihuì
holiday	jiéqìng
hometown	lǎojiā
homework	gōngkè
honest, sincere	lǎoshí
honorable	guì
hope	xīwàng
horse	mǎ
hospital	yīyuàn
hot water	rèshuǐ
house	fángzi
how	zěnme
how many	duōshǎo
how many	jǐ
however	ránér
hug	yōngbào
humid	cháoshī
humid and stuffy	mēn

I

I, me	wǒ

ice hockey	bīngqiú
ice water	bīngshuǐ
ideas	yìjiàn
illness	bìng
important, pressing	yàojǐn
impression	yìnxiàng
in addition	érqiě
in addition	lìngwài
in fact, actually	qíshí
in order to prevent	yǐmiǎn
indeed, really	díquè
inexpensive	piányi
influence	yǐngxiǎng
inform	tōngzhī
information	zīliào
information booth	fúwùtái
insect	chóng
into	chéng
Italy	Yìdàlì

J

jacket	jiákè
Japan	Rìběn
jeans	niúzǎikù
jet lag, time difference	shíchā
joint venture	hézī
junior high school	chūzhōng
just	gāng

K

keep an eye on	liúyì
key (door)	yàoshi
kind, type, sort	zhǒng
kindergarten	yòuéryuán
kiss	qīn
kitchen	chúfáng
knee	qī
knife	dāo
know	zhīdào
knowledge	zhīshì
Korea	Hánguó
kungfu	gōngfu

L

lake	hú
lamp	dēng
last month	shàngge yuè
last week	shàngge xīngqī
last year	qùnián
last, the final	zuìhòu
laundry room	xǐyīfáng
law	fǎxué
lawyer	lǜshī
lay off, to fire	jiěgù
least	zhìshǎo
leaves	yèzi
left	zuǒ
left hand	zuǒshǒu
leg	tuǐ
letter	xìn
life	shēnghuó
light, thin	báo
lightbulb	dēngpào
like	xǐhuan
like a drowned rat	luòtāng jī
linguistics	yǔyánxué
lion	shīzi
listen to	tīng
literature	wénxué
little while, in a moment	yīhuǐr
live	zhù
lively and exciting	rènào
living room	kètīng
local	dāngdì
local police station	pàichūsuǒ
lock	suǒ
long time	jiǔ
long time no see	hǎojiǔ bújiàn
look like	hǎoxiàng
lose	diū
love	ài
lozenges	réndān

M

mah-jongg	májiàng

mail, to send	jì
make a fool of oneself	nào xiàohuà
make use of	shǐyòng
make, to cause	ràng
manager	jīnglǐ
many	duō
match, game, competition	bǐsài
math	shùxué
may I ask?	qǐngwèn
McDonald's	Màidānglǎo
meaning	yìsi
measure	liáng
meet	jiànmiàn
meet	yíngjiē
menu	càidān
meter	biǎo
meter (metric unit)	mǐ
method	bànfǎ
Mid-Autumn festival	Zhōngqiū jié
miles	lǐ
mineral water	kuàngquán shuǐ
mirror	jìngzi
miss an opportunity	cuòguò
miss, to want to	xiǎng
Miss, young woman	xiǎojie
mom	māma
Monday	xīngqī yī
money	qián
month	yuè
month after next	xiàxià ge yuè
month before last	shàngshàng ge yuè
moon cakes	yuèbǐng
more and more	yuè lái yuè
morning	zǎoshàng
most	zuì
mother	mǔqīn
mountain	shān
mouse	shǔ
mouth	zuǐ
mouth	zuǐba
Mr., husband	xiānsheng
Mrs., wife	tàitai

museum	bówùguǎn
music	yīnyuè
mutually, each other	hùxiāng

N

nationality	guójí
nearby	jìn
necktie	lǐngdài
need to, to have to	děi
need, to require	xūyào
neighbor	línjū
neighboring	gébì
never	cóng bù
never	cónglái
new	xīn
New York	Niǔyuē
next month	xiàge yuè
next week	xiàge xīngqī
next year	míngnián
no wonder	nánguài
noodles	miàntiáo
north	běi
north	běifāng
nose	bízi
not	bù
not bad	bú cuò
now	xiànzài
number	shùmù
nurse	hùshì

O

o'clock	zhōng
occupation	zhíyè
ocean	hǎi yáng
of course	dāngrán
an official	guānyuán
often	chángchang
Oh, my goodness!	Wǒ de tiān!
oh no! oh dear!	āiyā
oil	yóu
old-fashioned, not stylish	tǔ
older brother	gēge

older sister	jiějie
on	shàng
one's own	zìjǐ
open	zhǎnkāi
open, open-minded	kāifàng
opportunity	jīhuì
opposite	duìmiàn
or	huòzhe
order food (in a restaurant)	diǎn (cài)
ordinary mail	píngxìn
organization	jīguān
originally	běnlái
other	bié de
otherwise	yàobùrán
outside	wàibiān
outside	wàitóu
outstanding	yōuxiù
over again	chóng
overcoat	wàitào
overweight	chāozhòng

P

painting	huà
pants	chángkù
pants	kùzi
paper	zhǐ
parcel	bāoguǒ
parents	fùmǔ
Paris	Bālí
park	gōngyuán
park	yuán
paste, to stick	tiē
pay a visit	bàifǎng
pay attention to	zhùyì
pay respect to	zūnjìng
perfect, standard (language)	dìdao
perform	biǎoyǎn
perhaps	yěxǔ
person	rén
personal affairs	sīshì
pets	aìwù
photographer	shèyǐngshī

physics	wùlǐxué
pick, to choose	tiāo
plan	dǎsuàn
plan, to plan	jìhuà
plane	fēijī
plate [measure word]	pán
play (certain instruments)	lā
play or do a sport	dǎ
please, to invite	qǐng
point (as in decimal point)	diǎn
policeman	jǐngchá
political science	zhèngzhìxué
pond	chítáng
possible	kěnéng
pour	dào
practice	liàn
prepare	zhǔnbèi
presently	mùqián
pretty	piàoliang
previously, formerly	cóngqián
price	jiàqián
probably	dàgài
problem	wèntí
products	chǎnpǐn
promise, to agree	dāyìng
pronunciation, to pronounce	fāyīn
propose a toast	jìngjiǔ
public bus	gōnggòng qìchē

Q

quickly, at once	gǎnkuài

R

rabbit	tù
radio	shōuyīnjī
rain	xiàyǔ
rain	yǔ
raincoat	fēngyī
raise	yǎng
read	dú shū, kànshū
realistic	shíjì
realistically	shíjì shàng

really	zhēn
really, truly	zhēnde
recently, lately	zuìjìn
recognize, to know (a person)	rènshi
red	hóng
red gift envelope full of money	hóngbāo
regard (something as)	yǐwéi
register	guàhào
registered letter	guàhào xìn
relatively	bǐjiào
relax	fàngsōng
remain, to be left	shèngxia
report a crime	bào àn
reserve (a room or a table)	dìng
rest, the remainder	qíyú
restaurant	fànguǎnr
result, outcome	jiéguǒ
résumé	lǚlìbiǎo
retail sales person	diànyuán
retire	tuìxiū
rice	mǐfàn
ride astride	qí
ride, to sit (for transportation)	zuò
ridicule	qǔxiào
right	yòu
river	hé
roast, to barbeque	kǎo
rock	shítou
room	fángjiān
room	wūzi
round	yuán
row	huá
rug	dìtǎn
run	pǎobù
Russia	Éguó

S

sailor	hǎiyuán
same pronunciation	tóngyīn
satisfied	mǎnyì
Saturday	xīnqī liù
scar	bā

science	kēxué
score, grade	chéngjī
sculptures	diāokè
seafood	hǎixiān
second place finisher	yàjūn
secretary	mìshū
see	jiàn
see guests to the door	sòngkè
self	zìjǐ
self-service	zìzhù
sell	mài
send by land	lùyùn
send by sea	shuǐyùn
serious	yánzhòng
shady and cool	yīnliáng
shake hands	wòshǒu
shirt	chènshān
shiver, to tremble	fādǒu
shoes	xiézi
shorts	duǎnkù
should	yīnggāi
shower	línyù
(to get) sick	shēngbìng
single room	dānrén fáng
sink	xǐdícáo
situation	qíngkuàng
skating	huábīng
skirt	qúnzi
sky	tiān
slippers	tuōxié
slow	màn
smoke	xīyān
snake	shé
sneeze	dǎ pēntì
snow	xuě
soccer	zúqiú
socks	wàzi
sofa	shāfā
soft seat	ruǎnzuò
soft sleeper	ruǎnwò
software	ruǎnjiàn

son	érzi
soup	tāng
south	nán
south	nánfāng
South America	Nán Měizhōu
Spain	Xībānyá
speak	shuō
speak	shuōhuà
specialized	zhuānmén
speech	huà
spend money	huā (qián)
spot, site	chǎng
spring	chūn
spring break	chūnjià
stamp	yóupiào
standard	biāozhǔn
start	kāi shǐ
start class	shàngkè
start work	shàngbān
station	zhàn
steal	tōu
stir-fry	chǎo
stomach, tummy	dùzi
stop	tíng
store	shāngdiàn
straight	zhí
strange	guài
strange	qíguài
street	lù
strength	shílì
strong point	yōudiǎn
strong, healthy	zhuàng
student	xuéshēng
study	xué
study	xuéxí
subway	dìtiě
such, in this way	rúcǐ
succeed	chénggōng
suddenly	hūrán
summer	xià
summer	xiàtiān

Summer Palace	Yíhéyuán
sun	taìyáng
sun, day	rì
Sunday	xīngqītiān
sweater	máoyī
sweatshirt	yùndòngshān
symbolize	biǎoshì

T

T-shirt	hànshān
table	zhuōzi
taboo	jìnjì
taichi	tàijí quán
take	ná
talk	qiàtán
taxi	chūzūchē
teach	jiāo
teach in a school	jiāoshū
teacher, professor	lǎoshī
team	duì
technical	jìshù
television	diànshì
tell	gàosù
temperature	wēndù
temple	sì
ten cents	jiǎo
ten cents	máo
tennis	wǎngqiú
tennis shoes	qíuxié
thank you	xièxie
that	nà/nèi
the Bund in Shanghai	wàitān
the same	yīyàng
theater	jùyuàn
theater company	jùtuán
theatrical play	huàjù
there is no need	hébì
therefore	suǒyǐ
thermometer	wēndùjì
they, them (plural)	tāmen
thick	hòu

thief	zéi
thin	shòu, báo
thing	dōngxi
things, events	shìqing
think	xiǎng, juéde
this month	zhège yuè
this week	zhège xīngqī
this year	jīnnián
thoughtful, considerate	zhōudào
throat	hóulóng
Thursday	xīngqīsì
tiger	hǔ
time	shíjiān
time period	qījiān
times, era, epoch	shídài
today	jīntiān
toes	jiǎozhǐ
tomorrow	míngtiān
tongue	shétou
too	tài
top (shirt)	shàngyī
town in northern Shanxi province	Dàtóng
trade	màoyì
tradition	chuántǒng
traffic	jiāotōng
train	huǒchē
train station	huǒchēzhàn
translate	fānyì
transmit a broadcast	guǎngbō
traveler's checks	lǚxíng zhīpiào
treat a guests to a welcoming dinner	jiēfēng
tree	shù
Tuesday	xīngqīèr
turn	zhuǎn

U

U.S. currency	měijīn
umbrella	yǔsǎn
understand	dǒng
understand	liǎojiě

underwear	nèiyī
up and down	Shàng xià
upstairs	lóushàng
use	yòng

V

vacant	kòngquē
vacation, holiday	jiàrì
valley	shāngǔ
vegetables	qīngcài
very	hěn
very	tǐng
Vietnam	Yuènán
violin	xiǎotíqín
visa	qiānzhèng
visit, to look around	cānguān
vocation	zhíyè
vomit	tù

W

waitress	fúwùyuán
walk	zǒulù
wall	qiáng
want to, to plan to	yào
warm	nuǎnhuo
watch	kàn
we, us	wǒmen
wear, to bring	dài
weather forecast	qìxiàng yùbào
wedding ceremony	hūnlǐ
wedding invitation	xǐtiē
Wednesday	xīngqīsān
week	xīngqī
week after next	xiàxià ge xīngqī
week before last	shàngshàng ge xīngqī
welcome	huānyíng
west	xī
west	xīfāng
what	shénme
what's up?	zěnme huíshì?
which	nǎ
white	bái

whole	mǎn
window	chuānghù
windy	guāfēng
winter	dōng
wish	xīwàng
with	gēn
with grace and ease	dàfang
withdraw money	qǔqián
wolf	láng
wonderful	jīngcǎi
words, characters	zì
work unit	dānwèi
work, job	gōngzuò
worry	dānxīn
worship	jìbài
would rather	níngyuàn
wrap	bāo
writer	zuòjiā
wrong	cuò

Y

year after next	hòunián
year before last	qiánnián
yellow	huáng
yesterday	zuótiān
you	nǐ
you're welcome	bù gǎndāng
you (formal)	nín
you (plural)	nǐmen
younger brother	dìdi
younger sister	mèimei

Z

zoo	dòngwù yuán

INDEX

NOTES